LIVING IN NETWORKS

How do personal networks emerge from social contexts? How do these evolve during the course of a lifetime? How are relationships established, maintained, connected, disrupted? How does the structure of a network evolve as people face transitions and events? Based on a classic text originally published in France and that has become the standard on the empirical study of social networks there, for the first time, a network analysis perspective is extended from contexts and social circles to relationships and life events through empirical studies. Following in the tradition of personal network studies, this contribution to the field of structural analysis in sociology offers both a synthesis of knowledge and original results from two immense surveys carried out in France. This volume proposes an original theory grounded in relational dynamics, offering novel perspectives on individual social relations over the course of a lifetime through the context of personal networks, access to social resources, and inequalities.

Claire Bidart is Research Director in the French National Centre for Scientific Research (CNRS) and Aix-Marseille University.

Alain Degenne was Research Director in the French National Centre for Scientific Research (CNRS). He is the co-author with Michel Forsé of *Introducing Social Networks* (1999).

Michel Grossetti is Research Director in the French National Centre for Scientific Research (CNRS) and the School of Advanced Studies in the Social Sciences (EHESS).

STRUCTURAL ANALYSIS IN THE SOCIAL SCIENCES

Edited by Mark Granovetter

The series Structural Analysis in the Social Sciences presents studies that analyze social behavior and institutions by reference to relations among such concrete social entities as persons, organizations, and nations. Relational analysis contrasts on the one hand with reductionist methodological individualism and on the other with macro-level determinism, whether based on technology, material conditions, economic conflict, adaptive evolution, or functional imperatives. In this more intellectually flexible, structural middle ground, analysts situate actors and their relations in a variety of contexts. Since the series began in 1987, its authors have variously focused on small groups, history, culture, politics, kinship, aesthetics, economics, and complex organizations, creatively theorizing how these shape and in turn are shaped by social relations. Their style and methods have ranged widely, from intense, long-term ethnographic observation to highly abstract mathematical models. Their disciplinary affiliations have included history, anthropology, sociology, political science, business, economics, mathematics, and computer science. Some have made explicit use of social network analysis, including many of the cutting-edge and standard works of that approach, whereas others have kept formal analysis in the background and used "networks" as a fruitful orienting metaphor. All have in common a sophisticated and revealing approach that forcefully illuminates our complex social world.

Recent Books in the Series

WIlliam Sims Bainbridge, *The Social Stucture of Online Communities*

Michael Kenney, *The Islamic State in Britain*

Wouter De Nooy, Andrej Mrvar, and Vladimir Batagelj, *Exploratory Social Network Analysis with Pajek: Revised and Expanded Edition for Updated Software*

Darius Mehri, *Iran Auto*

Navid Hassanpour, *Leading from the Periphery and Network Collective Action*

Cheol-Sung Lee, *When Solidarity Works*

Benjamin Cornwell, *Social Sequence Analysis*

Mariela Szwarcberg, *Mobilizing Poor Voters*

continued after the index

Living in Networks

The Dynamics of Social Relations

CLAIRE BIDART

French National Center for Scientific Research (CNRS)
and Aix-Marseille University

ALAIN DEGENNE

French National Center for Scientific Research (CNRS)

MICHEL GROSSETTI

French National Center for Scientific Research (CNRS)
and the School of Advanced Studies in the Social
Sciences (EHESS)

ANDREW WILSON

Translator

CAMBRIDGE
UNIVERSITY PRESS

CAMBRIDGE
UNIVERSITY PRESS

University Printing House, Cambridge CB2 8BS, United Kingdom

One Liberty Plaza, 20th Floor, New York, NY 10006, USA

477 Williamstown Road, Port Melbourne, VIC 3207, Australia

314–321, 3rd Floor, Plot 3, Splendor Forum, Jasola District Centre, New Delhi – 110025, India

79 Anson Road, #06-04/06, Singapore 079906

Cambridge University Press is part of the University of Cambridge.

It furthers the University's mission by disseminating knowledge in the pursuit of education, learning, and research at the highest international levels of excellence.

www.cambridge.org
Information on this title: www.cambridge.org/9781108841436
DOI: 10.1017/9781108882392

First published 2020

Translated and updated from the original French edition

Originally published in France as:
La vie en réseau: Dynamique des relations sociales
By Claire Bidart, Alain Degenne, and Michel Grossetti

© Presses Universitaires de France, 2011
6, avenue Reille, 75014 Paris

A catalogue record for this publication is available from the British Library.

Library of Congress Cataloging-in-Publication Data
Names: Bidart, Claire, author. | Degenne, Alain, author. | Grossetti, Michel, author.
Title: Living in networks : the dynamics of social relations / Claire Bidart, French National Center for Scientific Research (CNRS) and Aix Marseille University, Alain Degenne, French National Center for Scientific Research (CNRS), Michel Grossetti, French National Center for Scientific Research (CNRS) and the School of Advanced Studies in the Social Sciences (EHESS).
Description: Cambridge, United Kingdom ; New York, NY : Cambridge University Press, 2020. | Series: Structural analysis in the social sciences | "This book is the adaptation for English-speaking readers of a book published in French in 2011 under the title La vie en réseau. Dynamique des relations sociales (Presses Universitaires de France, 2011)"–Foreword. | Includes bibliographical references and index.
Identifiers: LCCN 2020012895 (print) | LCCN 2020012896 (ebook) | ISBN 9781108841436 (hardback) | ISBN 9781108794831 (paperback) | ISBN 9781108882392 (epub)
Subjects: LCSH: Social networks. | Social networks–France. | Interpersonal relations. | Interpersonal relations–France.
Classification: LCC HM741 .G756 2020 (print) | LCC HM741 (ebook) | DDC 302.3–dc23
LC record available at https://lccn.loc.gov/2020012895
LC ebook record available at https://lccn.loc.gov/2020012896

ISBN 978-1-108-84143-6 Hardback
ISBN 978-1-108-79483-1 Paperback

Contents

Figures

Tables

Preface

This is an English adaptation of a book published in French in 2011 under the title *La vie en réseau: Dynamique des relations sociales* (Presses Universitaires de France, 2011). In writing this book, our project was to build on our research in two French cities – a longitudinal survey begun in 1995 in the Caen agglomeration and a more classical survey conducted in 2001 in the Toulouse region. It was to present a synthesis of what we knew about personal networks, the sets of ties forming the environment of each person. Using long interviews repeated several years apart, the Caen survey included very detailed data of a new type for the study of personal networks; the Toulouse survey made it possible to make the link with more traditional surveys, both in France and in other countries. In particular, for comparative purposes, this survey used a method developed by Claude Fischer for a study conducted in the late 1970s in California[1]. As complementary approaches, these two surveys made it possible to generalize the results obtained by multiple comparisons with very varied surveys. We have focused on understanding interpersonal relationships and networks from a social science perspective, thus seeking to link the analysis of personal networks to the broader social sciences.

The book was well received in France and also read by colleagues from other countries who encouraged us to make an English version. When we started working on this version, we immediately rejected the idea of a simple translation and decided to revise our text to take into account the research conducted since the book was originally published. We also wanted to take into consideration the evolution of the problems, in particular, the development of communication technologies and digital social

---

[1] Claude S. Fischer, *To Dwell among Friends: Personal Networks in Town and City* (Chicago: University of Chicago Press, 1982).

networks. The continuation of the Caen panel by an additional survey wave and the realization of other surveys in the Toulouse region allowed us to maintain our line by permanently relying on firsthand data while mobilizing the considerable international literature on our subject.

This version is thus largely revised compared to the original work. Many passages have been reformulated to adapt them to an English-speaking readership, to integrate new bibliographical references, and to take into account the progress of our own research. In particular, we have introduced a new chapter to review the relational uses of new digital communication media and the evolution of relationships and networks in this context.

Acknowledgments

For this new version, we warmly thank Mark Granovetter, who took the risk of examining a somewhat unusual editorial project, encouraged us, and took the time to read the text carefully; our translator, Andrew Wilson, who accompanied us during this long work, agreeing to adapt his writing to international usage; and the two anonymous evaluators whose suggestions were very useful to us. The adaptation to English was made possible by the support of the Institute of Labour Economics & Industrial Sociology (LEST – UMR 7317), Aix Marseille University, CNRS, and the "laboratory of excellence" "Structuring of Social Worlds" (SSW – ANR-11-LABX-0066). We also thank the Presses Universitaires de France for having kindly accepted this adaptation.

More generally, many people have contributed to this book, some by agreeing to be asked about their backgrounds and relationships, others by participating in research as investigators or contributing to certain analyses, and others by giving us advice on preliminary versions of the text.

We cannot mention the names of the respondents in Toulouse and Caen because we must respect the anonymity we promised them, but we would like to thank them warmly for their time and for sharing often intimate information. We hope that our analyses will do some justice to the richness of their stories.

The Caen survey was designed and conducted by Claire Bidart, with Alain Degenne, Daniel Lavenu, Didier Le Gall, Lise Mounier, and Anne Pellissier. More occasionally, Dominique Beynier, Bertrand Fribourg, Cathel Kornig, Clotilde Lemarchand, Charlotte Letellier, Charlotte Lê Van, and Madeleine Royet helped us to carry out interviews. Paula Kervennic put together biographical calendars and intermediate files. Patrice Cacciuttolo and Léo Joubert contributed to the exploration and visualization of data processing on networks. Special thanks to Daniel Lavenu, who has carried out this research since its inception with rare enthusiasm and commitment.

The Toulouse survey was designed and conducted by Michel Grossetti. David Pontille assisted with sample development, survey tracking, and coding. Myriam Dereix and Marina Jean contacted the respondents and administered the questionnaires. Fabrice Fernandez, Hélène Marche, Paul Roche, Jean-Baptiste Grossetti, and Quentin Grossetti carried out complementary codings. Alexis Ferrand, Claude Fischer, and Barry Wellman made very useful remarks on the comparison between France and the United States.

Graphical representations of the networks were made with an original tool developed by Léo Joubert for adapting data to the package "visNetwork" of R.

Among the attentive proofreaders of the French version were Jean-François Barthe, Ainhoa de Federico de la Rua, Florence Maillochon, Philippe Méhaut, Guillaume Pérocheau, and Eric Verdier. Their comments and advice were valuable. We are particularly grateful to them. Mark Granovetter and Claude Fischer made very useful comments on this new version. For their patience during the long journey of writing and adapting this book, we would like to thank Annick, Véronique, and Jean-Claude.

Introduction

Social networks are currently attracting increasing attention from com-
mentators of all kinds: from academic journals in various disciplines to
employment agencies, via social workers and internet service providers, the
notion of the network society is rapidly becoming established. This notion
is undoubtedly not unconnected with the increasing affirmation of the
individual dimension of social life, in contrast to the influence of institutions and authorities, which appeared to be dominant before the 1970s.
Rather than being determined by their origins, their position in the social
structure, and their culture, individuals are now regarded as strategists and
masters of their own destinies. As such, they have become reacquainted
with the risk of fragility and solitude and are expressing their need for
social relations by attaching great importance to the network dimension,
which is supposed to reconcile society and individual freedom. As actors in
their own personal lives, individuals like to think they are also actors in
their social lives and are supposed to try to surround themselves with the
"right people." But what is the situation in reality? Over and above this way
of thinking and the injunctions to "get networked," what actual practices
are adopted in constructing social ties? What are the dynamics of this
construction process? How do interpersonal relations emerge, change, and
fade away? What is the structure of "real" networks, those used by ordinary
people, who sometimes act reflexively and strategically but are also frequently governed by the environments in which they live and the vagaries
of their lives?

   The subject of this book is social relations, the concrete ties that are
established between individuals and the networks these ties constitute. It
puts into practice a sociology taking into account relational dynamics.
Family members, friends, neighbors, business or work colleagues, romantic
partners, vague acquaintances: all play a part in people's lives, helping,

1

influencing, and giving them ideas, but also preventing them from doing certain things. Some they entrust with little secrets and problems; with others they share leisure time and evenings out. Each individual's vision of the world and of himself – the moods and the confidence he has in the future – depend to a great extent on this network of persons with whom he discusses, argues, works, has fun, and faces life's difficulties. When this network changes, following the severing of a tie or the arrival of a new person, life also changes to a greater or lesser extent. Equally, a significant change in life has repercussions on the individual's network: he sees less of certain friends and more of others who more closely match new concerns and desires. Some of them help to find work or somewhere to live, sometimes by giving useful information, sometimes simply by pointing in the direction of someone else who can help. If the individual has money problems, he knows there are some he can call on to get out of a fix or to provide more substantial assistance. Some may even be able to give his life a new direction through the advice they give or the example they set. For their part, these people know they can also rely on him up to a certain point, even if only for a brief chat. He feels close, intimately or emotionally committed, to some of them, while regarding the others as mere acquaintances whose absence would scarcely affect his mood. All these people constitute one's personal network, which is more or less narrow or extended depending on the degree of intimacy by which one chooses to define it.

Interpersonal relations, indeed everything that constitutes everyday sociability, may appear of little significance compared to the major social and political issues. However, what is not seen may be just as important as what is emphasized in social life. Studies of social networks carried out over several decades have revealed the importance of interpersonal relations in economic activities, social movements, politics, and many other areas of social life.[1]

More than that, however, interpersonal relations are the basic building blocks of social cohesion, which is derived not solely from the fact that people talk and spend time with each other in one-off interactions but also from the vestiges of these interactions, which persist in time and constitute relationships. Simmel, one of the founders of sociology, perceived this to be the case in the very early days of the discipline:

---

[1] For a general summary of these studies, see, for example: A. Degenne, M. Forsé, *Introducing Social Networks* (London: Sage, 1999).

Beyond its first origin, all sociation rests on a relationship's effect which survives the emergence of the relationship. An action between men may be engendered by love or greed of gain, obedience or hatred, sociability or lust for domination alone, but this action usually does not exhaust the creative mood which, on the contrary, somehow lives on in the sociological situation it has produced. Gratitude is definitely such a continuance. It is an ideal living-on of a relation which may have ended long ago, and with it, the act of giving and receiving. If every grateful action, which lingers on from good turns received in the past, were suddenly eliminated, society (at least as we know it) would break apart . . . . But "benefit" is not limited to a person's giving things to another: we also thank the artist or poet who does not even know us. This fact creates innumerable connections, ideal and concrete, loose and firm, among those who are filled with gratitude toward the same giver. In fact, we do not thank somebody only for what he does: the feeling with which we often react to the mere existence of a person, must itself be designated as gratitude. We are grateful to him only because he exists, because we experience him.[2]

Thus, taken in their entirety, these vestiges "make" society. Relationships, and the networks they constitute, form the basic framework of social life.

Interpersonal relations are often perceived as a world of freedom and equality that stands in contrast to the constraints of organizations, groups, or even families. A society structured by largely involuntary associations and the constraints that accompany them is replaced, it is argued, by a world of ties freely chosen between equals on the basis of affinities of all sorts. However, even friendship has a social dimension: it is recognized, is subject to norms, and conforms to certain rules.[3] Relationships are also sometimes perceived as a shameful aspect of collective life: thus clientelism, "string-pulling," "wheeling and dealing" are all denounced, along with all the other shortcuts that enable individuals to circumvent common rules and obtain small, unjustified privileges. In both cases, relations between individuals are contrasted with the regulated and hierarchized social worlds. Nevertheless, there are many links between the two, even though there are sometimes tensions between them.

As the social sciences (essentially anthropology and sociology) have attempted over almost a century to get a grip on these varying perceptions, hundreds of studies have accumulated findings that turn out to be astonishingly consistent.[4] It is now known, for example, that relationships are

---

[2] G. Simmel, K. H. Wolff, *The Sociology of Georg Simmel* (Glencoe: Free Press, 1950), 388–389.

[3] Graham Allan, *A Sociology of Friendship and Kinship* (London: G. Allen & Unwin, 1979).

[4] For a history of the analysis of social networks, see Linton Freeman, *The Development of Social Network Analysis: A Study in the Sociology of Science* (Vancouver: Empirical Press, 2004).

not independent of social hierarchies: the wealthiest or most highly qualified individuals have more relationships than others and derive more advantages from them. It is also known that the interplay of elective affinities tends to produce ties between individuals who resemble each other, have similar levels of education, come from similar social backgrounds, and are similar in age. It is also known that relationships are enormously influential in areas as different as access to employment, entrepreneurship, mental health, the ability to overcome ordeals such as illness, bereavement, unemployment, and family breakdowns as well as expressing happiness or deciding to start a family.

The aim of this book is to offer an overview of social relations and their dynamics at the level of individuals and their social surroundings. We draw, first, on two surveys we carried out and, second, on the accumulated findings of the tradition of social network analysis or, more specifically, of studies of "personal" networks (an individual's relationships), which include data that we have analyzed specially. However, before we present further details of the data and of the book and its organization, we need to clarify what we understand by relationships and networks and how this aspect of the social world is linked to other entities such as groups, organizations, and "social circles" in general.

RELATIONSHIPS, NETWORKS, AND CIRCLES

What is a social relationship between two individuals? Throughout the book, as in most studies of social networks, this expression denotes the existence of an association that goes beyond mere interaction, is sustained over time, and has developed beyond one-off exchanges. When someone goes into a grocer's shop where he is not a regular customer and buys a packet of detergent, the exchange he has with the shopkeeper is based on the various codes of politeness and civility in use in a given space and time, which determine the things it is preferable to say ("hello," "please," etc.) and to do or not do (in a small grocer's shop at the present time, one does not go behind the counter to serve oneself unless invited to do so by the shopkeeper). Such an interaction in no way implies a relationship as we define it here, since the codes used make no reference to previous interactions between the same individuals and would also be used with a different grocer. Let us now imagine that the same shopper goes to buy bread at the baker's with whom he always has a little chat about life in the neighborhood and whom he also encounters at meetings of a parent-teacher association. This time, the exchange will take a more personal turn and will make reference, explicitly or implicitly, to past interactions, to what each knows of the other, and to what he is expecting of the exchange. With another baker or parent, the exchange would be different. Finally, let us take the case of a mother-daughter relationship: apart from the fact that the bond between them will generally be immediately perceptible from the outside, it will have many complex dimensions and an intimacy and intensity that even years spent on a psychoanalyst's couch would probably not be sufficient to explain to the protagonists themselves.

We will discuss in greater detail in Chapter 1 the problem of defining the scope of relationships and the sociological questions this raises. It is sufficient here to note that, of the three examples described above, only the last two will concern us directly. In our definition, relationships are exchanges that last and cannot be reduced to a functional or one-off interaction. It includes family ties, romantic partners, and all types of relationships – whether elective or more obligatory – with friends, partners, and other intimates as well as with mere acquaintances, neighbors, colleagues, etc. Moreover, relationships do not appear suddenly out of nowhere and are not isolated from each other; rather, they knit different circles together, mixing together their actions, influences, and characteristics. At the very beginning, each of them takes shape within a specific environment. Two people meet somewhere, under certain circumstances, in a particular place and at a particular time. These places and times are not without implications for the development of a relationship and for its nature and quality. Someone encountered at a dance will not, on the face of things, play the same role in our lives as a person we know from work. Subsequently, if the relationship becomes firmer, the activities undertaken, the places visited together, the routines established for meeting, and the shared circles of friends and acquaintances will all change. Each person will introduce the other to new people, places, and knowledge; they will try out leisure activities together and share a growing intimacy. The situations and spaces explored together will imbue the relationship with a particular color and tonality that will imprint themselves on the memory. It is important, therefore, not to separate relationships artificially from the contexts in which they emerged and developed. This is not to say that a relationship should forever retain its place of origin label or be reduced to the characteristics of the situations and spaces explored: as we shall see, its particular characteristics may indeed be a product of the way in which it breaks free from those same situations and spaces. Nevertheless, it is impossible to deny the influence of these contexts on the very existence of the ties that emerge and develop within them and on the characteristics that develop as the relationship evolves.

Interpersonal relations are not simply the specific result of practices linked to sociability. They form the very basis of a fundamental element of the social world, namely social networks. Each of our relationships is, after all, connected to others; together, they form a network that surrounds us, and which, if the connections are pursued one after the other, links each individual to the rest of society. Thus, it is possible to imagine a vast network that, link by link, connects the entire world. Each individual's network is just a tiny portion of this vast global social network.[5] However, our analysis is not located at this level. We are concerned rather with the processes whereby social circles are constituted and evolve and with the personal networks made up of all the direct relationships an individual enters into. Made up of relationships old and new, work- or leisure-related, of a romantic or merely friendly nature, family-based or sports-related, such networks have a form and structure that has an impact on each of their constituent links. A childhood friend, who does not know any of the new acquaintances and with whom the person meets up once a year for lengthy one-to-one discussions, will not have the same place in her life, the same influence over her actions, or the same feeling of belonging to a group as a team of work colleagues with whom she eats lunch every day next to the office.

Networks are an essential component of the social world. Although they can be defined in extremely simple terms as sets of relationships, their structures and dynamics are very complex and they play a central part in most social processes. The analyses published here belong to the tradition of "social network analysis," which can be defined as a broad range of approaches in which the emphasis is on networks as lasting structures produced by interactions. We have drawn on the methods used in this tradition to list interpersonal relationships and reconstitute networks. The analyses produced by these methods are much more precise than studies of sociability considered as a generic practice.

---

[5] In order to obviate any possible confusion, it should be noted that, according to the definition of the notion of social network that we are using, and which is the standard one in the social sciences, so-called social networking sites such as Facebook are not in themselves social networks, even though the relationships that are formed and made visible there may match the definition of social relations used here (although this is not always the case). In our view, such sites are "aids to sociability" or, in more theoretical terms, "mediation mechanisms." This is discussed in greater depth and empirically in Chapter 12.

Nevertheless, in contrast to many analyses of social networks, which focus on the structure of the networks and tend to reduce relationships to mere channels for the transmission of resources, our study has two specific characteristics. Firstly, our aim is to investigate relationships in all their complexity, as the basic units of networks. Secondly, we take as our starting point the principle that the social world cannot be reduced to a network and that it contains other forms with which networks and relationships interact. Thus, around these relationships and networks are other groupings, which may be more or less fluid, more or less structured, more or less ephemeral or durable. We introduce here the dimension of "social circles." This notion is well established in sociology even though it has been somewhat neglected.[6] A social circle is a set of individuals, bonds, "shared motivations," and norms that are mutually recognized as shared, even though their boundaries are not always very firmly fixed. They cannot be reduced to the sum of the interpersonal relationships that are present in them nor limited to networks; rather, they are defined by particular habits and norms, motivations, identities, sometimes even names, that transcend the characteristics of the persons and connections of which they are constituted. Kadushin (1968) attributed the following characteristics to social circles: "(1) A circle may have a chain or network of indirect interaction such that most members of a circle are linked to other members, at least through a third party. It is thus not a pure face-to-face group. (2) The network exists because members of the circle share common interests – political or cultural. (3) The circle is not formal."[7] This third characteristic excludes, for Kadushin, formal organizations, while we prefer to consider them as one of the possible kinds of social circles. Kadushin's definition helps to distinguish social circles from groups (in circles members do not directly know all others) and from networks (as there are common interests underlying the circle).

Some of these social circles are institutionalized and are sometimes very highly organized and hierarchized, with their official rules, membership cards, flags, and medals. Others are more informal and fluid and are sometimes imperceptible from the outside. A large circle of friends, a basketball team, a company, an association, a neighborhood facing a new housing project, or some regulars at a pub who defend ideas or a lifestyle are all examples of these "social circles," the reality of which transcends the

[6] Simmel, Wolff, *The Sociology of Georg Simmel.*
[7] C. Kadushin, "Power, Influence and Social Circles: A New Methodology for Studying Opinion Makers," *American Sociological Review* 33(5) (1968), 692.

individuals that constitute them and the ties that bind them. Individuals may leave, others may join and friendships may break up but the circle's "spirit" will remain intact. When talking about a circle to which they belong, people say "we." These kinds of circles produce norms, opinions, specific knowledge, and sometimes linguistic codes that are likely to influence habits, thinking, and life choices. By providing examples of how to live that are more specific and accessible than the great mythical, political, or cultural models, they can be used by individuals as reference frameworks or action models. For Célestin Bouglé, a sociologist active at the beginning of the twentieth century, a social circle was created when the passengers in a coach, for example, caught sight of a rival coach or of a bandit; suddenly animated by a common will, the passengers, who had previously been ignoring each other or daydreaming in their own seats, would start to talk to each other, get organized, and attempt to achieve a shared objective, namely to win the race or defend themselves.[8] This rather antiquated but very apposite example shows that the boundaries, membership, and strict definition of a social circle are less important than the strength of the "common motivation" that drives its members and gives them a sense of "togetherness," at least for a time. This helps to differentiate the notion of "social circle" from that of "group."

Relationships, networks, and social circles intermingle without overlapping completely. Relationships exist more or less independently of the circles to which their protagonists belong. Firstly, when they are initially forged within a circle, they may survive that circle's disappearance (e.g., two students may remain in contact after leaving university). Secondly, even when they remain rooted within a particular circle, they frequently extend beyond its boundaries. If we take the example of two work colleagues, we can say that a relationship exists between them as soon as their interactions become specific and go beyond their professional roles and they are no longer wholly substitutable one for the other (like the baker mentioned above). The relationship will have become partially independent of the circle in which it first developed and will now form part of a network. For their part, circles cannot be reduced to bundles of relationships, as shared motives go beyond individuals and their ties. Thus, these various social forms – relationships, networks, and social circles – constitute each person's relational environment. The dynamic association

---

[8] C. Bouglé, "Qu'est-ce que la sociologie?," *Revue de Paris* (1897), 3–32.

between them is the object of the sociology of relational dynamics that we are putting into practice here.

AN INTERMEDIATE LEVEL OF ACTION AND INTERPRETATION

One of this book's key objectives is to show that individuals do not exist in isolation and that their actions are not driven by desires forged autonomously in a burst of creativity focused entirely on themselves. The elements that shape their decisions, the avenues open to them, the constraints that limit their actions, the routines that guide them, the range of possible options and the ideas they have are influenced by social factors structured on a large scale: national legislation, the education system, the labor market, gender roles, etc. Moreover, although they are much less analyzed in the social sciences, resource and constraint systems operating on a smaller scale and at an intermediate level – namely, those emanating from individuals' personal networks – are undoubtedly just as influential. Individuals are not isolated, and their identities and actions are guided by a relational environment that cannot be reduced either to the determinism of large-scale social structures or to one-off interactions. The relationship between society and the individual is made up of interconnections and interdependencies, of configurations of interpersonal relations, and the networks and social circles that form society's constituent matrix.

In looking for explanations for life in society at the level of individuals and their networks and subjecting their trajectories and their evolution to detailed scrutiny, we will inevitably also discern some of the effects of the macro-level social structures that classic sociology holds so dear (social groups, age groups, gender, territories, etc.). However, we will gain a clearer understanding of how these effects operate by locating our analysis at the level of the world that can be apprehended by individuals, while at the same time assessing in what ways the construction and evolution of their personal networks and affiliations help to reinforce or weaken these social differentiations. For individuals, after all, their network constitutes a social milieu that is both flexible and accessible, because it is located at a reasonable distance. This social form is situated at an intermediate level between social structures and institutions, on the one hand, and individuals, on the other. It is made up of a series of relationships that have temporal depth and are interconnected in a particular configuration.

Those around an individual – his friends, colleagues, and leisure companions – can provide personified examples of how to live that are within his reach and comparable for him. They can "set an example" and offer interesting images and new ideas. They can also show him very clearly what he must avoid if he is not to suffer the same failures, thereby acting as warnings. They can, of course, help him or support him in very direct and practical ways, by lending him tools or money or giving him a little of their time. This help may or may not be mutual. It may be symmetrical or differentiated (when the same benefit is not expected on both sides, for example, in a doctor-patient or a parent-child relationship). In some cases, people can help as effectively as the institutions established for that purpose. They may also open up access to these institutions, act as stepping stones in order to facilitate his integration into the wider society, and give him access to crucial resources, sometimes by directing him to other people, depending on the scope of the network. They also hold out mirrors to him, show him what he is for them, what he is not, what he might be and help him to define, position and project himself.

However, it should not be forgotten that an individuals' network also defines constraints – a set of limitations and duties that are likely to lead to renunciations. The people providing assistance are also the ones who often expect services, time, and forms of recognition in return; the people one likes also bar the way to certain avenues and choices. An individual's relational environment is made up of various types of relationships and commitments, many of them double-sided. It is, above all, plural, more or less mixed, sometimes discordant and liable to include a range of different opinions. This relational environment does not take the form of a simple list of relationships or an indeterminate group; rather, it is a precise configuration of more or less interconnected relationships, whose structuring, whether it be tight or loose, dispersed or centralized, has specific characteristics that are very important and discriminating. It is this configuration that constitutes an individual's personal network. These relationships and this network are not set in stone; they do not emerge randomly out of nothing, nor are they permanent. Rather, they are constantly being reconstructed over the course of the person's life. Furthermore, individuals are actively involved in these interactions; they act on their networks, choose their friends, maintain or cut off contact with their families, stop seeing friends from previous periods of their lives, and reactivate connections that they cherish or which they think might be useful to them. It is this dynamic aspect of the interactive processes between relationships, networks, social circles, and life trajectories that is the focus of this book.

A FUNDAMENTALLY DYNAMIC INTERPRETATION

Relationships emerge, evolve, decline, come to an end, start up again, change, and take on different qualities. Some are "given" to us at birth (parents, elder siblings, other family), even though circumstances may part us from them sooner or later or we may ourselves decide to leave them behind. Other relationships develop over the course of our lives, emerging out of the milieus we frequent: at school, in our neighborhoods, at work, in our most mundane activities, or from the meetings that occur during collective events, whether planned or unplanned (festivals, social movements, catastrophes), or when people are introduced to us by friends or family members. Frequently, what is initially just a vague acquaintance, a member of a particular circle who comes to our attention as part of a group or in the course of some activity or other, gradually turns into a more definite, closer, more interpersonal relationship. That relationship may also break up following a move, a change in lifestyle, or a disagreement, or be revived, for similar reasons. One of the aims of this book is to explore in detail all the microprocesses that are at work as relationships are permanently constructed and reconstructed. The study of relational dynamics examines processes as they unfold rather than static links between inert substances. Consequently, it enables us to "unfreeze" static, substantialist categories and recreate the fluidity and mutability of the various elements involved.[9] When new relationships develop or others disappear, the balance, coherence, and structure of an entire personal network are affected. A couple's separation, for example, has significant effects on each of the partners' networks, with some relationships (family-in-law, some of the spouse's friends) disappearing and others (single friends) coming to the fore. A quarrel with a friend who connected us with several circles can prove to be devastating, just as an apparently insignificant encounter can open up new worlds. Thus, it is insufficient to consider the history of relationships alone; we also need to examine the overall dynamics of an individual's network. We will focus, in particular, on the evolution of networks over a lifetime, and, more specifically, on the interactions between the variations in networks and biographical changes. For example, how do relationships and networks change during the transition to adult life, when a person starts working, when two partners set up home together, when the first child is born, when a couple divorces, or when

---

[9] M. Emirbayer, "Manifesto for a Relational Sociology," *The American Journal of Sociology* 103(2) (1997), 281–317

someone retires? The evolution of relationships and networks goes hand in hand with that of the social circles in which one is involved to a greater or lesser extent. Membership of a new circle usually generates new relationships, even though they may initially at least be limited to opportunities. Conversely, a person's choice of affiliations is very often influenced by existing relationships: it is often through the intercession of a friend that one joins a group or an activity. Thus, the evolution of interpersonal relationships is also involved in the emergence of circles and their reconstitution or disappearance. Consequently, at the same time that we are analyzing the dynamic of relationships and networks, we also have to examine the changes affecting the circles to which individuals belong. These changes are dependent, in part, on the institutional milestones that punctuate our lives (school, work, retirement, etc.) as well as on more specific stages of individual trajectories (setting up home with a partner, birth of children, new leisure activity, moving house) and more unforeseen events that may lead to reconfigurations of an individual's affiliations (accident, change of career, divorce). All these dynamics are reflected in changes in the relational environment within which relationships, networks, and circles are linked together in various ways over the course of an individual's life.

SOURCES

The material for this book is drawn mainly from two original studies carried out in France in the 1990s and 2000s. We use a convention that is standard practice in personal network analysis: "Ego" denotes the individual surveyed and "Alter" the individuals he or she mentions.

The Toulouse Survey

The first of these studies is a systematic transposition of a method used in a "classic" survey of personal networks conducted in California by Claude Fischer in 1977 to a population of 1050 individuals in the southwest of France (Toulouse and the surrounding region).[10] The target population was composed of 399 adult individuals living in the Toulouse urban area and in the small rural communities located an hour by car from the city.

---

[10] C. S. Fischer, *To Dwell Among Friends. Personal Networks in Town and City* (The University of Chicago Press, 1982).

The method relies on the name generators used in 1977 by Claude Fischer's team in the San Francisco area.

Here is the list of name generators used:

(1) "When people go out of town for a while, they sometimes ask someone to take care of their house – for example, to water the plants, collect the mail, feed the animals, or just keep an eye on it. If you went out of town, would you ask someone to take care of your house for that period of time?"

(2) "Some people never talk about their work or their education with others, neither at work (or university) nor elsewhere. Other people discuss things like decisions they have to make, professional problems they have to solve, and ways to improve how they work. Is there someone with whom you talk about your work?"

(3) "In the last three months, have friends helped you with household tasks like painting, moving furniture, cooking, washing, or doing major or minor repairs?"

(4) "In which of the following activities have you participated in the last three months?"
    - Having someone over for lunch or dinner
    - Going to someone's house for lunch or dinner
    - Having someone over for a visit
    - Going to someone's home for a visit
    - Meeting someone you know outside the home (e.g., restaurant, bar, park, club)
    - Other activities

    If so, can you tell me with whom you may have shared these activities?"

(5) "Sometimes, people discuss recreational activities or pastimes they have in common. Do you discuss this type of thing? If so, with whom do you do it regularly?"

(6) "Do you have a partner or a best friend, whom you meet very often (outside the home)?"

(7) "When you have personal problems – for example, regarding someone close or something important to you – ... with whom do you discuss them?"

(8) "Oftentimes, people rely on the advice of someone they know in order to make important decisions – for example, decisions regarding family or work. Is there someone whose advice you would consider seriously in making important decisions? If so, whose advice would you consider?"

(9) "If you needed a large amount of money, what would you do – would you ask someone you know to loan it to you; would you ask for a loan at a bank; would you do something else? What would you do in an emergency situation – is there someone (else) whom you would be likely to ask for some or all of the money?"

Once the list of names (first names, last names, or pseudonyms) was established, it was submitted to those interviewed with the question: "Is someone important to you missing here?" 24.1 percent of the respondents did not add any name, while the others added from 1 to 47 names, which makes a mean number of 4 added names. Then, the complete list was resubmitted to the respondents, asking them to characterize the relations ("family," "friends," "neighbors," etc.). Finally, a subsample of a maximum of 5 people mentioned by each respondent was selected by the investigator (the names first mentioned in response to generators 1, 4, 5, 7, and 9), about whom further questions were asked.

The 399 interviewees named 10,932 people, of whom 1,624 – who made up the subsample constituted by the above procedure – were questioned further. Respondents also cited 305 persons with whom they were no longer related, and 249 of them were asked additional questions. We thus have several datasets: a population of 399 respondents, a population of 10,932 "active" social relationships, 1,624 who were questioned in greater detail, and a population of 249 "disappeared" relationships, about whom additional questions were also asked. The survey received funding from the Plan Urbanisme Construction and Architecture, a French interministerial agency attached to the Ministry for the Environment, Sustainable Development and Energy, and the Centre Prospective de la Gendarmerie Nationale (National Gendarmerie Futurology Centre). The research was conducted by the Interdisciplinary Laboratory Solidarities, Societies and Territories (CNRS and the University of Toulouse).

The Caen Panel

The second study is a longitudinal survey, carried out over a period of nine years, of a population of young people who were interviewed every three years between 1995 and 2004 (with a partial re-interrogation in 2015). The aim of this survey was to investigate the relationships between socialization processes and the evolution of personal networks. It provides more detailed information on the dynamic of relationships and networks.

It is a qualitative survey of a cohort of young people who were living in Caen, in Normandy (France), at the time of the first wave of the survey. The sampling criterions were gender and the course of study. The young people contacted were in the senior year of general high school (*lycée général*), vocational high school (*lycée professionnel*), or on various labor market integration programs; each group contained more or less even numbers of boys and girls. The survey started just before a turning point for them, that is, the French baccalaureate (*baccalauréat*)[11] or the end of a training course. At that time, they were aged between seventeen and twenty-three. They were first contacted at school, in separate classes, in order to avoid common members in their networks. The face-to-face questionnaires and interviews were conducted in their homes.

The first wave was conducted in 1995, and eighty-seven persons were interviewed; the second wave was conducted in 1998, and seventy-four of them were re-interviewed; the third wave was conducted in 2001, and sixty-six of them were re-interviewed; the fourth wave was conducted in 2004, and sixty of them were re-interviewed. In 2015, a partial additional wave was conducted with twenty of them.

First, factual biographical details were recorded on standardized questionnaires and calendars outlining their trajectories over the three years since the previous wave of the survey, focusing on education, training, and employment but also on family, home, leisure activities, etc.

Personal networks were constructed using a specific "contextual name generator" tool. After asking one or two questions about all the possible contexts (more than fifty were proposed), they were asked:

In (name of context – e.g., work), who are the people you know a little better, with whom you talk a bit more?

---

[11] The French education system is divided into five main parts: nursery school (usually for children aged 3–5), primary school (6–11), middle school (12–15), high school (16–18), higher education (18 and older). The ages indicated are theoretical: some pupils may repeat, others skip classes. The baccalaureate is a diploma, obtained on the basis of a national examination, which ends high school and allows access to university. The average age at which the baccalaureate is taken is 18 for the economic and social sciences courses (from which part of the Caen sample is drawn) and 21 for the vocational courses (another part of the sample). The success rate in 1995 was 73 percent for general courses and 76 percent for vocational courses. The baccalaureate is an important qualification for young French people (the exam is perceived as difficult) and discriminating (having or not having the baccalaureate leads to very different opportunities for access to employment and to considerable inequalities in salary levels). Above all, it marks the threshold of the transition from the high school years (homogeneity) to entry into adult life (more hierarchical environments) and thus plays an important role for young people.

The answers to these questions were used to single out the individuals (Alter) in a given context who were identified personally by the respondents (Ego). The aim was to build the widest possible networks, reporting all activated ties in all life contexts. Two filter questions were used in order to distinguish strong ties from weak ties in each context: (1) Do you see any of them outside of (the context – e.g., work)? (2) Are any of them important to you, whether you see them elsewhere or not? If the respondent replied "yes" to one of these questions, then the relationship was considered to be a strong tie.

The questions were repeated for each context (current contexts and former contexts from which a relationship was still maintained). The list of first names generated in this way provided the basis for constructing the personal network. With this procedure, the average size of the networks was 37.6 Alters, the largest being 131 and the smallest 6. Information sheets were then compiled on the social characteristics of all those Alters and on the characteristics of the relationships between Ego and his/her Alters.

At the end, the names (of strong ties only, for time reasons) were placed around a circle and the respondent was asked to draw lines representing the connections between the Alters who knew each other (according to Ego) in order to measure network density. Social circles were also investigated in detail when activities involved more than two people.

Then the interviewer went back to his office to compare these data about the trajectory and the network with those collected three years before. A few days after, semi-structured interviews were conducted, consisting of narratives and explanations by respondents of the biographical and relational changes that had happened between the waves of the survey and of discussions on various matters of opinion.

Because of the multiplicity of spheres that were tackled, and the time involved in collecting network data, the interviews lasted between four and ten hours and were usually conducted over several meetings held several days apart. Throughout the 4 major waves of this survey, a total of 287 personal networks were constructed, 7,096 Alters were listed, and 10,804 relationships were described (the same Alter could be cited in several survey waves and their relationship may have changed), of which 6,716 were strong ties and 4,088 weak ties.

This survey was launched by Claire Bidart, Alain Degenne, Lise Mounier, Daniel Lavenu, Didier Le Gall, and Anne Pellissier, and involved the CNRS, Caen University, and Aix-Marseille University (LEST – Institute of Labour Economics and Industrial Sociology). It was funded by the Lower

Normandy Regional Department of Health and Social Affairs (DRASS), the Calvados Regional Department of Health and Social Affairs, the Lower Normandy Regional Department of Employment and Vocational Training, the Town Council of Caen, the Interministerial Commission on the Integration of Young People, France-Télécom R&D, the National Family Allowance Office (CNAF), and the Labex SMS "Structuring of Social Worlds" (Toulouse).[12]

In some chapters, we also draw on other studies we have carried out, which are concerned with a particular aspect of relationships or a particular population.

National Surveys

In addition to these firsthand sources, we also used secondary analyses of various national surveys. In particular, surveys of the National Institute of Statistics and Economic Studies – INSEE included questions designed to obtain information on the respondents' relationships:

The survey "Contacts entre les personnes/Interpersonal contacts" was conducted in 1983 by INSEE and the National Institute of Demographic Studies – INED. It investigated 8,104 households, recording all contacts (excluding work-related discussions) a person had for a week as listed in his or her schedule.

The "Enquête Permanente sur les Conditions de Vie des ménages/ Permanent Survey on Household Living Conditions" (INSEE) was conducted in 1997. It involved 10,203 respondents, and included a question on respondents' three best friends as well as one about the people with whom informants spoke for least five minutes for a week.

Finally, we make constant reference to studies conducted within the American tradition of social network analysis, particularly those concerned with "personal" networks. It is not within the scope of this book to present all the studies conducted on these issues, and it is impossible to cite them all. We have made every effort to combine these various sources with as much rigor as possible, a task that was made much easier by the very high degree of convergence on most of the questions addressed here. The surveys on personal networks require respondents to provide information about their lives that is sometimes very personal. Their anonymity has

---

[12] For further information on this survey, see http://halshs.archives-ouvertes.fr/halshs-00164797.

obviously been maintained most rigorously. When cases are mentioned in the book, the first names are fictitious. A brief description of their social characteristics is mentioned in the appendix.

STAGES IN THE EXPLORATION OF RELATIONSHIPS AND PERSONAL NETWORKS

Our analyses will be developed in a sequence that starts at the lowest, most "micro" levels and proceeds toward increasingly larger units. Interpretation is simply easier this way. The first part of the book (Chapters 1 and 2) is devoted to establishing the principles and tools for the study of relational dynamics. In the second part (Chapters 3–7), we seek to analyze very precisely the dynamics of relationships and networks; the aim here is to understand, using an original approach and data, how networks are "constructed." The third part (Chapters 8–11) examines the place and effects of these networks and relationships in the various social spheres; it is more strongly linked to studies that focus, in particular, on relational resources. Chapter 12 examines offline and online networks, focusing particularly on the question of the changes that "social networks" such as Facebook are assumed to have brought about.[13] The book concludes with an examination of what role networks play in the wider society. Do they reproduce inequalities and possibly even reinforce them? Do they, even so, provide some small spaces in which social constraints and divisions are loosened to some degree? And as far as the social sciences are concerned, do they serve as a sort of intermediate level of observation or are they a relatively autonomous dimension of life in society, with its own logics and dynamics?

Thus, by attempting to link together various dimensions of sociology, this book seeks to demonstrate the specific contributions that the study of relational dynamics might make. However, it also has several original features that set it apart from the tradition of personal network analysis. Firstly, it gives serious consideration to the question of the relationships on which networks are based. These relationships have "depth" and content – they are not mere lines between individuals. Our approach connects these two dimensions very precisely. It also connects networks and relationships with other social entities that are not reducible to them, such as social circles. In so doing, it does not base the entire structuring of the social world on social networks alone, which do not constitute a total, exclusive

---

[13] Chapter 12 has been added for this edition.

explanation of the social world, its divisions, and coherences. Contexts, institutions, social norms, as well as individual attributes, continue to be of relevance to the history of society and that of the people of which it is made up. Rather, personal networks constitute an intermediate level that contributes to the development of social trajectories and to the explanation thereof. Furthermore, relationships and networks are not investigated solely from the point of view of the resources they provide; rather, we ask what types of relationships and networks – with what characteristics, contents, and configurations – are likely to provide resources, among other things.

Secondly, the book focuses on the dynamic of relationships and networks, which are regarded not as fixed entities but rather as dimensions in a perpetual flow of change. It is this dynamic that shapes their configuration at any given moment. Changes in personal networks and relationships are investigated in conjunction with biographical transitions and the events that punctuate them. The structuring of networks is not analyzed in isolation from the histories that shape them and which they in turn influence. Finally, the combination of qualitative, quantitative, and structural methods ensures that the object of investigation is viewed from a number of different angles and in various dimensions. We hope that our analyses will be able to build bridges between various strands of the social sciences, well beyond specialists in networks.

PART I

FOUNDATIONS OF A SOCIOLOGY OF
RELATIONAL DYNAMICS

Understanding Relationships

Relationships are not all the same. Some are linked to daily life, others are brought into play at more exceptional times; some are important, others are insignificant or occasional. After the initial encounter, the links between the individuals concerned acquire their own "content," their "common motivation." The subject of this section is the various sorts of relationships and their modes of existence. The differences observed between relationships are very closely linked to the questions asked in surveys. After all, network analysts generally begin by constructing lists of relationships on the basis of "name generators." For example, questions such as "Who are your best friends?" or "Who did you speak to last week?" produce a list of names or first names. Some generators are intended to capture as many names of individuals linked to the interviewee as possible, while others are aimed at closer, more intense relationships.

Relationships always come with stories attached to them. But how do these stories arise? What is important? Some one-off interactions are memorable and leave a strong impression, but they do not constitute a relationship. An exchange of a few sentences, a certain affinity, or maybe a joke remain in the memory, but no lasting link has been forged. The difference between a relationship and an interaction is that an interaction is a one-off event, whereas a relationship is a series of interactions between the same individuals. If these interactions are repeated and become incorporated into certain routines, they may give rise to familiarity, mutual recognition, and expectations. In many cases, however, this series of interactions remains defined by the role more than by an attachment between individuals. Thus, one can go regularly to the same shop or club without a relationship ever developing, because each time this happens it is as if it were for the first time. The shopkeeper remains a shopkeeper, the customer a customer. Sometimes, by dint of repetition, but especially when an event or an encounter in another context causes those involved to step out of their roles, the new shared experience has the effect of changing the interactions that follow. A new layer of potential exchanges is opened up, the relational space expands and a story begins to take shape and unfold. This process can be spread out over time or may sometimes be very short if precipitated by an event or crisis.[1]

CHARACTERIZING RELATIONSHIPS

Once the relationship is firmly established, various types of interactions will help to sustain it and keep it going. People talk to each other, face to face or on the telephone, they play tennis, they do each other favors, invite each other to dinner, and so on. Measurement of these interactions, of their frequency and variety, is useful in characterizing the relationship. Nevertheless, it is important always to separate these measurements, which relate to interactions, from those concerning the intensity of the relationship. After all, one can have very significant or affective relationships with people whom one sees just once a year or, conversely, have relationships that are neither intense nor personal with people one sees every day. Similarly, an exchange of small services does not automatically signify great commitment or a highly personal relationship. Thus, we will take care to distinguish between the "formal" dimension of interactions, their frequency and the exchanges to which they give rise, on the one hand, and, on the other, the substantive dimension of the relationships that they bring into play, while at the same time examining the linkages between the two aspects. For example, certain experiences or exchanges may alter the quality of a relationship. Thus, some people state that the transition from mere "chumminess" to real friendship dates from a vacation taken together or from crucial help given at a critical time. This being so, these same individuals will know other people with whom such exchanges have not taken place but whom they nevertheless describe as friends. Consequently, it is through questioning that the links between interactions and the qualities of relationships have to be investigated.

The knowledge each has of the other and of past interactions may not be symmetrical. One may know the other better than he/she knows him/her, whether because the other opens up more easily, because one is more "interested" in the other and more readily remembers what he/she learns

---

[1] Claire Bidart has examined these processes in the case of friendship: C. Bidart, *L'amitié, un lien social* (Paris: La Découverte, 1997).

about him/her, or because one has the advantage of outside information about the other. However, it is clear that a unilateral acquaintance cannot be considered a relationship. We may feel we have intimate knowledge of certain individuals with a high media profile (celebrities, politicians, etc.), but if we have not interacted with them, they do not know us and we do not have a relationship with them. If we have interacted (by getting them to give us their autograph, for example) but the person in question does not recognize us, there is no relationship either. The word "recognition" has several meanings, all of which may be involved in the construction of a relationship. A person recognizes our face and identifies us. A person recognizes our value and accords us a place in her world. A person is grateful to us in recognition of the help we have given her. The first case is essential if mere interaction is to develop further into a relationship, the second is closely associated with it, and the third may very well never happen even in some very important relationships. Thus, in order to become a relationship, knowledge of another person must be accompanied by interactions that will show, in particular, that we recognize that person as someone with whom we can associate. Thus, to recognize a person is to show a commitment to that person, with the minimum requirement being simply to admit the existence of a relationship, which is itself maintained over time. Thus, a word expressing commitment will represent a step toward other exchanges that, as they accumulate, will create the depth and the history that turns the interaction into a relationship.

Hence, a relationship implies mutual history, knowledge, and commitment. Here also, two meanings of the term are combined. Commitment is a sort of promise, an indication that the relationship is going to continue to be of interest to us in the future, that the recognition of another person will be maintained. By projecting this relationship into the future, it is being given a temporal dimension. The story has begun. Commitment is also a way of affirming that one is personally involved, willing to give "of one's self" and ready to accept one's responsibilities. In recognizing and affirming a relationship with another person, it is an individual's identity that is being involved.

This commitment to another person is usually accompanied by an affective or emotional dimension. We value – to varying degrees – the people with whom we have relationships, we seek out their presence, we look forward to seeing them; for some of them, we may have feelings of friendship or even love. One may also, for various reasons, have relationships with people whom one does not value. Such enforced relationships may be linked to one's family (the relationship between a woman and her mother-in-law can be very strained, but it is still a relationship, the product essentially of their roles within the family), one's work (we try to remain polite with those colleagues whom we find disagreeable but have to deal with nevertheless), one's neighborhood, etc. These enforced relationships are interpersonal relationships insofar as they involve repeated inter-actions, mutual knowledge, and a form of commitment, however minimal or formal. All things considered, however, interpersonal relationships have a positive affective dimension. Sociologists have tended to ignore this dimension, doubtless intimidated by its proximity to questions that tend to be the province of psychologists, the difficulty of dealing with these very subjective data that are difficult to gather and measure, or even by the lack of academic credit accorded to these questions in the dominant approaches to their discipline.

It would seem safer to infer the strength of a relationship from more "objective" or at least more factual information (in both cases, of course, any judgments are based on the statements of those concerned), such as the frequency of meetings or the possibility for mutual assistance. How-ever, as we have already noted, such an inference is unwarranted and deprives us of the value of investigating the linkage between the practical and affective aspects of a relationship. It is, after all, perfectly possible to examine affects from a sociological perspective without entering into complex considerations. For example, asking two young women if they feel close to each other, if they are real friends or just buddies, or even what the nature of the tie between them is, may be sufficient to draw conclusions about the quality of the tie and its affective character without reducing them to any particular type of exchange. Thus, it can be seen that this affective dimension is absolutely central to the existence of the relationship and even to the most effective aspects of its strength.[2]

Asking questions about the "mainspring" of the tie between two indi-viduals, about the motivating force that "makes it tick," is a way of adding flesh to the bones of the relationship. This dimension is very seldom tackled head on. The mainspring of a relationship is what constitutes the attraction and commitment between two individuals, what keeps them together, over and above the various qualities of the relationship.[3] This

[2] D. Krackhardt, "The Strength of Strong Ties: The Importance of Philos in Organization," in N. Nohria and R. G. Eccles (eds.) *Networks and Organization: Structure, Form, and Action* (Cambridge, MA: Harvard Business School Press, 1992), pp. 216–239.

[3] C. Bidart, "En búsqueda del contenido de las redes sociales: los 'móviles' de las relaciones, A la recherche de la substance des relations: le ressort du lien," *REDES* 16 (2009). http://revista-redes.rediris.es/pdf-vol16/vol16_7.pdf.

Table 1.1 *Frequency of responses selected over the four waves of the Caen panel survey*

What brings you together:	%
A family tie above all	28
Friends, buddies in common	15
Our children (only in waves 3 and 4)	1
One or more shared activities (including work or study)	13
You help each other	3
You can confide in each other	7
An emotional attachment primarily (friendship . . .)	25
The simple pleasure of being together	19

mainspring, or motivating force, has its roots in part in the individuals' backgrounds and qualities and in the interactions and ties between them. However, it cannot be reduced to these elements. One of the questions put to the Caen panel sums up this notion of mainspring: "Finally, what brings you together, is it mainly . . .?" (Table 1.1) There followed a list of twelve items from which interviewees could select a maximum of two responses.[4]

These response items require some clarification:

- In some cases, a family tie constitutes the relationship's sole motivating force: it is "only" a family tie, which on some occasions is mentioned almost as an automatic reflex (if an uncle is mentioned, it is sometimes awkward not to mention the aunt); in other cases, the family tie is accompanied by other relational mainsprings (emotional attachment, personal qualities, etc.). However, with this response the family role takes precedence and is the dominant force sustaining the relationship.
- Another relational mainspring has its roots in another shared part of the individual's network, namely "buddies in common." This response shows the multiplier effect produced by a network, which grows by creating new relationships from the existing ones.
- The fact that children (usually of the same age) can constitute the main motivating force in a relationship was not suggested until the third wave of the survey, the participants having previously been too

---

[4] These items were constructed on the basis of the first wave of the survey, when the response was open-ended and then coded. From the second wave onward, respondents were asked to choose from the list. The two possible responses have been merged here, as have the four waves of the survey.

young. In this case as well, the mainspring has its roots in other relationships that establish connections.

- The shared activities response also places the relationship into its context. Whether it be school, university, work, or leisure, the relationship has at its heart a shared activity.
- Mutual aid may be the initial motivating force behind a relationship, but the fact that it applies to only a small share of the relationships here suggests we should be wary of the "utilitarian" vision of relationships. The exchange and resource dimension dominates the relational content here.
- The possible sharing of confidences puts the emphasis on the degree of intimacy in the mutual exchanges. Here too, the relationship is above all a vector for support, provided in this case by listening to very private words and enabling self-disclosure.
- Emotional attachment comes in second, but in first place if family is excluded. Thus, the majority of relationships are a question of feelings, which may seem obvious but is worth emphasizing.
- The "simple pleasure of being together" also emphasizes the free gift and conviviality that relationships provide above all.
- The importance of a shared past shows the importance of a relationship's history, which may still be shaping a current relationship.
- The friend's qualities are sometimes mentioned as the main motivating force, in which case the relationship really does revolve around the interpersonal dimension.
- The "not much, nothing" item shows that some relationships are mentioned rather by convention. This applies particularly when they are mentioned in "bundles," for example, within groups of buddies or families.

This brief look at the mainsprings of the relationships, as those involved see them, shows that the substance of relationships is very diverse. Examination of some of their qualities will help to characterize relationships more precisely.

Relationships may have their roots in a single context or in several contexts simultaneously. This multiplexity shows that a network can superpose different social circles and combine various contexts, even for the same relationship. But at what point can we say that a relationship is multiplex? When it moves out of the place where the individuals concerned first met? When the variety of topics discussed goes beyond the register of the initial context? When the contexts in which shared activities and exchanges take place proliferate? When motivating forces emerge that place greater emphasis on personal qualities? Obviously, there is no one answer to this question and some situations are ambiguous. Some contexts, such as work and neighborhood, are spaces in which relationships are fairly commonly located, giving rise to designations for the clearly identified relational roles of colleague and neighbor. However, contexts can be defined on the basis of many criteria other than these roles or the initial settings; these include places currently frequented, shared activities, and so on. It depends on the relationships under investigation.

Multiplexity is connected with the intensity of ties. In the Toulouse survey, multiplexity is measured by the number of contexts for which the same person is mentioned. Family members, friends, and close relationships are generally more multiplex than neighbors, colleagues, or mere acquaintances. In the Caen panel, this multiplexity is also measured by the number of contexts in which a relationship is mentioned, but also by the multiplicity of shared activities and by the interviewee's declaration that he/she spends time with that person outside of the context. This last point is, incidentally, one of the two criteria used to differentiate strong from weak ties. For each of the names mentioned, interviewees were asked if they considered that person to be important or if they saw him/her outside of the context in question. This questioning was based on the hypothesis that a tie capable of freeing itself from the original context by becoming more multiplex is more particularized and personalized and thereby becomes stronger. If the relationship was declared important or moved outside of the context, it was regarded as a strong tie. Use of these two criteria enabled us to verify the hypothesis of a link between multiplexity and the strength of a tie: 82 percent of the relationships regarded as important are indeed multiplex ones. This said, the two criteria do not overlap completely since, despite everything, 18 percent of important ties are not multiplex (these tend to be family ties, although not exclusively so). Moreover, 36.6 percent of non-important ties are actually multiplex. Thus, the two notions of a tie's strength, on the one hand, and its multiplexity, on the other, are not exactly one and the same thing. Certain specialized ties may acquire great intensity (a former professional partnership, for example) whereas more multiplex relationships may turn out to be lacking in intensity (e.g., relatively peripheral friends in a group of young people).

Efforts have always been made, to varying extents, to assess the strength of ties. Obviously, certain relationships involve considerable attention and affection, whereas others remain at a minimum level of recognition. Trust and emotional intensity were two of the criteria used by Granovetter to define the more general notion of the "strength of a tie."[5] We will have an opportunity to reconsider this notion, which incorporates various aspects of relationships, but we can say here that everything we have just touched on can be highly variable in its intensity, whether we are dealing with the knowledge, commitment, emotional dimension, mainspring, or multiplexity associated with the tie in question. These variations in intensity are complex and utilize a mix of registers involving a number of different dimensions. Nevertheless, most network analysts have attempted to combine the criteria that seem to them most relevant in order to form two broad categories: "strong" ties and "weak" ties. The idea is to differentiate those relationships that constitute a "cluster" of close associates around the individual from those that form a wider "halo" around him, connecting him to the wider society. The problem is that it is difficult to compare surveys in this respect, since the criteria used are not the same and are sometimes even left very vague. It sometimes seems that the frequency of meetings or the level of mutual support provided are regarded as the primary criteria, while in other cases it is suggested that certain roles, notably those of family and friends, give the tie greater strength. In some surveys, the name generators immediately target the strongest ties, the most intense "core" of a network, by giving interviewees the choice of naming the people they consider "closest" to them.[6] Thus, once they have been identified more or less methodically, strong and weak ties constitute two levels of relationship that can be fruitfully compared.

One of the points our two surveys have in common is that they reconstruct a significantly wider network. Afterwards, the respondents were asked to describe the ties very precisely. In this method, the intensity of the tie is not confused with the forms of interactions and the link between these two dimensions can be posed in the form of a question, as we indicated above. Consequently, we preferred to begin by constructing the

---

[5] Mark Granovetter gave this distinction between strong and weak ties a key position in his theory of the strength of weak ties. M. S. Granovetter, "The Strength of Weak Ties," *The American Journal of Sociology* 78 (1973), 1360–1380.

[6] This is the case, for example, with Barry Wellman, who asks interviewees to name "the people that you feel closest to." B. Wellman, "The Community Question: The Intimate Networks of East Yorkers," *The American Journal of Sociology* 84(5) (1979), 1201–1231. It is also the case with Ronald Burt, who analyzed the General Social Survey in the United States, in which respondents were asked to list "who are the people with whom you have discussed important personal matters." R. S. Burt, "Network Items and the General Social Survey," *Social Networks* 6 (1984), 293–339. In both of these cases, the analysts are concerned more with the "core" of very close associates than with the wider "halo" of an individual's extended network.

entire network on the basis of the contexts; we then identified the individuals the respondents regarded as important, asked them if they considered them to be close friends, buddies, or mere acquaintances, and had them specify the motivating force behind the ties, etc. We then examined how many times they saw them in a year, what activities they shared with them, if they had already helped them or influenced them in their decisions, if they would be willing to share a flat with them, etc.

RELATIONSHIPS IN NETWORKS AND CIRCLES

Let us now look beyond the characteristics of relationships considered as singular entities and examine the way in which they combine together to become part of networks and circles. The first question is that of the scale of an individual's relational environment.

One of the ways of getting an idea of variations in intensity and of their consequences for our perception of relationships and the size of networks is to ask oneself the apparently simple question of how many people one knows. What does it mean to know a person? Where does a relationship begin? At what point does one stop being part of an interaction between strangers or playing a prescribed role? These are actually not simple questions. If the threshold were to be set at the lowest possible point, then coexistence of any kind would ultimately be regarded as a relationship and one could be linked to the planet's six or seven billion other inhabitants. This, as it were, is the ground zero of relational intensity. One commonly used way of setting a minimum threshold is to require that each person knows the other's name. However, studies have shown that there is an "anonymous swathe" of people whom one can locate in terms of where they live and what they do for a living but whose name one does not know.[7] For example, when elderly people are asked about people whom they could ask to help them should a problem arise, it is not uncommon for them to give answers such as "the little lady who lives on the corner of the street" or "the nurse who comes every other day, she's so kind." Conversely, there are some people whom we know by name but whom we do not regard as acquaintances. Nevertheless, memorizing someone's name is a useful criterion for identifying ties, which may be very weak. How many people do we know in this sense? Various experiments have been carried out, for example, by encouraging people to remember names

---

[7] J. K. Eckert, *The Unseen Elderly: A Study of Marginally Subsistent Hotel Dwellers* (San Diego: Campanile Press, 1980).

with the telephone book.[8] Obviously, the results depend on the method used, but they range between 600 and 6,000 names depending also on country, town, and the social status of the individuals questioned; it turns out that the number of people one knows or has known is around 5,000 on average. Thus, if we use knowing one another's name as the criterion for defining an individual's relational environment, then that world is very densely populated. However, many of these relationships obviously operate at a minimal level of commitment and knowledge. We would not dare to ask even a very simple favor of most of these people. So let us take another, more demanding criterion, namely the number of people we could ask to introduce us to someone we do not know. This is a favor that commits a person: to introduce someone is often also to act as guarantor, to vouch for his or her qualities. It is estimated that, in general, the number of people meeting this criterion is on the order of 200 on average.[9] The anthropologist and biologist Robin Dunbar put the size of "natural human groups" at no more than 150 individuals, due to cognitive constraints.[10]

In many surveys of personal networks, such as that conducted by Fischer, name generators are used. Between 15 and 30 names are obtained on average by this method (18.5 in Fischer's case, 27 for the Toulouse survey).[11] For the Caen panel, using a name generator based on all life contexts, the average number of relationships per respondent, and taking all waves of the survey together, is 37.6 (the people whom one knows or with whom one speaks in each of these contexts). The average number of strong ties (multiplex or important ones) is 23.4, while the average number of weak ties (neither multiplex nor declared to be important) is 14.2. Again, in this Caen panel survey, the interviews in each wave of the survey always opened with the following question: "Who are the people who are currently important to you, who matter to you?" On average, 10.4 names were

[8] I. de Sola Pool, "Contacts and Influence," *Social Networks* 1 (1978), 5–51, reprinted in M. Kochen (ed.), *The Small World* (Norwood: Ablex Publishing Corporation, 1989); L. Freeman, C. R. Thompson, "Estimating Acquaintanceship Volume," in M. Kochen (ed.) *The Small World* (Norwood: Ablex Publishing, 1989), pp. 147–158; H. R. Bernard, E. C. Johnsen, P. D. Killworth, C. McCarty, G. A. Shelley, "Estimating the Size of Personal Networks," *Social Networks* 12(4) (1990), 289–312.

[9] P. D. Killworth, H. R. Bernard, "The Reversal Small World Experiment," *Social Networks* 1 (1978), 159–192,

[10] R. Dunbar, "Coevolution of Neocortex Size, Group Size and Language in Humans," *Behavioral and Brain Sciences* 16 (1993), 681–735.

[11] The difference between the number of names in the US survey and that of Toulouse is due to the fact that in the US survey, investigators stopped at the first eight or ten names, while in the Toulouse survey, investigators noted every name cited by the respondents.

mentioned in response to this point-blank question, which is similar to the name generators that target the core of networks of close relationships. And if the aim is to identify the more intense ties, then the name generators used in surveys of the type conducted by Fischer include some that target, for example, the people with whom the interviewee discusses personal problems or asks for advice when making important decisions. On average, such questions generate just two or three names. A result of the same order is obtained when the name generator focuses on interviewees' confidants, the people to whom they are willing to entrust serious, secret things that can affect their lives. In these cases also, the number of ties falls to a handful, three on average.[12]

The various criteria for measuring the intensity of ties usually tend to go along the same lines, but this is not always the case. When the individuals in question live far away from each other, the criteria for measuring intensity, such as intimacy or affective quality, are disconnected from those used to measure actual practices, such as the frequency of exchanges or the importance of any material support. The strongest ties, as measured by the intrinsic criteria of affective intensity, tend to be more frequent in geographically distant relationships than in those that are in the neighborhood. We will examine the spatial aspect of relationship networks in greater detail in Chapter 8, but we can state here and now what this difference signifies, which is that only "strong" ties as measured by the intrinsic criteria withstand distance. This also confirms that the various criteria usually used to assess the "strength of ties" must be differentiated from each other. By shifting the cursor of relationship intensity in this way, we have moved from several thousand to just a few names, around 1,000 times fewer. Thus, our idea of a person's network differs considerably depending on the criteria we adopt to identify the relationships. The choice and construction of the types of name generators are absolutely crucial in network analyses and go hand in hand with very specific hypotheses and research objects.[13]

---

[12] A. Ferrand, L. Mounier, "Social Discourse and Normative Influences," in A. Spira, N. Bajos and the ACSF Group (eds.) *Sexual Behaviour and AIDS* (Dartmouth: Aldershot, 1994), pp. 140–148. http://halshs.archives-ouvertes.fr/halshs-00257614/fr/.

[13] See, in particular, H. R. Bernard, G. A. Shelley, P. Killworth, "How Much of a Network Does the GSS and RSW Dredge Up," *Social Networks* 9 (1987), 49–61; A. Marin, "Are Respondents More Likely to List Alters with Certain Characteristics? Implications for Name Generator Data," *Social Networks* 26 (2004), 289–307; C. Bidart, J. Charbonneau, "How to Generate Personal Networks: Issues and Tools for a Sociological Perspective," *Field Methods* 23(3) (2011), 266–286.

The case of the family is a rather particular one. After all, the members of our family constitute a more or less clearly defined and finite unit that is governed by the rules of kinship. We cannot extend it simply on a whim, even though we might declare that a friend is "like a brother to us" or that certain family ties, such as those in reconstituted families, have certain similarities with the relationships between friends. Moreover, the relationship between a mother and her daughter is obviously not fully delineated by the social rules and prescriptions that define the mother-daughter role. The interactions between them may be harmonious or conflictive, close or strained. Some authors speak of the relative "liberalization" of family relationships: modernity is said to be turning family ties and obligations into primarily elective and affective relationships.[14] However, although kinship today undoubtedly forms the basis for a more diverse range of relationships than used to be accepted in the past, it is still a structural, anthropological tie that is not readily negotiable.

Above all, it is important to separate those aspects of family relationships that are a product of family roles from those produced by the development of a family relationship over time, that is, by its history. To that end, we can attempt to isolate these two dimensions from each other: the one that reflects the symbolic, anthropological, and structural roles of parents and their children or of brothers and sisters, uncles and aunts, etc., and the one that reflects the temporary and evolving experience of kinship and of interactions with family members.[15] Family relationships develop on two different levels: that of family position, which remains unalterable and unconditional regardless of what happens, and that of the history of the relationship, which gives it a variable intensity and causes it to evolve and be sensitive to events. Relationships change at the various stages of the life course. In particular, when young people become adults, they construct a relationship with their parents that becomes increasingly interpersonal. The fixity of family position and the role it determines is gradually overlaid by an increasingly substantial relational dimension that is based more and more on interpersonal interactions and developments. This is not to say that the relationship replaces the formal role, rather that it envelops and coexists with it. This new relationship "between adults" is constructed both within the family role and with the addition of an increasing dyadic relational dimension. This is the story told, for example, by Emeline, one

---

[14] See, for example, the work by François de Singly in France.
[15] C. Bidart, A. Pellissier, "Entre parents et enfants: liens et relations à l'épreuve du cheminement vers la vie adulte," *Recherches et Prévisions* 90 (2007), 29–39.

of the young people in the Caen panel who observed how her aunt Odile's view of her changed. Initially, her aunt simply "pigeonholed" her as a child in the family:

For her, I was absolutely just a part of the family structure. I didn't particularly stand out in my family. She used to bawl me out sometimes, because at that time she was still pigeonholing me as a teenager, along with her own sons. It's completely different now. We have great conversations. So I like her a lot. And now I really stand out as an individual relative to my family.

This individualization develops in tandem with the adult relationship, not outside it but above and beyond it.

The ways of characterizing relationships listed above concern the relationship itself – its intensity, its diversity, and its qualities. However, it is also useful to characterize a relationship in terms of the attributes of the parties involved and, in particular, to compare these attributes in order to assess their degree of similarity. Such a characterization is located at the level of the dyad, which comprises the two individuals connected by the tie. In general, homophily is defined as the tendency to maintain relationships with individuals who are similar to oneself, at least on one level. Homophily or similarity may concern a large number of characteristics. A relationship may be homophilic in terms of age (i.e., there is little difference in age between the two individuals), gender (two men or two women), level of education (both parties are graduates), etc. The friends may be similar by one criterion but not according to another. This dimension of relationships is very important, since it provides a starting point for addressing the question of social cohesion and segregation processes. The effects of homophily are generally quite pronounced but they vary depending on context, social category, and type of relationship. The fact that people tend to keep company with others similar to themselves, including when it comes to "voluntary" relationships, is evidence of the strength of the social divisions in question, as well as of the unequal distribution of that strength in society.[16] Thus, the degree of segregation and self-regulation varies depending on the sector and constituent element in question. We will return to the question of homophily in Chapter 9. The important thing here is to be aware that a relationship is characterized by its own qualities but also by the distance between the characteristics of the

---

[16] An extensive literature has developed around these phenomena. See, in particular: L. M. Verbrugge: "Multiplexity in Adult Friendship," *Social Forces* (1979), 1286–1309 and M. McPherson, L. Smith-Lovin, J. M. Cook: "Birds of a Feather: Homophily in Social Networks," *Annual Review of Sociology* 27 (2001), 415–444.

individuals that it connects. On a larger scale, this preference for people like oneself sheds light on and reinforces social divisions and the various effects of segregation.

Nevertheless, homophily is far from being the rule and, fortunately, conflicting tendencies disrupt its unifying tendency. Thus, partners can be characterized not by their similarity or dissimilarity but by their complementarity. Many relationships are, after all, based at least initially on complementary roles: doctor-patient, teacher-pupil, and so on. This complementarity can be instituted or formalized, but it may also be more informal and based on subtle character traits or skills. Selectors for team sport are constantly searching for complementarities. This is a relatively unexplored aspect of social relationships but it may be very important in pairing or matching situations. Thus, each context is a combination of homophily and diversity, with social institutions and contexts helping to define selection processes and specific balances. Thus, the school system contributes to strict segregation by age but tends, conversely, to mix boys and girls. It also claims to mix social classes, as long as catchment areas are respected and residential segregation is not too strong. This example points to the social and political issues surrounding this question of homophily.

Except for certain particular roles, exchanges of services do not provide the main motivation for relationships. It may even seem offensive to mention the idea that they might be motivated by self-interest or that the exchanges of services should be evenly balanced. In most cases, as we saw with the Caen panel, a relationship exists for itself, particularly for the affective tie or just for "the simple pleasure of being together," while mutual assistance is the motivation for the tie in only 3.7 percent of relationships. This puts it far behind all the other more "disinterested" motives. And yet, even though a relationship may not be based on or explained by exchanges of goods or services, this does not preclude many diverse forms of assistance from circulating within it, whether they be material (mutual assistance) or more symbolic (influence). Households help each other out, with neighbors and friends lending each other tools, looking after children, and watering house plants or gardens during holidays; households belonging to the same family also provide services for each other but, in addition, generally take care of people in difficulty and may possibly also lend each other money. More broadly, giving advice or sometimes even simply lending a sympathetic ear con-stitutes an exchange of resources that helps to reassure, comfort, and make people feel like others, approved and recognized. Thus, certain "significant others"[17] may shape our lives without us thinking to say that they "helped" us directly. Furthermore, from our point of view, the term "resources" has its "dark" side, since it can imply constraints. After all, relationships generally result in constraints on behavior by directly preventing us from doing certain things, creating obligations, requiring time and attention, dissuading us, and so on. We will return to these aspects of relationships in Chapter 10.

Interpersonal relations (and the networks that they constitute) are combined with affiliation to collective entities that we call sets, groups, or social circles as the case may be. We do not intend to enter here into a debate on collective entities in the social world. In what follows, we will be taking into consideration only those groups of which individuals are able to recognize themselves as members. We use the term "social circle" to denote these groups. The individuals belonging to a social circle are aware of being part of that circle and can recognize those who are also part of it and those who are not. This excludes lists of individuals drawn up without this being brought to their attention, for example, on some websites. Social circles have boundaries, however fluid and shifting they may be, an inside and an outside, forms of collective identification (the fact that members can say "we") and a designation. Its members share certain resources that define the circle relative to what is external to it: being a member of a family, a group, an organization, or a nation is to have a certain number of duties toward the other members and a right to the resources shared within the circle. Some of these resources define the parameters for the exchanges between members, their rights and obligations, as well as the way in which they are supposed to exercise them. These are mediation resources. They are the formal or informal rules, the stories about the circle, which, woven together, form a sort of collective narrative, as well as the tangible coordination mechanisms (internal means of communication, for example). This definition is a very broad one. Circles can be very small (pairs of friends) or very large (a nation); they may be very loosely organized (a group of friends) or highly structured (a company); they may last a long time (a church) or be short-lived (the people involved in a protest movement, for example). Logically, there is no reason why a relationship, which is a dyad or pair of individuals who have a sustained relationship for a certain period of time, cannot be regarded as constituting a particular kind of circle. Nevertheless, there is a fundamental difference between a circle

---

[17] G. H. Mead, *Mind, Self, and Society*, ed. Charles W. Morris (Chicago: The University of Chicago Press, 1934).

comprising two individuals and a circle consisting of any number of people. In the first case, if one of the individuals withdraws from the circle or disappears, then the circle disappears at the same time, whereas a circle with more members can survive perfectly well if one of its members leaves, even though the departure will change it.

Circles can be differentiated from each other by the way in which they are likely to influence the formation of relationships among their members. First of all, there are those circles in which membership is generally "inherited," such as families, clans, nations, and neighborhoods. Then there are "utilitarian" circles that are based on pursuit of an objective outside the circle itself, for example, companies or associations that have a specific goal. In this case, it is the objective being pursued (production, game, etc.) that leads the individuals to become members of the circle. To this category will be assigned all cases in which individuals become aware of having a common interest and come together in order to defend or promote it. Finally, there are "identification" circles, whose objective is based on an idea (religions, philosophical circles, and groups of supporters or "fans" can all be put into this category). In this case, the objective of participation seems to be the participation itself. From this point of view, even regulars in a bar can constitute a social circle. This last distinction is interesting, since the cohesion between the members of a circle of the second type (utilitarian circle) is not the same as the cohesion that exists between the members of a circle of the third type (identification circle). A relationship that is linked primarily to the existence of an external objective, such as a relationship between colleagues, can be closely dependent on their company's ups and downs. It will not necessarily survive if the company goes bankrupt or if one of the members leaves the company. On the other hand, a relationship based largely on participation for its own sake will more readily find an autonomous motive for its continued existence. There are of course intermediate cases, that is, circles that have an objective and that also inspire identification from their members. Cases in which individuals who were not in any way predestined to find themselves brought together but who share one or more experience and consequently learn things about each other will be assigned to a fourth type of circle. Participants on an organized trip, prisoners of war, hostages, spectators at a sporting event or opera, passengers on a long airplane flight, people living in a new residential development, etc. might be included in this category. They are brought together more or less by chance, but they have certain issues to deal with together (getting to tourist sites, surviving, sharing a festive atmosphere, etc.), they share experiences, observe each

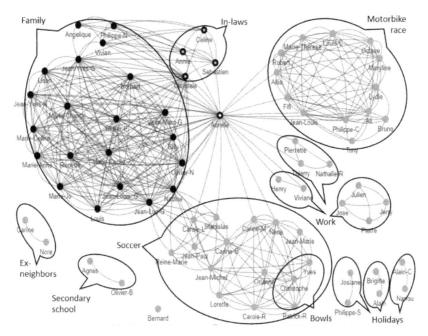

Fig. 1.1 The network of Joseph in the Caen panel (wave 4)

other, exchange views, and learn about each other. It is a context in which relationships can be forged and maintained even after the initial experience.

Let us give a more concrete example based on our data. Figure 1.1 depicts the members of the network that had developed around Joseph, one of the young people in the Caen panel, in the fourth wave of the survey. Joseph himself does not appear on it, since it is his network and he is by definition linked to all his friends. The lines represent the relationships between the people with whom Joseph keeps company. We have plotted the social circles in which these individuals participate with Joseph. Of course, some of these social circles extend beyond the people with whom Joseph spends time: many more people work in his company, for example, but the only people who appear here are those he knows in each of the different contexts. In some cases, the context has disappeared but Joseph maintains contact with some of the people he knew in those contexts, such as his ex-neighbors and people he met on holidays.

The first thing to note is the large family circle, supplemented by his partner's family (in-laws). Aurélie, Joseph's partner, occupies a rather particular position in that she is connected to almost all the circles except for the ones consisting of Joseph's school friends, ex-neighbors, holiday acquaintances, and one of the three circles linked to Joseph's work.

The family and neighbor circles belong to the first type of circle: Joseph did not choose them; they were given to him. The work-related circles are based on pursuit of an external objective. The soccer and bowls (*petanque*) circles (the latter game involves just some of his soccer buddies) also exist to fulfill an objective (playing sports or games), but the fact that they include friends who are not, strictly speaking, players (the girls, in particular) indicates that they also exist for purely social reasons. With those whom he calls his "soccer gang," Joseph does not just play soccer but also maintains friendly relations for their own sake (the pleasure of meeting up, having dinner together, etc.). Thus, these circles combine the two types of motive. Finally, other circles are based on shared experiences, including vacations and the motorcycle endurance race, where Joseph has met friends. Thus, most of the relationships unfold within circles, at least for a time, and are characterized by the roles assigned in that context. The roles vary in significance, depending on the circle in question. In the family, they are strongly defined and the linkage between circle and relationship is very strong. In a company, they are moderately well defined while among a bunch of friends they may be implicit and more flexible, but in many cases, they do exist nevertheless. Relationships may remain very closely linked to these circles, but they can also become independent of them, disconnecting themselves more from the circle as they develop their own "rules of relevancy."[18]

Relationships constitute a relevant entity since they exist to some extent beyond circles. Even a highly specialized relationship, defined by a particular circle, can become an interpersonal relationship when the protagonists begin to move away from the roles assigned to them by their position in the circle and to add other interactions to them and become partially non-substitutable for each other. From one point of view, a relationship constitutes a departure from a role. As it develops, a relation comes in tension with the circle or circles in which it was originally located and finds its own dynamic, one that is separate from the circle's. In order to explain this tension, we can use the notions of embeddedness and decoupling. Drawing on the work of Harrison White,[19] albeit with a few

---

[18] G. Allan, *A Sociology of Friendship and Kinship* (London: G. Allen & Unwin, 1979).

[19] H. C. White, *Identity and Control: How Social Formations Emerge* (Princeton: Princeton University Press, 2008).

modifications,[20] we will use the term "embeddedness" to denote the dependence of one social formation (in this case an interpersonal relationship) on another (in this case a circle) and "decoupling" to denote the reciprocal dynamic tending toward autonomy. By extension, we will use the same terms to denote the processes leading to increased dependency and autonomy. A relation becomes autonomous when it becomes uncoupled from the circles in which it first developed, that is when it is no longer reducible to them.

Forms of Regulation

Everyone is accustomed to having exchanges with people in various contexts that seem to arise "naturally." If somebody stops a person in the street in order to ask his way, he is going to obey certain rules of politeness that mean the person will not run away but will agree to listen to him. If somebody makes inquiries of a shopkeeper or craftsperson, here too there will be a sort of trust arising from the fact that this person is well established, which in turn means that the potential customer quite naturally expects a good quality of service and that the tradesperson knows he will be fairly remunerated for his work. If somebody is a member of a sports club, the other members will expect him to behave in accordance with the club rules. Finally, with his partner, his family, and his friends, mutual knowledge has been acquired and over time habits have become established that enable them to understand each other without having to spell things out, thereby facilitating exchanges. All this seems so self-evident that one is no longer aware that these are in fact forms of relationship regulation, whether they be universal, instituted, or acquired over the course of time within a restricted circle. If these forms of regulation did not exist, all interactions would require prior negotiation of the conditions under which they were to proceed. To borrow the terminology used by economists, this would give rise to considerable transaction costs. This is why all societies have developed and institutionalized relational roles and conventions that are universally recognized and ensure that interactions are always accompanied by a certain degree of trust, without which it would be necessary to renegotiate the conditions of each exchange afresh.

---

[20] M. Grossetti, *Sociologie de l'imprévisible. Dynamiques de l'activité et des formes sociales* (Paris: Presses Universitaires de France, 2004).

The notion of trust is a very complex one and may give rise to typologies of varying degrees of sophistication. Some authors, for example, make a distinction between voluntary trust (which results from a reflexive choice, a calculation) and assured trust (which is taken for granted in a given context),[21] or even the trust that results from an institution or a contract, from collective pressure, or from experience of another person's reliability. This trust is constructed over time and evolves in the course of learning processes and reconstitutions that make it a dynamic process. For Georg Simmel,[22] trust is midway between knowledge and ignorance of a person. While it is true that trust leads to a reduction in uncertainty about other people, it is not limited to experience, since it also makes it possible to anticipate what will happen, thereby making experience unnecessary. After all, the trust one grants extends commitment beyond mere extrapolation from experience by attenuating uncertainties about others.

Thus, trust is based on a variety of factors; some are highly institutional, collective, and structural, others more dyadic, constructed out of the history of the interactions between the two parties. Our first type includes everything relating to the knowledge shared by all members of an entire society, such as language, the rules of politeness, customs, etc. They are generally acquired through socialization and prove to be fairly stable and shared, so that individuals can "count on them." This same type also includes all the material and legal arrangements that contribute to the organization of life in society and provide support for people in their daily lives. If a person starts to behave aggressively, one can remind him of the rules of politeness and also threaten to take him to court. Similarly, doctor-patient relations are not based solely on social roles but are also shaped by legislation (with which doctors must comply) and various mechanisms, procedures, and arrangements (the doctor's office and its instruments, the medical association, internet health forums, etc.). Here, the institutional arrangements serve to mediate trust. We also include in this type instituted social roles, which, in the interactions that bring them into play, constitute a way of creating the trust that makes a specific interaction possible. Adoption of a role (shopkeeper, doctor, teacher, expert) defines the conditions under which an interaction takes place. Kinship is also governed by rules and a more or less implicit hierarchy. At the same time, a role to some

---

[21] N. Luhmann, *Trust and Power* (Chichester: Wiley, 1979); S. N. Eisenstadt, L. Roniger, *Patrons, Clients and Friends: Interpersonal Relations and the Structure of Trust in Society* (Cambridge: Cambridge University Press, 1984).

[22] G. Simmel, *The Philosophy of Money* (London: Routledge, 1990 [1900]).

extent fixes the conditions under which an interaction takes place and inhibits the development of forms of exchange other than those prescribed by the role. It is difficult, for example, for a pupil to become friends with a teacher or a patient with a doctor. Here, trust is linked to the legitimacy and complementarity of the roles. We also assign to this category the trust established through participation in a circle in which the rules and customs of the larger circles of which it is a part are recognized but where habits and rules specific to the smaller circle may also develop. This can be easily illustrated by observing, for example, how a religious circle, a family, or even a group of young people functions. These "cradles of trust" are based on shared membership in circles of varying size and type, of which they constitute the concrete, palpable part that is "within arm's reach."

A second type of trust arises more directly from the effects of the network itself. For example, a person might trust someone because he or she is a close relation of somebody they trust or on whom they can exert pressure. Here, trust is linked to the structural effects of interrelationships.

The third type is based on knowledge acquired through similarities or shared experiences that are not confined to role performance. This is more intimate, "dyadic" knowledge that is difficult to transmit. If the other person seems to be one of our own kind or if we have personally experienced their qualities, then we bestow on them a trust that is associated only with the two of us, with what we have both accumulated over time. It is often this kind of knowledge that is emphasized when we talk of relationships, but it would be harmful to neglect the other kinds.

These types are not exclusive but exist in a state of tension with each other. On the face of it, all relationships draw to varying degrees on these different forms of trust. The trust between parents and children, for example, is rooted both in references to established roles and in shared experiences. Conversely, even in the case of a very loving couple, their relationship cannot be reduced to love alone, since it is impossible to ignore the fact that, in most cases, one of the two partners belongs to the woman's circle and the other to the man's circle and that the roles associated with these circles will necessarily "catch up" with them at some point.[23] Romantic relationships are also shaped by all the collective references to romantic love that have accumulated since the nineteenth century.

---

[23] E. Bott, *Family and Social Network: Roles, Norms and External Relationships in Ordinary Urban Families* (New York: Free Press, 1971 [1957]).

The same applies to friendship.[24] Thus, even in an interpersonal relationship, trust cannot be reduced to its strictly dyadic dimension but is generally also influenced by institutional, structural, and cultural factors. Even a relationship such as friendship is at least to some extent "embedded" in social expectations, in links with other relationships in the network, in cultural representations of what friends owe each other, and so on.[25]

Thus, all relationships are shaped to some degree by points of reference that are more or less general and fixed and which subject them to the influence of systems of regulation. Even if we are inclined to believe that a relationship is absolutely unique, it is not totally improvised or wholly devoid of context or reference points. Even in the case of friendly relationships in which the two parties concerned are not accountable to anyone (unlike a romantic relationship, which very quickly comes up against the social frame of reference), their limits, conditions, and expectations are defined by (usually implicit) "rules of relevance."[26] Thus, different types of relationships come within the orbits of different systems of regulation. We will adopt, with a few minor modifications, the typology of forms of relationship regulation developed by Alexis Ferrand.[27] In Figure 1.2, each vertex of the triangle acts as a hub representing one of the systems of relationship regulation. The closer the relationship is to one of the vertices, the more important this type of regulation is.

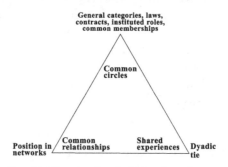

Fig. 1.2 The triangle of relational regulations

[24] A. Vincent-Buffault, *L'exercice de l'amitié. Pour une histoire des pratiques amicales aux XVIIIe et XIXe siècles* (Paris: Seuil, 1995).

[25] R. Paine, "Anthropological Approaches to Friendship," *Journal of the Institute of Man* 1 (1970), 139–159; A. Silver, "Friendship and Trust As Moral Ideals: An Historical Approach," *Archives Européennes de Sociologie* 30 (1989), 274–297.

[26] Allan, *A Sociology of Friendship and Kinship*.

[27] A. Ferrand, *Confidents. Une analyse structurale de réseaux sociaux* (L'Harmattan, 2007).

Membership of circles common to both partners in the relationship (top vertex) means it is possible to rely on categories, laws, or regulations and established roles that are specific to these circles, which may be very wide (institutions, a nation, a linguistic or cultural area, etc.) or much narrower (an association or the nuclear family, for example). Roles and formal rules, together with all the mechanisms, procedures, and arrangements associated with them, more or less determine the nature of the interaction, depending on each case. Sometimes legislation even dictates certain aspects of it. For certain roles, some of the interactions are fairly strictly determined by collective procedures and arrangements (parent-child, doctor-patient, etc.). For others, the rules or norms are simply a resource or constraint, a kind of support for the relationship (sports partner, leisure club, internet forum, etc.). The relational roles encompass those elements of the interactions determined by these established regulations. In the parent-child relationship, for example, the relational role defines the assistance one owes the other, but the interactions and content of the relationship generally go well beyond that. The resources associated with relational roles can be drawn on in various coordination processes. If the term "mediation" is used to denote all the processes during which individuals "accommodate themselves" to others, then the term "mediation resources" can be used to denote everything that makes circles a tangible presence in everyday life.[28] The first major type of trust described above equates to this type of regulation.

An individual's position in social networks (left-hand vertex) gives rise to specific constraints and resources associated with the shared relationships (members of one's partner's family whom one is obliged to see because they are part of one's partner's close relationships, for example) or, more broadly, with the overall structure of these networks (an intermediary through whom one can get in touch with people who are important to us). This equates to the second type of trust.

Finally, situated at the right-hand vertex is what is specific to the two parties involved in the relationship and their shared history, what might be called the strictly dyadic dimension of the tie. To take up once again the notion of mediation resources, we might say that these are "dyadic" resources, that is, they are of value only to the two people

---

[28] M. Grossetti, "Réseaux sociaux et ressources de médiation," in V. Liquette (ed.) *Médiations*, Les essentiels d'Hermès (Paris: CNRS éditions, 2010), pp. 103–120.

in the relationship. This is the basis for the third type of trust described above.

It is true that if a relationship is made up of exchanges whose modalities are dictated entirely by common membership of a religion, for example (the parties meet at services and in prayer groups, but the communication stops there) or a company (they work in the same department and the exchanges are confined to work-related matters), then the history of the relationship will be of little relevance. Similarly, if a relationship between a shopkeeper and a client or between a doctor and patient has no object other than the professional relationship, then the relationship will not develop very far and its history will be of little interest for a study such as ours. However, not all relationships are "pure," in the sense of being assigned to one or other of these types. Many relationships are shaped by a role and a history, or by a history and a contractual framework. Moreover, a relationship will develop according to this pattern: If each of the different interactions that constitute a relationship were to be represented by a point in the triangle, then they would form a trajectory that would move nearer to one or other of the vertices of the triangle at varying stages of the relationships. A relationship between two colleagues, for example, will begin near the top vertex, since the exchanges will be dictated by the requirements of their work. Gradually, their shared experiences will accumulate and their knowledge about each other will become more important than the professional environment in establishing the trust that links them. After a certain time, they may become true friends and the fact that they work together will become one opportunity for exchanges alongside many others. In this case, the relationship will move toward the right-hand vertex of the triangle. However, it is also possible that, after a period during which friendly relations developed, they will fall out over work-related issues or find themselves competing with each other for promotion and consequently revert to purely professional exchanges and stop seeing each other outside of work. Nevertheless, they can remain an important part of each other's professional network.

*

*   *

Thus, relationships are forged in contexts that influence their history, qualities, intensity, motivations, and the similarities between the partners. Sooner or later, however, they may start to exist independently of these original contexts, moving away from the social role and drawing closer to the network-regulated hub or to the one more focused on interpersonal relationships.

If we try to synthetize now what constitute relationships, one may imagine a meeting in the street: two friends (let's call them James and Luke) are out for a walk together, and they run into another person (let's call him Mark). James knows Mark, and he tries to explain his relationship to Luke after a while. We imagine this dialogue:

LUKE: "Who was that?"
JAMES: "He's a buddy of mine . . . a good guy. He's doing a computer course. I met him on a course a few years ago. And then I lost touch with him when I left Paris. When I came back, I met up with him again at the golf club. My wife also helped his daughter, who was having problems with math. We mainly see each other for a game of golf, but sometimes we invite them over to our place. I also call him when I'm having problems with my computer."

This very commonplace little dialogue already contains many of the aspects of social relations that were examined in this chapter. Firstly, their attitudes and words differ from the generic codes on which people rely when interacting with someone they do not know. For example, they call each other by their first names (which they therefore knew already) and their exchanges revolve around a plan to "meet up" that they both seem to take for granted. James then fills in the backstory by giving details of the times and situations he has shared with Mark. A relationship always has a story attached to it. James and Mark got to know each other through an institutional framework, namely the circle formed by the course they were attending, where the interactions between them were regulated by the complementarity of their roles (trainer-learner in computing). When this contextual framework disappeared at the end of the course, their relationship came to an end. They might never have seen each other again, even though James says they had hit it off. Moreover, this is what must have happened with most of the other course participants. It was pure chance that James returned to Paris and that they met again at the same golf club. Chance is important. Here it brought James and Mark together before they had to take the initiative and make other arrangements to meet up.

However, let us suppose that Mark, or James, has a back problem and can no longer play golf. Will they continue to see each other? In other words, has their relationship become sufficiently independent of the circumstances that have so far kept it up to date so that it remains alive and is more than just a relationship based on memory? If golf no longer provides the main opportunities for them to meet up, perhaps mutual assistance, whether with gardening or computer problems, will take over. Or maybe the mere pleasure of being together will be enough to inspire them to meet up. Clearly a relationship is caught up in the interplay between the contexts in which it is constantly being renewed and on which it depends. It is not until it begins to exist independently of those contexts and is able to survive outside of them that it becomes primarily an interpersonal attachment.

However, they met again in a different shared context, the golf club, which is a more flexible circle in which they play on equal terms and their relationship is based more on similarity than complementarity. Their knowledge of each other and the recognition they accord each other were changed as a result. The relationship became more multiplex. A network effect came into play when James's wife started to help Mark's daughter with her math. As a result, the relationship was now positioned more toward the relational vertex of the triangle. The commitment started to be shared and it was two families that were now associated. Invitations to each other's home are an indication of this development. However, the dyadic dimension also becomes apparent in James's affective description of the relationship, when he declares to Luke that Mark is now "a very good buddy." Thus, we are illustrating here the stages through which a relationship emerges and becomes established. By going beyond the interactions strictly prescribed by the individuals' roles, leaving the initial context of the meeting, accumulating experiences and forging a history, increasing their knowledge of each other, and constructing a form of trust that goes beyond this knowledge and reduces uncertainty, a relationship becomes decoupled from its various contexts. Its qualities (intensity, multiplexity, homogeneity, functionality, etc.) will be intrinsically linked to these processes and this is why we place relational dynamics at the heart of this book.

2

Analyzing Networks

The social world could be described simply in terms of relationships and the groups of which many are a part. Many sociologists adopted this approach in the past or are still doing so today. However, to do so is to ignore a very important social structure, one that cannot be reduced to the form of a group but results from the interconnecting of relationships. Relationships, as we have seen, are not always connected to groups: they may have first developed in the course of group activities but then become independent of those activities and are maintained even when the group ceases to exist. However, even when relationships remain strongly "embedded" in groups, once interconnected, they cross boundaries; there are so many groups of such varied sizes that their boundaries intertwine in all directions. John knows a member of his family who knows one of his colleagues who knows a political activist. This constitutes a chain that is not closed in upon itself (John does not know the political activist) but may serve as a channel for the transmission of certain resources, whether they be "cognitive" (information, value judgments, or theories, for example) or more material (money, objects of various kinds). This chain of relationships is very different from a group: it has no boundaries, no resources shared by all its members, no specific rules, and no means of group identification. The individuals who are "connected" to each other by the network are generally not aware of being linked in this way. Even the individuals who responded to our questions in order to construct their own personal networks were surprised at the end of the interview: they had never considered their own personal networks, but became more aware of the groups to which they belonged in the course of the interview. This simple form (a system of relationships), which may be highly complex in its structures and prove to be of crucial importance in many social situations, is what we call a social network.

In most studies in social network analysis, the entities interconnected with each other in a social network are people or organizations. We will be focusing here on networks made up of people, and more particularly, on the relationships centered on one individual, what are known generally as personal networks. Thus, we are leaving aside the large-scale network approaches that seek, by experimental means, to assess the number of intermediaries one has to go through in order to reach a target and hence to demonstrate that we are living in a "small world."[1] Nor will we be examining "complete" networks, which map the whole of the interconnections between the members of a finite, delimited, tightly defined group, such as a school class, a sports club, or a corporation.[2] These studies are very interesting but fall outside our subject, which is the dynamic of personal networks.

The Caen and Toulouse surveys that constitute the main basis for the analyses presented in this book are studies of personal networks. In such surveys – using standard criteria for representativeness or other, more specific ones – a sample of individuals is put together who are not necessarily connected with each other (it may even be preferable for them not to be connected so that their respective networks do not overlap); a personal network is then reconstituted around each of the individuals selected. Obviously, in light of what we saw in Chapter 1 regarding the variable intensity of relationships, a minimum degree of intensity needs to be selected; it should not be too low (merely knowing a person's name, for example), since that would cause the number of connections to be investigated to proliferate and give an insufficiently precise picture of individuals' relational environments and social integration.

Investigation of personal networks based on sociability and interpersonal relations (who one goes out with, who one speaks to, relationships that thrive on mutual assistance, etc.) produces robust results that can be easily linked to more standard analyses of social inequalities or forms of solidarity. After all, an individual's personal network bears the traces of the worlds he has traversed and in which he met the people who constitute his network – those who "bear witness," as it were, to his history. It includes his parents, childhood friends, and sometimes a relationship kept alive

---

[1] See, for example, S. Milgram, "The Small World Problem," *Psychology Today* 1 (1967), 61–67; D. J. Watts, S. H. Strogatz, "Collective Dynamics of 'Small-World' Networks," *Nature* 393(1) (1998), 440–442.

[2] See, for example, E. Lazega, *The Collegial Phenomenon: The Social Mechanisms of Cooperation among Peers in a Corporate Law Partnership* (Oxford: Oxford University Press, 2001).

from a far-off holiday camp or journey, to which have been added, more recently, work colleagues, spouse's friends, leisure time partners, etc. These still-active links reflect the various environments in which the individual has moved and in which he has constructed these relationships. Moreover, each relationship also opens up its own "little world," a segment of society to which it gives access. Each new friend introduces new contexts, social circles, and knowledge and also brings with him different partners and different knowledge. As an individual builds up his network of relationships, he begins to move in more or less diversified social spaces. Moreover, it is by meeting and interacting with others that an individual begins to perceive social distinctions, learns where to locate himself within them, how to draw close or distance himself from certain people, and how to negotiate his place in society. Thus, this dynamic is part of an individual's socialization processes, since it helps to construct his mode of social integration and forms his "social base." The study of personal networks, their distribution, temporal strata, diversity, and degrees of interconnection helps us to construct a sort of dynamic social cartography of the ways in which individuals move through and settle in social worlds. In order to better understand the particular characteristics of personal network analysis, a few examples will be briefly explored below.

FORMS OF PERSONAL NETWORKS

Networks are not merely shapeless collections of relationships. They show a certain degree of regularity in both size and composition. They also have a structure, which may vary in density and degree of segmentation or cohesiveness. This structure, which is partly linked to the social circles but cannot be reduced to them, has specific effects beyond the relationships that make up the network. In order to describe this structure, let us take the example of Etienne who, when we meet him for the first time, is studying for his vocational baccalaureate and living with his parents but getting ready to leave them to live with his girlfriend Christelle.

Beyond a simple list of Etienne's relationships, interesting additional information is provided by displaying who knows each other among the people connected to Etienne. It is no longer necessary, then, to include Etienne in the graph; in fact, for clarity's sake, it is actually desirable to remove him, since by definition he is linked to all his own network's members. The links between the people mentioned by Etienne can then be displayed. As mentioned in the presentation of the sources in the

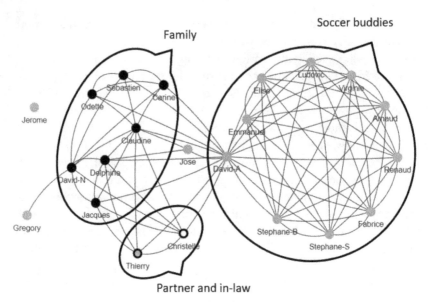

Fig. 2.1 The network of Etienne in the Caen panel (wave 1)

Introduction, only strong ties (i.e., multiplex ties and ties declared as important for Ego) are used in drawing this network.[3]

The first people to be identified in Figure 2.1 are Etienne's family, represented with black circles. The core of his family is made up of his mother Claudine, his father Jacques and his sister Delphine. It can be seen that his mother spends more time with the other members of the family than his father, which is often the case. His cousin David-N goes to the same high school as Etienne and thus spends time with Etienne and his friend Gregory. José is his sister's boyfriend. The central position occupied by his friend David-A is also worthy of note. He is the only person who links up with Etienne's family. He is an old school friend; as a child he used to go to Etienne's house and therefore knows all his family. He plays soccer and is thus part of the large group of "soccer buddies" – all the boys who play soccer together while the girls "just watch," according to Etienne. These soccer buddies are also school friends, thus combining the two contexts. Christelle is Etienne's girlfriend, what we call his partner;[4] he has introduced her, and her brother Thierry, to the important members of

---

[3] This decision was only a matter of saving time during the (already very long) interviews.

[4] We use this term to denote romantic relationships which, depending on the case (and age), may refer to a boyfriend or girlfriend, a spouse, a lover, a fiancé, etc.

his own family. Jérôme is an old friend from junior high school; he does not mix with the others and Etienne sees him by himself. Gregory is a friend from primary school with whom he met up again in senior high school; apart from Etienne, he is in touch only with his cousin David-A. This description highlights the structure of the system by providing us with additional information that enables us to go beyond the simple list of people in the network. In particular, it shows us the degree of cohesion within the network and the particular position occupied by certain more central individuals who act as links between different groups, such as David-N, or those, like Jérôme, who are not part of a group but just form a dyad with Ego. The distinctive role played in the development of this structure by the duration of each tie and by shared activities should also be noted.

SIZE AND COMPOSITION OF PERSONAL NETWORKS

As we saw in Chapter 1, the size of a personal network can vary from just a few units to several thousand, depending on the threshold selected for inclusion of a relationship. Thus, there is no intrinsic size for networks. Both of the surveys used in this book are located at the level of what we have called current ties – that is, those that constitute a person's social environment, the relationships with people the respondents know and with whom they talk "a little more" in the various contexts of their lives (Caen survey), or those with whom they have certain types of exchanges (Toulouse survey). The average size of personal networks in the Toulouse survey was 27 (range from 3 to 141). In the Caen survey, the average was 37.6. The largest network in the Caen survey is that of Agnès in the second wave, with a total of 131 relationships, while the smallest is Sonia's in the fourth wave, which consisted of just 6 relationships. Vast, diversified networks that extend into various spheres of the social world make resources, knowledge, and emotional support available on a much larger scale than do more restricted networks centered around a single social sphere. For example, if we compare the networks of Agnès and Sonia (Figure 2.2), it is not difficult to imagine the differences in lifestyle, sociability, and diversity of their social environments.

Agnès is the daughter of a bank executive and a hospital manager. At the time of the fourth wave of the survey, she is working in sales for a clothing company in Saint Malo in Brittany, having previously been an advertising manager near Paris. Her work and the fact of having moved around have not prevented her from maintaining a very extensive network. Her partner

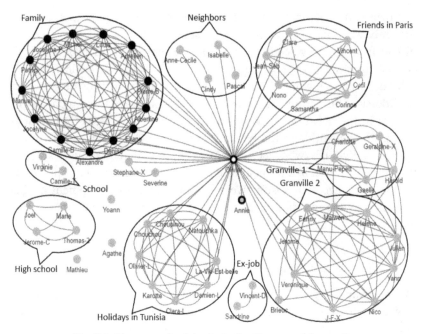

Fig. 2.2 The network of Agnès in the Caen panel (wave 4)

Olivier occupies a central position in it. He connects Agnès's large family clique and his own mother, Annie (his stepfather is not very important to Agnès so he does not appear in the network of her strong ties). Olivier is also connected to several groups of Agnès's friends: the "Paris" group on the bottom right-hand side of the graph, which includes Vincent, Corinne, Clara, Nono, etc.; the two "Granville"[5] groups above, one including Harold, Gaëlle, Géraldine, etc., and the other with Hélène, Nico, Brieuc, etc., with Maïwen, Hélène, and Yann connecting both groups; the "Tunisia" group whom she met on a trip, with Chouchou, Karotte, Natouchka, etc. (the importance of nicknames for some young people is evident here); and the "neighbors" group, with Anne-Cécile, Cindy, Isabelle, and Pascal. Thus, Olivier is very much a part of these relational groups, which he shares with Agnès. On the other hand, he does not see other friends she has kept up with from the past: Camille and Virginie, whom she met in primary school; Agathe, Mathieu, and Yoann, whom she

---

[5] Granville is a small town on the Normandy coast, where Agnès lived and now spends holidays.

knew in high school but now sees separately; another group from her senior year at high school, Thomas, Jérôme, Joël, and Marie; as well as Vincent and Sandrine, friends from a previous job. Thus, the circles from Agnès's past are somewhat more remote; she sees those friends separately, whereas the more recent circles are shared with Olivier. Agnès's social interactions are very diversified; they are both firmly rooted, enabling her to maintain relationships first developed during her schooldays, and sufficiently adaptable for her to forge important relationships during a trip abroad, weekends in Granville, and her time in Paris. These social interactions are rich, partly resistant to changes in her life, and they enable her both to maintain very long-established ties and make new ones very quickly. In all these respects her network is typical of the higher social categories.

The network of Sonia, the daughter of commercial employees, presents a completely different picture (Figure 2.3). She takes part in several training programs for young unemployed people during the course of the survey, but she does not work. She is in receipt of welfare benefits, some of which she gives to her mother, whose resources are diminishing. Her network is limited to her mother, with whom she lives; Dominique, a female friend of her mother; Solange, her former child minder; and a neighboring family, who are also older. Sonia has not kept up with any school friends or people she met in her training programs, she has lost touch with other friends of her mother after a row, and has not had any romantic relationships. Even her family ties have slackened, which she attributes to her father (he was violent and committed suicide after a protracted and bitter divorce) and

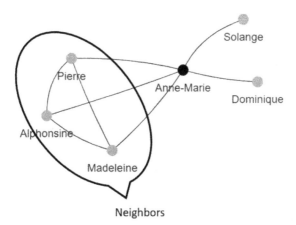

Fig. 2.3 The network of Sonia in the Caen panel (wave 4)

the idea that she and her mother are seen as "less than nothing" by their family. The precariousness of Sonia's resources is not difficult to imagine, particularly as her process of disaffiliation would likely continue if her mother were to die or fall out with her. The contrast between these two networks illustrates the social gap between Sonia and Agnès. The number and, above all, the diversity of relationships are important factors in the constitution, extent, and solidity of the social resources available to an individual through his or her network.

As might be expected, the size of networks varies according to the social characteristics of those surveyed. In the Toulouse survey, those in managerial positions listed more names than manual or clerical workers (about twenty-three compared with nineteen in response to the name generators), as did those who had remained in school until at least the baccalaureate compared with those who had left school earlier (thirty and eighteen respectively). Thus, the number of relationships acts as a sort of resource and is correlated with the other indicators of resources, such as level of education and occupational category. This question will be examined in detail in Chapter 11.

Once the size of a network has been analyzed, the logical next step is to analyze the list of relationships that constitute it. There are a number of possibilities. The composition of a network can be analyzed in terms of activities, frequency of contacts, contexts in which meetings take place, mode of contact, relational intensity, closeness, etc. Two standard approaches are outlined here: distribution by roles and distribution by exchanges. The categories linked to the standard relational roles (family, neighbors, colleagues, etc.) are seldom satisfactory but they are well understood by respondents and serve as an initial filter for relationships that might produce some interesting results. In the Toulouse survey, we asked the respondents to classify their relationships by suggesting categories similar to those that had been used in the American survey that was the model for the French survey and which served as the basis for a comparison (Table 2.1). The distributions obtained are fairly similar.

In order to shed more light on these trends, it is useful to give separate consideration to the lists produced by the different name generators, which, as we have seen, are constructed for the most part on the basis of various types of exchange (giving advice, lending money, etc.). Examination of the number of names produced by each generator shows, first, that for each category a fairly high share of respondents mention no names at all. The cases range from 14 percent mentioning no name for discussions of personal problems to 49 percent for help with household tasks.

Table 2.1 *Classification of the relationships cited (%)*

Classification	Toulouse survey (2001)	San Francisco survey (1982)[a]
Family	40[b]	42
Colleagues	8	10
Neighbors	4	10
Community associations	5	6
Friends	28	23
Others	15	6

[a] C. S. Fischer, *To Dwell among Friends: Personal Networks in Town and City* (Chicago: The University of Chicago Press, 1982), 41.
[b] In both cases, families account for around two-fifths of all relationships. For example, in the Toulouse survey, 40 percent of all relationships on average were family-based.

Thus, not all types of support are available to everyone. Only the questions on leisure time, outings, or trips almost always generate some names (6 percent mention no name for leisure activities and 0 percent for outings). Some generators produce many names (18.5 names on average for outings, 5 for discussions about work, and 6 for leisure activities), whereas others produce significantly fewer (1.5 for help with accommodation and 1.8 for advice on important decisions). Thus, the total number of names mentioned in these networks depends more on the most "productive" generators than on the others. Thus, the above-mentioned correlations between the total number of relationships cited and indicators such as occupation or educational level result from just some of the name generators. The one on outings, which produces many more names than the others, is highly discriminating.

Thus, the most productive name generators (outings, discussion of work, and leisure activities) are those that reveal the greatest differences between educational levels. Other tendencies are more specific. For example, the fact that women mention more people with whom they are able to discuss personal problems is unconnected with the other social characteristics. Finally, some generators produce lists whose size decreases with interviewees' age. This applies to questions on leisure activities, personal problems, and requests for advice on important decisions. In the case of leisure activities, it is the respondents under age twenty-five, in particular, who mention a lot of names. These results give us an idea of the relationships corresponding to the names mentioned in the Toulouse survey. There is a mixture of "strong" ties (which are to be found particularly among the people they ask for advice on important decisions, those they ask for loans, and those with whom they discuss personal problems) and "weak" ties (which are more numerous among those with whom interviewees go out for a meal or to the cinema, those they ask to take in their post when they are away, those with whom they talk about leisure activities, etc., but without being strongly involved with them).

INDICES TO DESCRIBE NETWORK STRUCTURE

The forms of network characterization outlined above could be applied to a simple list of relationships. In order to make full use of the notion of network, however, we have to go beyond mere lists and analyze the structure formed by the interconnected relationships. After all, a network is more than a mere list of names or collection of relationships. It forms a system, in the sense that these connections interact with each other, have reciprocal effects on each other, and are organized in a way that is not neutral but affects each of the constituent relationships. It is important, therefore, to extend its representation to the links that exist between members of the network: do the people one knows also know each other? The interconnections that make a person's relational environment more or less dense – the gaps between parts of the network, the bridges that link them, the centrality of certain ties, all the elements of a network's overall organization – have their own effects on each relationship and on the network's general qualities. The forms taken by its structures influence the modes of socialization. A network organized around a single sphere, such as a professional milieu or a village, for example, is relatively homogeneous and strongly interconnected. As a result, it is firmly rooted in that particular social world; its integration into its local environment is very strong but confined to that environment. When individuals move away, they may very well find themselves deprived of resources. A heterogeneous, dispersed network, conversely, constructed over the life course of an individual who has moved and changed jobs frequently, will be made up of a number of different ties, each one separate from the other. The individual in question is less well integrated into a milieu but is also less dependent on it. He is able to adapt more easily to moves, changes, and altered situations and may even allow himself to exploit the different facets of his identity. The shape of the social circles opened up by the network – whether they are concentrated and intertwined or, conversely, diversified and fragmented, whether or not they are interconnected – determines the variety and influence of the "little worlds" to which an individual has access and hence his modes of social integration. Thus, a social network is a structured form and the organization of this complex system has its own particular significance. Consequently, it is important to describe social networks using very precise methodologies and to eschew mere metaphorical approaches. These indicators are well known among social network analysts, but their application to personal networks is less familiar to those who specialize in complete networks, thus it may be useful to clarify them here.

A fairly simple structural parameter for networks is density, the standard indicator for which is the number of relationships observed compared with the number of possible relationships for a given set of individuals. In studies of personal networks like ours, density is estimated by asking interviewees to say, for each of the individuals they mention, whether, in their view, he or she knows the others. In the Toulouse survey, the estimated average density is 0.46. In the American survey it reproduces, the average was fairly similar (0.44). As in the American survey, density is slightly correlated with multiplexity and with the proportion of relationships described as close (strong ties). This numerical indicator can shed some very useful light on social situations. Density is, after all, a possible indicator of network fragmentation. Thus, in the survey by Fischer cited in the Foreword, the average density of personal networks is lower in urban than in rural environments. This may be explained by the fact that the groups of people with whom an individual comes into contact in the various contexts of urban life (neighborhood, work, leisure activities, etc.) are less interconnected than the groups found in rural environments. Network density decreases when population density in a person's social environment increases.

Network density is also linked to other factors, as Fischer himself noted. A network's composition, and, in particular, the share of family members in it, plays an important role. Not all members of a family may see each other regularly, but at least they know each other. Thus, a network of which a significant share consists of family members will be denser than a network made up largely of friends. Even though the young people in the Caen panel lived in the same town and were at the same stage in their lives, the survey brought to light networks of quite variable density. Names in this survey that were generated by social contexts and average density (0.28) were lower than in the Toulouse survey.[6] Similarly, engaging in

---

[6] It is not surprising that network density in the Toulouse survey is around 50 percent (which means that half of the possible connections between the Alters in the network are

group activities that involve a high level of relational cohesion, such as certain sports and cultural activities, encourages "group" relations and network density. Conversely, the fact of having recently moved means there will be "gaps" between groups of friends in one place and those in another, although some individuals may manage to bridge those gaps. As they enter adult life, with its differentiations and diverse patterns of activity, people are often led to separate their friends out according to the different social spheres they frequent, or even to see them in pairs without linking them all up. We will return to this point when we discuss the changes that take place in networks over the life course.

Centrality is a measure that makes a connection, as it were, between a network's structure and the position of each of its members. The simplest indicator – degree centrality – is the sum of the ties between one network member and the others. Thus, each Alter has his or her own centrality. A very central Alter will have many connections with other Alters, while a peripheral Alter will have few such connections or will even be isolated if he or she is not connected to another Alter (although it should be remembered of course that he/she is connected to Ego at least). Measuring centrality makes it possible to identify differentiated positions within a network and thus to detect some key individuals. There are, after all, networks whose high density is due to the fact that all the individuals in them are fairly central, with many connections with others, and there are other networks whose same high density is due to certain individuals whose centrality is extremely high (they keep company with all the other Alters) while others are isolated.

This initial measure is supplemented by other indicators of centrality. Closeness centrality is the inverse of the (shortest) distance that separates an Alter from all the other Alters in the network, whether directly or not. It is estimated by calculating the length of the paths separating two Alters, expressed in terms of the number of relationships (or "steps") between them. This measure indicates that the Alters are more or less likely to talk to each other directly, without any intermediary. Intermediarity or betweenness centrality indicates an Alter's ability to act as an intermediary for other Alters, to position himself on their path. Thus, an individual may

---

made), whereas it is significantly lower in the Caen survey. After all, the two surveys used different data-gathering procedures. In the Toulouse survey, interviewees were asked to indicate if there were links between five of the people mentioned. In the Caen survey, the question referred to all the strong links in the network as a whole. Thus, there were more links to be considered and the density between them was lower.

not be very central (in terms of degree) but constitute a sort of "obligatory crossing point" for two Alters seeking to communicate with each other. More complex analyses can also be carried out. For example, the centrality of those to whom an individual is connected can be taken into account: a person's prestige is greater if he is connected with individuals who themselves have a great deal of prestige. If he is connected to individuals who are themselves very central, then his "area of influence" is further extended by that of those close to him. These indicators and the methods used to calculate them are detailed in a number of books and articles.[7]

Other indicators are commonly used in network analysis. For example, counting the number of "triangles" (i.e., sets of three Alters) that have either zero or one, two, or three ties between them makes it possible to ascertain whether individuals who could be connected are indeed linked and, if so, to what extent. The share of triangles with three edges is an indicator of the transitivity of the ties. The number of isolated individuals (an Alter who is not connected to anyone) is important since it tells us whether a small or large number of Alters spend time on their own with Ego. The number of components indicates whether the network comprises several sub-networks, each one separate from the others and with no connection between them, or whether there is just one component and a path still exists between two Alters, however long it may be. There are also indicators that are less intuitive but which provide information on the network's structure. We will not discuss the reciprocity of relationships here. Generally, in studies of personal networks, only Ego is interviewed; consequently, Alter's perspective on the relationship is unknown to us. In our view, moreover, a relationship that has no element of reciprocity about it is not really a relationship.

A STRUCTURAL TYPOLOGY OF PERSONAL NETWORKS

We have developed a typology of networks based on the Caen panel. The starting point is resolutely structural. Our aim was to identify, firstly, networks with similar general structures (rather than comparing isolated indicators) in order subsequently to test the sociological relevance of these groupings. This approach is constructed inductively. Using the 287 networks identified in the course of the 4 waves of the Caen survey, we began by constructing classes of networks; only subsequently did we examine the

---

[7] L. C. Freeman, "Centrality in Social Networks Conceptual Clarification," *Social Networks* 1 (1978), 215–239; A. Degenne, M. Forsé, *Introducing Social Networks* (London: Sage, 1999).

Table 2.2 *Characteristics of four types of network*

Variable	Dense type	Centered type	Dissociated type	Composite type
Size	23.4–7.3[a]	18.9–24.8	26.3–31.3	16.3–19.5
Density	0.33–0.38	0.27–0.32	0.14–0.19	0.24–0.28
Closeness centrality	0.50–0.55	0.52–0.55	0.19–0.24	0.38–0.43
Betweenness centrality	0.19–0.24	0.50–0.57	0.08–0.14	0.17–0.26
No. of three-edged triangles	0.12–0.16	0.06–0.09	0.02–0.03	0.05–0.07
No. of components	1.18–1.39	1.04–1.34	2.13–2.68	1.40–1.75
No. of isolated individuals	0.06–0.10	0.03–0.05	0.22–0.31	0.10–0.16

[a] The two figures in each square represent the variable's 95 percent bounds for the estimation of the mean for a variable and the network type in question, that is, there is a 95 percent probability that the mean lies between these bounds (if the distribution is Gaussian).

sociological characteristics that the individual members of these networks had in common. A procedure of this kind undoubtedly lends greater force to the proof than a more deductive procedure that takes sociological categories as its starting point in order to test the structural differences associated with them.

To construct classes of networks, we used the following indicators: network size, density, median of the closeness centrality, betweenness centralization (ratio between variation in betweenness centrality and maximum variation in betweenness centrality for a network of this size), share of three-edged triangles, number of components, and number of isolated Alters. We then made a tree classification based upon distances between pairs of observations.[8] This enabled us to identify homogeneous cores and to gather the other networks around them to constitute classes.

This classification identifies four major, contrasting types that give a very clear picture of the main "ways of structuring" one's network that have emerged from this analysis. For the seven indicators, the table below gives the range of values equating to each of the four major types, which we have called the dense type, centered type, dissociated type and composite type (Table 2.2).

Even though some ranges may overlap, the various types are very clearly differentiated.

[8] We have normalized the indicators; distance is the square of the Euclidian distance and the algorithm is that used in Ward's method.

- In networks of the *dense type*, the density is very high and distributed among all the Alters. Networks of this type are more transitive.
- In the *centered type*, the connections are concentrated on one very central individual, while the others may be much more scattered. Above all, these networks have a greater degree of intermediarity or "betweenness."
- The *dissociated type* is the most clearly characterized: it comprises the networks that are largest in size and have the lowest values for density, centrality, betweenness, and transitivity and the largest number of components and isolated individuals.
- The *composite type* is characterized by a certain heterogeneity of structure, with various sub-groups. However, it is also very clearly differentiated from the others in terms of the indicators adopted here: it comprises the networks that are smallest in size and in second place for density, centrality, betweenness, and transitivity. It has many components and isolated individuals.

The centered and dense types are a little more mixed together. It is noteworthy that these 4 types are sufficient to classify the 287 networks satisfactorily. The dense type comprises 97 networks (34 percent of the total), the centered type 66 (23 percent), the dissociated type 63 (22 percent) and the composite type 61 (21 percent). Examples will show how these networks have become structured as such, along with life stories. Dense networks generally contain a large clique, that is, a group in which all the possible connections have been made, possibly with a few individuals gravitating around it. No one Alter is especially central relative to the others and the connections are fairly well distributed, even though there are sometimes a few less dense outgrowths on the margins of these large cliques. These networks tend to be those found at the beginning of the survey, in waves 1 and 2. Thus, they comprise the youngest individuals, most of them from the vocational baccalaureate path, having just completed their secondary education or in the first year of higher education. The majority of these young people are from working-class backgrounds. Some are living with their parents, others with a partner. There are high shares of economically inactive individuals and clerical or manual workers, and the women slightly outnumber the men. These networks are fairly typical of working-class modes of sociability, which are relatively intense and dense; they favor strong ties, which tend to be mixed together, with family and friends often appearing alongside each other in networks in which "everybody knows everybody else."

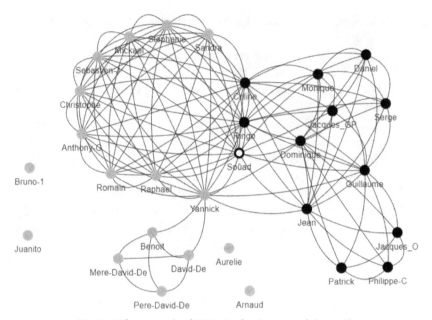

Fig. 2.4 The network of Kévin in the Caen panel (wave 1)

One example of this is the network of Kévin, a young man of gypsy origin who is in a labor market integration program during the first wave of the survey (Figure 2.4).

He is sharing an apartment with Sébastien, the brother of his childhood friend Christophe, but subsequently returns to his parents' house. His young aunt Céline is married to Ringo, one of the friends in his group; this couple connects his family with his friends, at least as much as his own "fiancée" Souâd, who was introduced to him by Stéphanie, the sister of Christophe and Sébastien. His "gang" also includes Sébastien's girlfriend Sandra, Romain whom he met at his kick boxing club, Mickaël, another friend from his childhood, and Raphaël who is Sébastien's brother-in-law. "My friends, they're my family in a way," said Kévin, thus combining the two. His friends from the earlier stages of his vocational education (Benoît, David-De, and his parents) are connected to the rest of the network only through Yannick, and Arnaud is now living in another town, Le Havre. Kévin also meets with Aurélie, whom he first encountered in his labor market integration program, and Bruno, his trainer, on their own. Thus, in Kévin's network, there are many links between most of the individual members.

In the centered networks, it is above all the betweenness centralization that is very strong. After all, the centrality is very evidently concentrated on a particular Alter who connects the various parts of the network which, without him, would be completely cut off from each other. Thus, he acts as a structural "bridge" between the various parts of the network. The network has medium density; the average of the centralities is relatively low, but above all, it is very unequal, since it is concentrated on one individual. There are relatively few isolated individuals, since even the peripheral individuals are connected to this very central Alter. As might be expected, this central individual is usually Ego's partner. Ego keeps company with everybody with him or her, as a couple. Nevertheless, it may be someone else. For Joël, for example, it is his childhood friend Yann, who connects his family with his various groups of friends. For Fleur, it is her great friend Magali, who shares all her relationships; for Patrick, it is his sister's husband who is central. In Etienne's network, which we examined earlier, it is not his girlfriend who is central but rather his friend David-A who, he says, "is a bit like a member of the family. We take him everywhere and our friendship has become stronger." David-A connects Etienne's family, his girlfriend's family, soccer buddies, and school friends.

This type of centered network tends to appear in the final, fourth wave of the survey, in which the young people are older; they also come mainly from the intermediate social classes, and they are relatively poorly qualified. Most of them are women, employed in intermediate occupations, living with a partner and generally well-established in adult life. It is this last point that principally characterizes them, whether they be middle-class women who started work immediately after completing the vocational baccalaureate, working-class women without qualifications but with children or women from the higher social classes who also started their working lives at an early age. Thus, these centered networks are principally networks of adults already established in their married and professional lives. Agnès's network, already mentioned above, is one of these, as is Violette's in wave 4 of the Caen survey. Violette has been working since she completed the vocational baccalaureate; she is working as an accountant in a taxi firm, living in Paris with Stéphane and expecting a baby.

As Figure 2.5 shows, Stéphane is an intermediary between Violette's family (on the left) with his own family (above), to whom Violette is becoming increasingly close:

The fact that we're going to have a baby together means our life as a couple is taking shape. I'm going to be part of their family now.

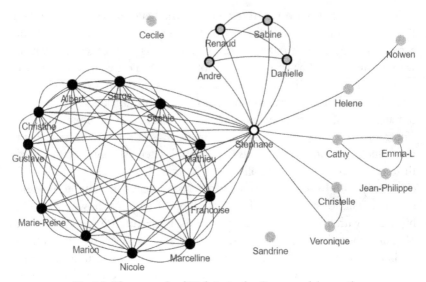

Fig. 2.5 The network of Violette in the Caen panel (wave 4)

Stéphane is also connected to most of the friends, including Hélène, Violette's oldest childhood friend. Although Hélène lives in Dijon, she is now more important to Violette (and connected with Stéphane) than Cécile or Sandrine, whom Violette got to know later and sees on her own from time to time. Nolwen practices dance with Hélène, who introduced her to Violette.

In the dissociated networks, the number of Alters is relatively high but the number of connections between them is low. Consequently, the Alters are relatively dispersed: Ego does not mix friends and family nor his friends with each other and he sees some of them on their own. These networks may comprise cliques but they are separated from each other and surrounded by isolated individuals. There is a greater degree of fragmentation between the various life contexts, and a number of structural holes. These are networks formed toward the end of the survey period, in waves 3 or 4. A large share of these people completed the social and economic baccalaureate and have higher education qualifications. Most of them come from the higher social classes. At the time of the survey wave, they had finished their studies and were now working but living alone; they had no romantic attachments or children. They had postponed getting married until a later date. These were also the most mobile young people,

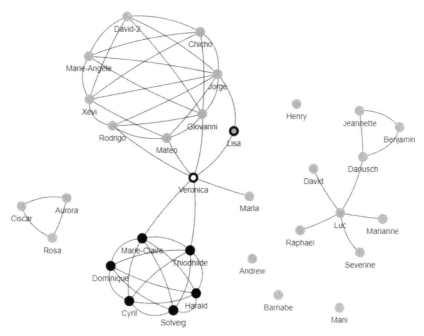

Fig. 2.6 The network of Nicolas in the Caen panel (wave 3)

particularly those who had traveled a lot; some were living abroad, such as Elodie in Boston or Nicolas who, in wave 3, was living in Spain (Figure 2.6).

Nicolas maintains links with his family in France as well as with childhood friends from Caen, such as Luc, his lifelong friend, and others whom he still mentions "out of nostalgia," even though he hardly sees them anymore, such as Dariusch, Benjamin, and Jeannette, or a lot of Luc's friends, whom he now sees only with him, such as Marianne or Raphaël. Séverine is an ex-girlfriend who previously had an affair with his brother and now with Luc. Andrew is a friend he met in the United States whom he still admires enormously although he regrets not writing to him more often. During the time he spent in England as a participant in the European Union's Erasmus exchange program, Nicolas met Jorge, a young Spaniard, and with him a whole group of foreign friends and housemates (Giovanni, Xevi, etc.). It was in this group that he met Véronica, a young Italian who became his girlfriend and came to live with him in Spain. It was Jorge who encouraged Nicolas to go and live in Spain. Most of his current Spanish friends, who form a group that meets mainly in a bar, were

introduced to him by Jorge and have now combined with friends from the
Erasmus program to form a clique. Rosa, Ciscar, and Aurora are work
colleagues of Nicolas's. Nicolas's network is fragmented, partly because of
his peripatetic existence. Nevertheless, it is not totally constrained by
geographical distance, since some individuals who now live very far away
from each other remain connected. As Nicolas puts it:

There have been a lot of goodbyes these last three years, but a lot of reunions as
well. This is because I've moved around a lot. And the people I get on with
generally, what we have in common is that they are foreigners as well, and
I think it's that difference that I like a lot.

The fragmentation of this type of network is linked to geographical
mobility as well as to the superimposition of different strata of existence
that are linked, to varying degrees, to periods of relational turmoil that are
not combined and remain separate from each other. While the Erasmus
friends and those from the Spanish bar are now linked by Jorge and
Nicolas himself, the friends from Caen (distant and from the past) and
those from his work in Spain (who are, nevertheless, recent and geographically close) remain separate. Other young people who have never left Caen
similarly maintain a certain degree of separation between the various
components of their networks and between different parts of their lives.

The composite networks have rather more complex structures that
combine heterogeneous elements: very dense cliques and less dense parts,
central individuals and others who are not, and isolated individuals as well.
Values for many of the indicators are average, but the most striking
observation is their heterogeneous distribution. Density is fairly low, while
centrality is average but unevenly distributed between a number of central
Alters and other, isolated individuals. We are dealing here with networks
that were present at the beginning of the survey, in waves 1 or 2, and with
others that remained unchanged in type right up to the fourth wave. Some
of these young people come from working-class backgrounds, others from
higher social classes, but most of them completed the economics and social
science baccalaureate. Those from the first wave have (of course) no higher
qualifications than the baccalaureate, while those from the fourth wave
have continued their education beyond high school. They live alone or
with their parents, although some of the older ones have a partner and
children. These networks are characterized both by the working-class
tendency to have some very dense cliques and that of the higher social
classes to keep the various parts of their networks separate from each other.
The processes of upward social mobility may perhaps be linked to these

types of networks, as in the case of Alice, the daughter of West Indian manual workers who became a business lawyer, or Alban, the son of a bricklayer and a housewife mother, who returned to university in order to become a dentist. However, they also include the trajectories of young people from working class backgrounds who have had a hard time of it, like Joël or Patrice, as well as young people from the higher social classes who are still in education, such as Emeline or Gaël.

Serge is the son of a forestry worker and a teacher who, after his vocational baccalaureate, got a job as a setter on a press in a sheet metal factory. His network includes both a strongly connected family clique, a girlfriend Carine whose only connection is with that family, two groups of friends, one of which is isolated and the other linked through Sylvain, his childhood friend, to his family and to another friend. There are four isolated individuals (Figure 2.7).

Thus, several ways of linking relational ties can be observed in these composite networks, which undoubtedly reflect the various contexts these

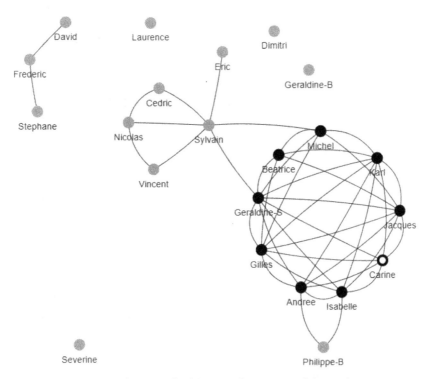

Fig. 2.7 The network of Serge in the Caen panel (wave 3)

young people have passed through in their lives, particularly in the course of their various geographical and social moves. Over time, some groups become diluted and people are introduced to each other; the composite networks reflect these asynchronous changes, with each sphere of life having its own temporality. These various processes are captured at different stages by the "snapshot" taken during each wave of the survey.

Analysis of the network structures reveals both their polarization around four fairly clearly differentiated types and the complexity of the temporal strata of which they are composed. The networks have a history and bear the trace of successive periods of relational turmoil and encounters, affiliations, and changing priorities. The links between these structures and our interviewees' individual attributes can also be observed. While gender seems to have little effect on the distribution of networks in this typology, class background, school career, and level of education, as well as age and position in the life cycle, exert a greater influence on network structure. In particular, a distinction can be observed between those young people who, regardless of their age, are still living the life of an adolescent (living with their parents, not in employment, no romantic relationship) and those who have entered fully into adult life. We are continuing our work on testing typologies that may be the most relevant both to synthesize complex realities and to be applicable to diverse kinds of data sets.[9]

ASSEMBLAGE AND COMPOSITION

A personal network is absolutely not a homogeneous, coherent entity, nor is it a stock of skillfully constructed and maintained capital. Rather, as we have seen, it is a lifetime's accumulation of relationships of all sorts, some of which represent strong and lasting commitments while others are merely ephemeral acquaintances. Some ties are imposed, at least up to a certain point (family, neighbors, colleagues), others are more voluntary ("friends," with all the ambiguity and diversity of meanings this notion may imply). Some relationships are part of everyday life, others are more or less dormant (not recently activated through an interaction). Nevertheless, this heterogeneous assemblage of relationships is of crucial importance. It constitutes the networked part of any individual's relational environment, the other part consisting of the social circles to which he belongs and to which many of those with whom he has relationships also

[9] C. Bidart, A. Degenne, M. Grossetti, "Personal Networks Typologies: A Structural Approach," *Social Networks* 54 (2018), 1–11.

belong. These men and women, close friends or vague acquaintances, whom he sees every day or just on special occasions, who may be similar to him or very different, are those who influence him, help him, and contribute to his "ontological security." With their "several voices," they mediate between himself and the social world.

For example, what Emmeline gets out of her important relationships is revealed by the contrasting set of motivating forces that underpin them. In some cases, she appreciates the fact that they are older, in others that they are the same age as her, and in yet others that they are younger than her. These are not contradictions but rather a reflection of her network's pluralist composition.

Hélène has experience from which I benefit, I find that enriching. She's taught me quite a lot professionally, and on a personal level we often have a good laugh about our partners. She anticipates things for me, she goes through things four years ahead of me. She's clearing the way for me, that's really how it is. Pascale and I, we're the same age, we have fairly similar attitudes to the world of work. So as well as the work side of things, we're quite similar in many ways and that's helped us swap ideas. We get on well because I have the impression that she's really my equal in what we're currently doing. Because all my other colleagues were much older people, with much more experience and maturity, it wasn't a huge gulf necessarily, but a small divide nevertheless. Claudine and Jean-Claude are long-standing friends of my parents, from the time my parents got married. They're the same – they had full adult status. Claudine likes young people a lot, and they're both really nice. Fred and I have a romantic relationship that's developing slowly. I haven't got to know him from all angles yet. And then Charlie, we haven't seen each other for two years, but we've stayed in touch just by writing to each other. That's testimony to a fairly subtle relationship.

Thus, there are a number of different forces driving these relationships and making the network a complex set of complementary ties. This plurality of experiences and motivations evokes the notion of "the plural actor."[10] After all, individuals are a combination of several social identities that are a product of the various contexts in which socialization took place and of the various groups to which they belong.[11] The members of their personal networks are the personifications of these various layers and contexts of their lives. Colette gives very clear expression to this plurality:

I have fairly different relations with people because I'm a different person, basically at any rate. I'll behave in one way with such and such a person but my behavior with another person will be different. There is not just one Colette. There are

[10] B. Lahire, *The Plural Actor* (Cambridge: Polity Press, 2011).
[11] M. Halbwachs, *On Collective Memory* (Chicago: The University of Chicago Press, 1992).

several Colettes. Depending on the person in front of me, different aspects of my character will come out.

From this point of view, individuals' networks provide a picture of their socialization, linking the social circles and the various issues at stake within them and bringing to mind the "little worlds" they have passed through in the course of their lives.

*

*   *

A sociology of relational dynamics opens up a rich area to analysis and interpretation, namely the "intermediate level" formed by personal networks. Socialization emerges as a process that is no longer solitary or guided by a few tutelary figures but rather one that is played out between individuals and their relational environment. One does not "grow up" alone but surrounded, led, reined in, and encouraged by the people whom one knows and by the complex system of ties that they form. This relational system has a structure that "makes sense" and has an origin and sociological significance. The size and composition of the network, as well as other original indicators derived from the structural analysis, such as density and centrality, prove both to be sensitive to sociological variables, such as level of education, and to have their own effects on individuals' destinies. The networks' structural characteristics are both dependent and independent variables; they are linked to social conditions and personal histories but they also shape and redistribute resources and trajectories. The structure of a network, whether it is dense or fragmented, centralized or composite, influences the cohesion of an individual's relational environment as a whole, its diversity, its unity, and its level of differentiation. As the product of an individual's passage through various milieus in the course of his life and a combination of plural identities, this structure clearly delineates the successive strata, foliations, and transformations of an individual life.

We have sought in this chapter to characterize personal networks and their variations. We have confined ourselves to a virtually static analysis, although the current description of each network has already led us to consider different temporal strata. A person's network is neither momentary nor set in stone. Each event in his life changes it, certain internal dynamics can cause it to change, even when the commitments within circles remain stable. In the following chapters, we adopt a dynamic approach to our analysis of relationships and networks.

PART II

NETWORKS AND THEIR DYNAMICS

3

Relationships Do Not Come Out of Nowhere

We begin with a statement that is obvious to all those who have studied social networks, namely, that no relationship originates outside of a social context. Friendships simply do not develop "out of nowhere." It is very rare for people to meet in a crowd or in the street in the absence of any shared context. And when this is the case, there is generally an event or an incident that brings the individuals together. This incident itself then becomes a context, since it establishes a framework made up of inter-actions, expectations, implicit rules, linguistic codes, various forms of involvement, etc. In any case, nobody walks down such and such a street at such and such a time simply by chance: urban movement patterns reveal differences between young rappers, mothers with strollers, elderly people, workers doing their evening shopping, etc. Thus, a good deal of implicit knowledge is used to draw "mental maps" and create the contexts in which lives unfold, with divisions that remain unconscious most of the time. Now, in order for an interaction to be initiated, it is important that the individuals in question share a minimum of common assumptions and codes of social conduct. This implicit knowledge, these divisions and these assumptions, are part of a context, a collective frame of reference. They vary depending on whether a person is encountered in his or her neigh-borhood, at an airport, at a training seminar, at a carnival, at a chess tournament, or at a football match. Each context defines populations: those who are present vs. those who are not, those who have been present longer than others, those who occupy such and such a position in it, those who engage in such and such an activity within it, and so on. There are various types of contexts: some are highly structured, with their official affiliations, hierarchies, and written rules, such as a company, for example. Others are much more fluid and implicit; they do not specify any real statuses but operate rather on the basis of tacit acknowledgements; examples might include an urban park, a bar, or a festival. Some may be regarded as circles, in the sense attributed to the term in the Introduction, while others are too evanescent or fluctuating for that.

Thus, contexts may be more or less highly structured. Furthermore, the forms that structuring takes affect the potential that exists for relationships to develop and the directions they might take. Divisions exist even within the same context. They may separate subpopulations that will find it difficult to meet each other. In a company, for example, different work schedules, the spatial distribution of the premises, differences between the various levels of the hierarchy, and the complementary nature of work tasks may isolate some categories of workers from others. In a neighborhood or village that appears, on the face of it, to be much less structured, divisions can be seen to emerge between long-term residents and newcomers, between tenants and homeowners, and between the most upscale parts of the neighborhood and the rest. Such divisions may determine the opportunities for meeting. Mixing with certain people or certain groups is not impossible, it's just more difficult and less likely to happen.

The relationships one has already established are another aspect of the context. It is difficult to make friends with someone who is in conflict with some of our closest friends or with members of our family. Apart from the fact that it originates in a context, an emerging relationship also takes its place within relational networks that already exist. Thus, in order to understand a relationship it is necessary to know what type of context and social circle it originated from, which will have important consequences for its characteristics and position within the network.[1] Relationships, networks, and contexts are, therefore, the entities in play in the dynamics that concern us here.

CONTEXTS, NETWORKS, AND RELATIONSHIPS INTERACT

A relationship originates in a context in which an encounter takes place. It may subsequently move into associational contexts other than those in which it originated, as when work colleagues go to the cinema together or become friends. This plurality of associational contexts, which also occurs when the range of activities is expanded and social circles become shared, gives a relationship additional dimensions, which is denoted by the term multiplexity. Furthermore, a relationship may be connected to other

---

[1] See, in particular, S. L. Feld, "The Focused Organization of Social Ties," *American Journal of Sociology* 86(5) (1981), 1015–1035; R. Adams, G. Allan (eds.), *Placing Friendship in Context* (Cambridge: Cambridge University Press, 1998).

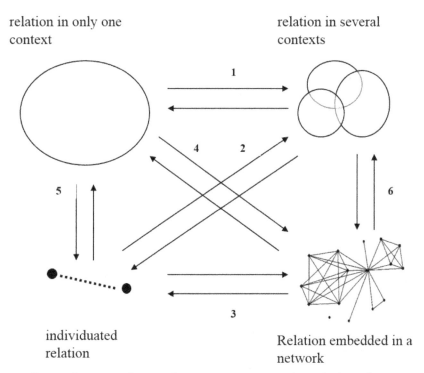

relation in only one
context

relation in several
contexts

individuated
relation

Relation embedded in a
network

Fig. 3.1 Dynamics of passage between contexts, networks, and relationships

relationships within an individual's personal network, which constitutes another dimension that plays a part in these relational dynamics. Networks differ from circles in that they link together a set of relationships without those relationships necessarily being in contact with each other or referring to a common "we." Figure 3.1 depicts these dimensions as well as the dynamics that combine them:

Each dimension is represented on one of the four corners of the diagram. The arrows positioned between these four corners represent the dynamics of the transition from one dimension to the other. For example, a relationship that was situated in just one context and subsequently becomes multiplex is represented by arrow 1, with the reverse transition also indicated. In some cases, a relationship is clearly situated on one of these corners but usually develops between the corners. These dynamics are listed below in opposing pairs.

Multiplexity/specialization (1): The first dynamic is the one that resituates the relationship from just one to several contexts, and vice versa. Firstly, there is an increase in multiplexity, through the addition of contexts and activities to the same relationship. This would apply, for example, to work colleagues who start going to the cinema together, join a chess club, go on holiday together, etc. Conversely, the dynamic may tend in the opposite direction, with a reduction from several contexts to just one, as part of a tendency toward specialization. This would be the case, for example, with two high school students who played music together and lived in the same neighborhood but who, having graduated from high school, relocated, and stopped playing music, now see each other only occasionally for dinner.

Individuation/embeddedness (2): Here, the move is from multiple social circles to a dyadic relationship, or vice versa. In some cases, the multiplicity of contexts in which encounters take place gives way to contacts involving just two people, for the sole purpose of seeing each other. Such is the case, for example, when two people become close friends and their exchanges no longer owe much to the circles in which the protagonists are involved. A relation becomes individuated when the two individuals concerned are no longer substitutable one for the other. The converse is a shift from a dyadic relationship to multiple circles, when two friends become involved together in various activities and social milieus.

Connection/dissociation (3): Individuals can also move from a dyadic relationship to a network, and vice versa. Any new relationship is situated in the personal networks of each of the two people involved. People frequently introduce new acquaintances into some of their other relationships, which helps to integrate the new relationship more firmly into the network. The converse is the move from a network to a dyadic relationship, as when two friends stop seeing their common friends and only spend time with each other, dissociating themselves from the network. Such dissociation is obviously relative, since each of the protagonists must take account of the other relationships in which he is involved.

Decoupling/embeddedness (4): Another dynamic is the move from a network to a single context and vice versa. It may so happen that individuals who maintain interpersonal relationships with each other engage in a shared activity together, give themselves a collective name, and draw up a set of rules, in short, form a circle. The converse is the move from a circle to a network, for example, when university students retain certain interpersonal ties after graduation but without doing anything all together or thinking of themselves as a group.

Decoupling/embeddedness of a relationship in a single context (5): In this case, we are dealing with a direct move from context to relationship, when a tie is "decoupled" and made independent of a circle. This may be because the circle no longer exists, as when two school friends continue to see each other after they have both left school, or because one of the protagonists has left the circle but they continue to see each other outside the circle. Under these circumstances, it is the increasing closeness or the affective aspect of the relationship that defines it, rather than the activity. However, the relationship may become autonomous even if the two protagonists remain members of the original circle. It is sufficient for their relationship to become particularized and for their mutual accommodation to become a more significant factor, like two work partners who form a friendly duo in which neither can easily dispense with the other. The converse is the shift from an autonomous relationship to a circle, as when one persuades a childhood friend to join an association of which one is already a member.

Decoupling/embeddedness of a network in several contexts (6): Finally, there is the case of the move from several social circles to a network, when interpersonal systems become dissociated from their contexts. This would apply, for example, to individuals involved in campaigning, leisure activities, or neighborhood associations who leave these social circles but continue to see each other. The converse is the move from a network to several social circles. This is the case in which a group of friends becomes involved in various group activities or voluntary associations.

Although these pairs of dynamics summarize fairly well the possible links between circles, networks, and relationships, they are not all equally represented in reality. Some are fundamental and common; others are exceptional or simply more unusual. Moreover, although they are presented here in isolation, this is done solely for the sake of clarity. In fact, as we shall see, they are often linked, interwoven, and complementary, overlapping each other to varying degrees. This general analytical framework enables us to investigate how relationships come into being, beginning with the contexts in which the initial encounters take place.

COLLECTIVE CONTEXTS CREATE MEETING OPPORTUNITIES

Before two people can meet, they have to be present in the same context, which already separates out the various populations to some extent. Some people will never be seen at a bridge club, others will never go to a boxing club. The young and the elderly, men and women, rich and poor, graduates and non-graduates tend to frequent different contexts. There are also differences depending on the time of day or night. Thus, contexts determine the specific opportunities for relationships to develop, simply because individuals spend time in them and have a greater probability of coming across such and such a type of person.

The various surveys included the question, "How did you get to know each other?" which gives an indication of the type of encounter that took place. In the Toulouse survey, as in the American survey whose method it adopts, respondents were asked, "How did you meet this person?" for each name listed in the subsample of relationships that was subjected to more detailed investigation. In the Caen survey, this question was asked for all the strong ties (multiplex relationships or those declared to be important). The data from these two surveys are presented in Table 3.1. It should be borne in mind, however, that in the case of the Caen panel the people surveyed were young. The categories that were constructed empirically on the basis of the responses were divided into three broad types: family, which constitutes a

Table 3.1 *The meeting contexts (Toulouse and Caen surveys)*[a]

Meeting context Toulouse survey	%	Meeting context Caen panel	%
Family	30.3	Family	24.2
Grew up together	1.1		
School	4.9	School	13.8
Post-18 education	4.9	Post-18 education	5.8
Work	13.6	Work	12.8
Voluntary associations	5.6	Voluntary associations	5.2
Neighbor	7.7	Neighbor	8.9
Total contexts	36.7	Total contexts	46
Through children	6.8	–	–
Through spouse	6.2	–	–
Through a friend	12.6	–	–
Total "through network"	25.7	Total 'through network'	31.2
		Leisure activities, outings	9.1
Other (chance, etc.)	6.3		1.2
Total "other"	6.3	Total 'other'	10.3
Total (1,606 relationships)	100	Total (4,233)	112.6

[a] In the Toulouse survey, 30.3 percent of the relationships mentioned originated within the family. In the Toulouse survey, relationships originating in leisure activities and outings were not included among the possible responses. In the Caen survey, 3,760 relationships were investigated but a total of 4,233 responses were obtained because several responses were possible. The item "grew up together" was not included here; the items "through children," "through spouse," and "through a friend" were not equally differentiated in the various waves of the survey, which is why they are left gathered together under the heading "through network."

particular context, contexts as defined in the Introduction, and networks themselves, as a relational context that helps to initiate new ties.

A majority of the relationships originated in "given" or ascribed contexts: family, colleagues, neighbors, etc. The family played a major role. It is a context that is everyday and at the same time particular, since everybody, or almost everybody, has a family. As far as one's own family is concerned, the boundaries are fixed and nobody can choose their parents. On the other hand, it is always possible to choose whether or not to have dealings with them. Of the existing family members, some maintain relationships with each other while others never see each other, even though they are undeniably part of the family. We are certainly dealing here with those with whom our interviewees have relationships. Family and relationships developed in childhood (family and school) account for more than a third of all relationships. Those with family members mainly involve the nuclear family (parents and siblings), who account for 70 percent of the total in the Toulouse survey.[2] If we also take into account the fact that children constitute 19 percent of the relationships, it becomes clear that the share of more distant relatives (uncles, aunts, cousins, etc.) is fairly low (about 11 percent) in that part of the relational environment captured by the survey procedure.

If the family and family-in-law are set aside and the people encountered in an "institutional" context (university, work, military service, voluntary associations, etc.) are added together, then the total for the Toulouse survey is almost 30 percent and more than 37 percent for the strong ties in the Caen survey (where the respondents were younger and their relationships more strongly connected with school). For young people, school (up to senior high school) and then work are the most prolific meeting contexts apart from family. Higher education constitutes a sort of parenthesis: it certainly generates a lot of ties but they do not last long after graduation and ultimately does not provide as many ties as education up to the end of high school. This was confirmed by Agnès, one of the young people in the Caen panel:

I've lost contact with all the friends I had at university but not with those who go back further. It's mainly because the friendships you have at university are not typical ones, they're something apart. At university, it's more a question of going to

---

[2] In this survey, family relationships were coded in detail after the event, but the data were not fully gathered, which made the estimations difficult. They should therefore be taken as a simple order of magnitude. In the Caen survey, the nuclear family accounted for 34 percent of Ego's family relationships (this proportion rose to 46 percent if only strong ties were considered), uncles, aunts, cousins, grandparents, and others were still very important (66 percent and 54 percent of strong family ties), whereas for these young interviewees children of course accounted for a smaller share.

parties, having a coffee, going for a drink, it's not at all the same thing as in high school, where you sit next to the same person for the whole of the school year. (So all those you're still in touch with are from your high school days?) Yes. University was a two-year digression. I learnt a lot of things, that's true, but it's a place where you have a lot of major turning points.

Contexts of the "club, association, religion" type are somewhat less rich as meeting contexts. Military service is not much mentioned (the surveys coincided with the period in which compulsory military service was coming to an end in France). The young people in the Caen panel were not involved in trade union or political activities. Consequently, they play no further part in our analyses. Relationships originating in respondents' neighborhoods account for around 8 percent of the total in both surveys.

Next in line are relationships that developed through network effects. In the Toulouse survey, the meeting context that most closely corresponds to these effects is that characterized as "introduced by a friend," which accounts for 12.6 percent of the total. The two other items, "introduced by spouse" and "through the children," also account for 13 percent of the total.[3] Taken as a whole, relationships originating in social connections account for a quarter of the situations. In Caen, relationships established "through network" (i.e., meetings that took place via an intermediary[4]) account for 28.8 percent of the total, to which can be added meetings "in a group" (2.4 percent); these younger respondents tended to operate in groups. The principal contexts in which meetings took place through an intermediary, whether an individual or a group, were the neighborhood, school, outings, leisure activities, and voluntary associations. University turned out to have a much less cumulative effect than school, with fewer meetings taking place through the medium of other acquaintances or of a group.

Uncategorized meetings, which might include chance meetings, accounted for only 6.3 percent of the total in the Toulouse survey. Thus, compared with the other types of meeting contexts, their role is more or

---

[3] We are aware that our classification is a little ambiguous, since these relationships could just as well result from integration into an existing family (e.g., in-laws) as from the interplay of social connections, in which a relationship develops with a friend of one's spouse or children. In both cases, moreover, the family circle is involved. Thus, both these meeting modes could be included in the first one ("family"), which we have reserved for the family of origin and for children. However, we preferred to retain all meetings that took place through the interplay of social connections as a single category.

[4] The distinction between "through family," "through spouse," and "through a friend" was not captured in the Caen survey equally in all the waves of the survey, which means the results cannot be given separately here.

less negligible, particularly since many of the interviewees answered "by chance" in respect of situations for which a sociologist might identify a structuring context. The "other" and "by chance" categories gave rise to only 1.2 percent of the ties in Caen. However, this survey also provides information on relationships originating in leisure activities, holidays, travel, nights out, and bars. Together they account for 9.1 percent of the total. These contexts, which are less highly structured, provided the young people in Caen with opportunities to meet others and gave them practical experience in maintaining relationships.

Thus, the Caen and Toulouse surveys are convergent. They are also consistent with the INSEE survey (EPCV–1997), in which respondents were asked to list various characteristics of their three "best friends," including the context in which they met them. These results clearly show that, taken together, institutions and social groups "produce" the majority of relationships, even the strongest ones, between individuals, at least when it comes to relationships like those captured in surveys of this kind.[5] This confirms the importance of context in establishing relationships. Even the most personal and closest of friendships, which we would like to believe are "detached" from instituted social frameworks, are in fact firmly entrenched within them.

However, it is not sufficient simply to be brought into contact with someone for a relationship to develop. Thus, the meeting contexts listed above are merely a starting point. The transition from interactions to relationships, as they were defined in Chapter 1, is a process that can take a considerable amount of time and go through various stages. Drawing on the analytical framework outlined in the introduction to this chapter, two major types of relationship-creating processes can be identified: that in which relationships gradually become detached from the original context and that in which relationships become connected with each other.

FROM CONTEXTS TO RELATIONSHIPS: INDIVIDUATION
AND DECOUPLING

The first type is the individuation of a relationship that originated in a particular context and which often goes through an initial increase in shared contexts, whether those contexts be more or less organized or more

---

[5] It should be noted that, in the case of the Toulouse survey, we are dealing with a subsample of five relationships within a larger set of some thirty relationships that constituted respondents' "normal" relational environment (see Introduction).

informal groups. Thus, individuals meet in a context, gradually come to share several contexts, and then spend time together just for the sake of seeing each other. Contexts have two additional qualities. Firstly, they ensure the relative social homogeneity of those who rub shoulders with them, which, to a greater or lesser extent, encourages relationships to develop. Secondly, they ensure that joint activities take place, thereby increasing the number of interactions and helping to establish more lasting ties. These two aspects – the relative homogeneity of those who spend time in a particular context and the shared activities – interact with each other. People engage in shared activities because they are in a particular context with others who are there for the same reasons and, conversely, they frequent specific contexts by engaging in a certain type of shared activity.

Depending on their social characteristics, contexts are more or less prolific when it comes to "producing" relationships. These differences are due in part to their structuring (population, spaces, temporal organization, social divisions), which facilitates exchanges to a greater or lesser degree; furthermore, as in the case of high school and university, they encourage homogeneity, or at least the formation of homogeneous groups, which play an important role in socialization. After all, besides the fact that contexts like those sort the populations that frequent them from those that do not and that they "produce" a greater or smaller number of ties depending on these social criteria, they also foster a certain degree of "clannishness" if only because people frequent them for similar reasons. Thus, a context constructs a social milieu, which in some cases is fairly homogeneous, in others more diversified. In a government ministry, for example, there will be a very high share of university graduates. At a rap festival young people will be in the majority, while at a car rally, men will be in the majority, and so on. In other milieus, such as in families or in neighborhoods, these various populations will tend to intermingle more. As we shall see, it is not sufficient to be birds of a feather in order to flock together. However, the fact that people recognize themselves as "similar to a certain extent" at least opens the first door. The person in question can then be regarded as "someone you can be around" if he shows signs that identify him favorably and make the first steps possible. Thus, in a public park, one will initially regard people of the same age and same "style" as oneself to be "people one can be around." In a company, one will turn first to individuals of equal status in the hierarchy and in the same department. These "criteria" may sometimes be very subtle. Some public places are identified by certain social groups as places they can go to. Young people in Caen, such as Elodie, made a very clear distinction:

We always meet in the same bars. There's Balto, which is opposite FNAC, we go there in the afternoon; in the evening, it's l'Univers and the Pub London. It's like a board game, there are squares and we land on every one.

To be in a particular context at a particular time is to acknowledge certain shared characteristics, ways of living, and values and to establish criteria for determining when one is "with one's own kind":

(What is it that keeps this group together?) They want to party and not work too hard, they hang out together to keep their spirits up while saying they're not going to do anything together, but with the others ... they guilt trip less, know what I mean (laughs)?

On the whole, people tend to prefer to form relationships with those who are "the same as oneself" in certain respects and to a certain degree. Consequently, contexts that ensure a certain degree of homogeneity within its population produce more relationships than much less closely defined contexts, such as the street or a crowd, even though, as we have seen, these are not exempt from social selection either. For example, a high school constitutes a world that is very highly structured on the basis of age: all the students are in the same age group, but more particularly at the same stage of their lives. They are all preparing for the examinations that will mark the end of their secondary education, which is an important factor common to them all. They also engage in similar leisure activities and their tastes in music, their attitudes, and their ways of dressing are also similar, even though here too, of course, divisions emerge, some of which are pursued to extremes. Merton[6] showed that the establishment of senior high schools in the United States had helped to create homogenous "small worlds" for the young people who attend them. These institutions had shaped lifestyles, created a "youth culture" and undoubtedly heralded the emergence of youth as an age group in its own right. We will return to this question in Chapter 9.

Over and above the way in which a context creates a certain homophily, additional divisions, preferences, and internal hierarchies also emerge. In a company, for example, divisions and affiliations are created on the basis of department, seniority, and various other criteria that are sometimes combined in very complex ways. Gaël, for example, had made two friends, Samuel and Sébastien, in his department at work. However, it was a criterion other than being in the same department, one combining age

---

[6] R. K. Merton, *Social Theory and Social Structure* (The Free Press, 1949).

and family situation, that served as a "filter" to single out these two from among all the employees in the department:

Even so, there are about twenty people in the maintenance department, but there are only three young people: me and these two. The others are a good ten years older, they have kids, they're married, they are older. These two, they're virtually the same age as me. (Was that the decisive factor that brought you together?) Yes. Later on, I invited them to my wedding. That really set the ball rolling, because Sébastien also got married that year. Then it was Samuel's turn the following year, we were both invited. Now we invite each other to dinner every two months.

Thus, once singled out from the group, these two colleagues were very quickly invited to share a very important ritual. In other cases, it is the immediate proximity at the workplace that is decisive, when the others have the office next door or are on the same corridor. Thus, for Agnès, sharing an office helped to change the poor impression she had had of Vincent:

When I met Vincent for the first time, it was at a job interview. And right from the start, we hated him, you know, rich kid and a lazy bugger. And in fact it turned out he was a bit odd. And then I was working in the same office as him, so that helps you to get to know each other a bit better. And I left X (the company) four months after he arrived, and in fact we continued to see each other outside that context because he left it as well and now we see each other really often. If we hadn't had that time working together in the same office. . .

However, contexts are also important because they provide the framework within which common tasks and goals are implemented through shared activities. After all, such activities are an important factor in bringing people together. Not only are they in each other's presence, in close proximity to each other, and therefore likely to take notice of each other, but they are also achieving something together. In high school, students do chemistry experiments or their history homework together, in a company, workers make a helicopter as a team. Such tasks will bring people closer together. Above all, they have to communicate with each other as soon as they have to finalize a project together. In order to succeed, they have to talk to each other, of course, but above all they have to make decisions, choices, and rulings, minimize conflict, manage their group or team, and organize the task at hand. In some contexts, this activity plays a central role. In a soccer club, it is normally the game that determines the players' presence, positions, and relationships, even though other issues do arise above and beyond what happens on the pitch. Musicians also typically develop a large share of their relationships around their passion, as Gaël explained:

As far as the music's concerned, there's no established group, we don't put on concerts, all that, but it's true that it's an activity that helps you sustain relationships. I think that, if we just hung out together and talked, it'd be nice, but with the music, there's something new each time, you want to go higher, do better and better. It's true it gives us a shared activity, it's good . . . .. It's really the activity that connects us as soon as we're all together.

And indeed, one-third of the activities that Gaël shares with all his ties revolve around music. The shared activities may be numerous and varied, which enables young people, in particular, to make distinctions within their relational circles. For them, sharing one activity or another is what mainly characterizes their relationships. Thus, Emeline separates out her high school friends:

I'm still involved in drama productions at high school. So there are people there who I have to talk to for two hours a week, because we're involved in a joint activity, we have to talk. Clarisse is doing a video workshop with me, so I used to see her there. Actually, Clarisse is in a slightly different situation because we come across each other in several places, at the theater, at the video workshops and then because she had an affair with a friend of mine, we used to see each other in other situations.

On the streets, on the other hand, there are few factors bringing people together,[7] which partly explains why very few relationships develop there spontaneously and the share of "institutional" contexts in the various meeting modes is so high. There are many other modes of structuration, usually implicit, between the two, which will tend to create both divisions and connections between the individuals concerned. Some activities have a significance beyond the activity itself, giving rise to shared concerns, communities of interests, or cultures. Thus, for some people, music is not only an activity but also a way of life. It can bring people together and also trigger various self-reinforcing processes, resulting in networks being extended, new ties being created, and the activity itself being further developed. Thus, for Patrick,

Graffiti and music are passions. And then there's the whole state of mind that goes hand in hand with hip-hop, which means that those who put a lot into it become fairly close. We tend to have the same sorts of interests, the same ways of behaving and thinking.

---

[7] It should be noted that there are no individuals in our samples who were living on the streets. For such individuals, the streets become the environment in which they live, in other words, a context.

Here too, there are often a number of triggering factors: existing ties that serve as go-betweens, shared activities, and common concerns. Collective events can also constitute specific contexts, marking a break with established structures. Thus, a strike at a factory, for example, may give rise to different rules, different hierarchies, and different forms of solidarity to those associated with the daily routine and which, combined with other factors, can create closer bonds between the members of a work group. A village festival, a house fire, or a crisis of some other kind may generate new and different contexts from which, out of the very upheavals they cause, specific relationships may emerge. Such events, which may occur regularly or only once, can influence the relational content, giving it a particular coloration. Some meetings take place, paradoxically, in conflictual circumstances. The issue at stake divides a group or a neighborhood and ties are established with those who are on "the same side." Thus, Emeline met Thibaut by singling him out in a tense situation:

There was a whole group of people on the bike ride .... The day hadn't gone off well because there were people who had had major problems with their bikes, which quickly got me irritated. As a result, I ended up talking with those two guys. It's funny, because I'd split off from people I used to see every day to hook up with people I didn't know. I didn't regret it, they were less annoying.

In some cases, it may also be the cumulation of several contexts that triggers the development of a relationship, while a single context would not have been sufficient. Thus, young people can often be heard saying they've come across each other previously, whether at school, during a leisure activity, or in their neighborhood, but that they did not "connect" at the time. Meeting up again through a mutual friend or when involved in another activity, sometimes several years later, may lead them to reconsider the individual in question and their relationship. The situation has changed, the combination of circumstances turns out to be a "coincidence" and this time the relationship takes shape.

A shared activity may initiate a relationship, but subsequently it may either remain central to it or fade into the background behind other aspects of the relationship. If we return to the question on the motivation for the relationship (what brings Ego and Alter together), one of the suggested responses was "one or more activities in common (including work and education)." Now, 13.2 percent of the responses on strong ties gave this sharing of an activity as the "common motivation." It was relatively recent relationships (in existence for two to three years) that were most firmly based on such activities, while really long-established ties depended very little on them; other more personal factors undoubtedly took over. In all these cases, the addition of factors bringing the individuals concerned closer together and enabling them to identify with each other helped the relationship to exist independently of the original context, to endow it with its own intrinsic qualities, and to single out one person from within the group.

EXPANSION OF THE NETWORK: MY FRIENDS' FRIENDS

A network may itself also form a relational context, since it provides opportunities to meet someone through an intermediary. In the INSEE survey, such meetings accounted for 24 percent of "best friends," 34 percent of friends in the Toulouse survey, and 39 percent of friends and 31 percent of strong ties in the Caen panel. Thus, networks are a very important breeding ground for relationships. Families themselves create family relationships, particularly through the mechanism of marriage: a sibling's spouse or a spouse's family become members of the family. Families can also add to an individual's network of friends, as happened in Gaël's case:

Fanny is the sister of my sister's best friend. We've known each other for a long time. When we were little, we knew each other but she wasn't really one of my friends. And then two years ago, we started seeing each other more often because our sisters were hanging out together and then we started going to the beach together. She's the one I tell most things to.

And it was through a series of indirect links that Gaël met his friend Thomas:

His mother and mine have been best friends for twenty-five years. Originally, our two fathers worked together as chemists in the same place. Now, Martine, his mother, sees my mother virtually every day.

As people grow up, it is friends who are more likely to become the intermediaries who introduce other friends, and Gaël continues to extend his network:

I got to know Alexandre solely through Jérôme, he was a friend of Jérôme's in primary school and junior high school, I think. So when there were parties where there was going to be quite a lot of people, Alexandre used to come and that's how afterwards . . . . We went on holidays together and so on.

These indirect relationships gradually build up, become stronger, and eventually become direct relationships. Gaël can now spend time with Alexandre without Jérôme, and even though Jérôme has faded into the background, he continues to see Alexandre.

Often, a connection made through a friend is reinforced by a shared activity, which helps to arouse interest and to lay the foundations for the relationship, as Gaël remembers of another friend:

Erwan's a friend of Jérôme's and we actually got talking because he plays rugby, and so do I. We spend the afternoon together sometimes.

In this case, the connection made through a friend combines with the "mutual motivation" of a shared activity. The context in itself is not always enough: it is through the addition of a second shared signal that a relationship truly begins to take shape. These two types of processes – individuation and connection – are not mutually exclusive but gain from being separated out for the purposes of the analysis.

Physical presence, similarities, activities, identities, events, connections: these are some of the factors that draw people together in a particular context and are likely to determine the potential for a more lasting relationship. Thus, these meeting contexts determine a relationship's origin and its initial characteristics. However, this relationship will not be limited to the circumstances in which it originated. Rather, it will become a true relationship by inventing its own history and forging its own characteristics.

FROM ORIGINATION TO DESIGNATION

Relationships originate in certain contexts, from which they may detach themselves, take on greater complexity, and change their nature. Once the meeting has taken place, they "live their own lives." The Toulouse survey does not provide the data required to go into individuals' histories in detail but it does offer some pointers. By comparing the contexts in which the relationships originated and the way in which the interviewees characterized them at the time of the survey, one can get an idea of how the relationships evolved.

At first sight, the main categories of ties appear to be stable. The family accounted for 44 percent of the originating contexts (family, through children, through spouse) and it reappeared as the current characterization in 43 percent of the relationships. Work provided the originating context for 10 percent of the relationships and colleagues likewise accounted for 10 percent of the current characterizations. There was a decline from 6 percent to 3 percent in the case of voluntary associations and from 16 percent to 12 percent for all "organized contexts" (work and voluntary associations). For neighbors, the figures were 8 percent and 9 percent respectively. However, this apparent stability conceals a considerable degree of change. While relationships rooted in the family of origin were still for the most regarded as family ties, only 70 percent of former neighbors were characterized as such; the figures for former colleagues and members of associations were 44 percent and 25 percent respectively. They had become "something else," mainly friends. Families had been extended through the addition of spouses, children, in-laws, and so on; these new additions accounted for one-third of all the family ties mentioned. Fifty-nine percent of current colleagues had not been first encountered at work (in most cases, the first meeting had actually taken place at university); the same applied to 30 percent of neighbors and 51 percent of association members, while 81 percent of friends had not been introduced by other friends. Apart from family relationships and those originating in childhood or university, 47 percent remained in their original context.[8] This proportion declined as the relationships matured (52 percent for relationships under 5 years old, 37 percent for those in existence for more than 20 years) and rose with age at first meeting (43 percent for relationships that started between the ages of 16 and 18, more than 50 percent after age 35), which is certainly consistent with the notion that relationships gradually detach themselves from the original context over time.

Some categories of meeting contexts have no counterpart in the designations, since the original contexts had, as it were, "disappeared" (childhood friends, school, university). The category that benefited from the "disappearance" of certain contexts was "friends" (without any further qualification), which accounted for 32 percent of the characterizations. Many relationships linked to "institutional contexts" had strengthened to such an extent that respondents generally checked "friend" or "family" as well in order to describe them (only 16 percent of the relationships in our sample do not include either of these two designations). Thus, the "family" and "friends" categories function as "attractors" toward which relationships tend to evolve. To become a member of a family or a friend is to forget, at least in part, the circumstances in which a relationship originated, with the relationship becoming detached from the original context.

*

*   *

---

[8] Neighbors by origin still characterized as neighbors, colleagues as colleagues, association members and "met through friends" who have become friends.

The majority of relationships originate in circles (family, organizations) from which they gradually become detached and then acquire their own dynamic. A significant share of social relationships are also produced directly, through social connections and the processes involved in the reproduction of networks. Other originating contexts are based more on shared concerns, in a neighborhood, for example. There are many cases in which it is the combination of several of these factors that crystallizes the relationship. Once established, relationships evolve, as we have seen. Some disappear, while others go from strength to strength until they are incorporated into the two major categories of "close relationships," namely, family and friends.

The sociology of relational dynamics as we understand it deals with relationships but also links them to other dimensions of the social world by revealing the dynamic of these links. By considering these relational dynamics at the interface with the contexts and circles out of which they emerged, we have already been able to identify some typical sequences, such as decoupling or embeddedness (of relationships or networks with regard to circles), an increase in multiplexity or specialization, connection or dissociation, etc. It is by affirming that relationships originate in social contexts and circles, that they join together in activities and are connected with each other in networks, and by taking to its ultimate conclusion the determination to link the relational dynamics with these various levels, that this sociology keeps its promises.

4

The Dynamics of Relationships

Relationships are born and develop but they also change and evolve over time. With experience of time spent together, the way in which people keep company and communicate with each other changes. The partners in a relationship get to know each other better. They add an activity to those they already share; they begin to invite each other to dinner and to tell each other personal things. Intimacy gradually unfolds. In most cases, "rules of relevance"[1] are implicitly established; these rules gradually evolve, defining what is possible and what would be shocking at each stage of the relationship. And one day, the partners introduce their partners or spouses to each other, followed possibly by other friends, who gradually become mutual friends. In this way, a network is gradually extended. In some cases, the new extensions form part of circles, for example, if the old and new friends take part in the same activity together or share a common motivation. In other cases, however, the extensions develop discretely, one by one, and are not included in a circle. The links with the other members of the network, with the groups and social circles, and with the activities and contexts, play a very large part in the development of relationships. A relationship may become more intense as much because it is combined with others as because it advances independently as the substance of the relationship itself evolves. It may disappear if the friends cease to like each other, if the spouses do not enjoy each other's company, if other friends supplant them, if group activities cease, or if certain contexts disappear. We are taking the gamble here of not separating relational dynamics from network dynamics, in order to try to discover the interactions between the two. Thus, we examine the various developments and dynamics that cause

[1] G. Allan, *A Sociology of Friendship and Kinship* (London: G. Allan & Unwin, 1979).

relationships to evolve within individuals' environments. To this end, we draw mainly on the Caen survey which, being longitudinal, provides information on changes over time.

MULTIPLEXITY: TAKING A RELATIONSHIP INTO DIFFERENT WORLDS

When the partners in a relationship share a range of activities in different contexts, that relationship can be said to have become a multiplex one. In this section, the dynamics of this multiplexity is considered. In the travel agency where she works, Sidonie runs into a certain number of colleagues every day. They say hello and sometimes exchange a few words out of politeness, but these interactions do not constitute a relationship. One day, she has to work on a customer file with Guy; this interaction changed the impression she had had of him and they subsequently became "very close." The relationship might have remained there, that is, the colleague might have just remained a colleague. However, the discovery of other points in common, in another sphere of life, extended the scope of the relationship. It had now expanded beyond its original context and become detached from its origins, thereby enriching the relationship: "Guy sings in a choir and he said to me: 'Look, if you'd like to come along, there are some tickets' . . . . So I went." Since then, Guy has no longer been just a colleague, he's also a singer. The relationship has opened up to other possible worlds: "Afterwards, we went to a restaurant and there we are – now he's a good friend." Still in the travel agency, Sidonie has also taken an important step with Audrey:

We began with work, in fact. There was nothing else, but one evening we decided to go and have a drink and then that was it. It was from that time when we went out together, when we really talked about things other than work, because at work it's always difficult to talk, it was then that we realized we had things in common. (Why Audrey?) There were several of us in the agency about the same age, twenty-four, twenty-five. And I think that's what brought us close. And Audrey more especially.

The history that built up subsequently between Sidonie and Audrey sets them apart from their other colleagues: they are no longer substitutable: "And then we had . . . I don't know, the same interests, the same things to share, a different kind of closeness from the others." A relationship developed between them as persons. They know each other in more ways than just through their roles and positions in the company. Their relationship's "rules of relevance," which give them an idea of what is conceivable, tolerable, and well regarded in their case, have evolved:

> Now in fact, we see each other every day, we have lunch together, we confide in each other, give each other advice, etc. And it's true she's someone who's important to me because, whatever the matter might be, I know I can turn to her.

This relationship has become independent of the work context and grown in intimacy and trust as a dyadic relationship. However, it may also, through a synergy effect, impact on the network by bringing in other relationships in its wake:

> In fact, when we began to meet outside work, the others sort of realized we were making arrangements to meet or were doing things together. So they said to us: "it would be nice to do things together." So there we are, Cédric, Thomas, Thibault, that's the work circle now, the young people of course.

This increase in shared activities led to the individuation of a relationship, which was subsequently connected with other relationships on the basis of a shared characteristic, in this case age, with the whole set of relationships now evolving in other contexts and forming a small social circle that shares work as well as leisure time. This is an example of the combining of these dynamics.

However, let us remain for the time being with the multiplex dynamic. Of all the relationships identified in the four waves of the Caen panel survey, 51 percent are multiplex.[2] This tendency to take relationships out of their initial context is unevenly distributed. The boys have a slight tendency to have more multiplex relationships than the girls, as do those of either sex from more privileged backgrounds and the more highly qualified and older of these young people. The degree of multiplexity also depends of course on the activities normally undertaken. Thus, a person who is not involved in any sporting, artistic, voluntary, or leisure activities may well engage only in sociability with his or her friends (going for a drink, chatting, etc.). On the other hand, someone who is involved in a range of leisure activities will be more likely to have multiplex relationships, if only because it adds one or more of these activities to his or her sociability. Thus, Patrick, one of our musicians, saw his relationships become increasingly multiplex as his musical activities developed.

---

[2] In the Caen panel survey, multiplexity was measured in three ways: by counting all the contexts (name generators) in which an Alter appeared; by the response to the question: "do you meet elsewhere?"; and by the existence of several different activities shared by Ego and Alter.

Multiplexity is also linked to the quality of a relationship: almost 80 percent of the relationships declared as important are multiplex, as are 89.1 percent of those declared as close friendships. On the other hand, only 67.4 percent of mere acquaintanceships are multiplex. Romantic relationships are of course the most multiplex, at 91.8 percent. However, fewer than 60 percent of relationships with the family or family-in-law are multiplex; such relationships are motivated by factors other than shared activities and milieus. Multiplex relationships also tend to be the oldest ones, typically childhood relationships that have lasted a long time rather than relationships embarked on more recently.

The gradual evolution of rules of relevance and the increasing sharing of contexts is sometimes reshaped by unforeseen events that have the effect of hastening the development of multiplexity. The roles and expectations are unsettled and the event then becomes a sort of additional exceptional context that knocks the relationship out of its routine and its normal course. The event may lie in one of the partner's life course, in the environment, in a personal crisis, or in a social crisis. A testing time of this kind for a relationship constitutes a sort of threshold and helps to strengthen the bond. It is a period of destabilization that takes the partners by surprise; they begin to talk more freely, thereby enabling themselves to establish an intimate relationship much more quickly than is usual. Confidence plays a crucial role. The partners have stepped out of their expected roles and entered a zone of uncertainty, in which social roles have been disturbed and the established order of interactions has broken down.[3] Moreover, examination of the definitions of friendship individuals give would suggest that the notions of drama and crisis are central. When asked "What in your opinion is a real friend?," the reply is very often: "Someone on whom one can always rely in a difficult situation." It is also evident that many friendships are born, or at least start to be regarded as friendships, at a time when both partners are going through a major personal crisis. In a work context, for example, in which each one has to stick to their role, such destabilization helps to open doors and establish relationships that quickly become predominantly interpersonal, as was the case for Antoine:

Yohann was my summer camp director and he became my confidant because I'd just lost my grandfather, about three months previously, and I fell apart at one

---

[3] See, in particular, G. Allan, *A Sociology of Friendship and Kinship* (London: G. Allen & Unwin, 1979); A. Silver, "Friendship and Trust As Moral Ideals: An Historical Approach," *Archives Européennes de Sociologie* 30 (1989), 274–297.

point and we talked about it, that did me good and since then we've got on well and he's told me I can drop in from time to time ... I confided in Yohann so much that I regard him as a friend, he knows so much about me. I trust him, he's straight up. If I have a problem one day, he's one of the people I'll go and talk to.

The normal scheme of things can also be destabilized in more collective circumstances and this too can help friendships emerge or become established. For example, besides the context of the work place, group travel, training courses, or even strikes, sequences develop that stand at some remove from everyday professional life and its rules and relational norms. It is true that, in such situations, social roles are very precisely defined, but they are disconnected from ordinary ones. It is in this sense that it is possible to speak here too of exceptional events and situations that create a situation of uncertainty in which temporary destabilization fosters the development of a closer relationship based on inter-individuality. Whether this destabilization of social roles occurs at a time of crisis or as a result of a less abrupt diversification of contexts, the important thing is this: as fixed social roles and behavioral norms are disrupted, individuals begin to reflect on their own qualities and to recognize each other as individuals. Thus, unforeseen events, and individual or social crises produce a terrain that is relatively detached from the major divisions and roles characteristic of the wider society and is conducive to the strengthening of friendships, particularly among young people.[4]

SPECIALIZATION: DOING FEWER THINGS TOGETHER

The opposite dynamic involves sharing fewer activities than in the past. There are several possible ways in which this might occur. In some cases, it is an activity itself that is abandoned. If a young person stops being involved in theater productions or playing basketball, he or she may maintain some of the relationships associated with those contexts even though they no longer share the activities in question. This sometimes constitutes a threat to relationships, weakening them to the point where they might eventually disappear. Paul acknowledges that his relationship with Stéphane changed in this way:

---

[4] B. Hess, "Friendship," in M. Riley (ed.) *Aging and Society*, vol. 3 (New York: Russell Sage Foundation, 1972); Z. Lopata, D. R. Maines (eds.), *Research in the Interweave of Social Roles: Friendship*, vol. 2 (Greenwich: JAI Press, 1981).

Now it's become a relationship in which we talk about work, things like that. Well, perhaps I should've continued some activities. At one time we played a bit of football with a few friends. I've also lost contact with Mathieu, for the same reason. We used to see each other regularly, we had a sort of schedule.

Restricting the shared activities may cause a relationship to weaken. However, it may also serve to strengthen it. Some relationships that used to combine leisure activities with a personal friendship may refocus on the friendship dimension only. In some cases, one of the partners moves a long way away, making it simply impossible to continue the activities. However, not all relationships disappear because of distance or the reduction in shared activities. Some, in fact, are strengthened by a new focus on personal exchanges, communication over a distance, and trust. Thus, Fleur no longer really shares any activities with Fabienne, whom she met at university, with whom she worked in youth leadership and shared voluntary activities, nights out, excursions, and holidays but who is now living a long way away from her. However, their correspondence indicates to Fleur that their relationship has evolved in a way that does not threaten its durability:

Her letters mean that Fabienne is still there. People always remain in my heart even if I don't see them, it's not the end of the world. (Is she a little less important?) It's not the same kind of importance at least. And then she showed that she could be there. When I was in Paris, she was the one who wrote to me every week.

Many relationships begin in one context, at school, in particular, and then go through a period of increasing multiplexity. Once the relationship is well established, the dynamic continues with a shift toward specialization, with the disappearance of shared activities or geographical distance precluding daily contact but not preventing the relationship from becoming more intense. This was the case for Didier and Stéphanie, for example:

We were in the same class in primary school, when we were about eight. We became really good friends when we were about thirteen or fourteen, we really hit it off and we were part of a small group of school friends, at that time we used to hang out at Stéphanie's place a lot after school, we used to go there to watch soaps on the TV, just like all young kids do.

The relationship both transcended school and merged with other relationships, thereby forming a circle.

We supported each other during the baccalaureate. It was then that our relationship took on real depth.

The experience of doing the baccalaureate[5] examinations intensified their relationship, which continued and was further strengthened during holidays spent together, despite the geographical distance between them:

When we'd finished high school, Stéphanie left Caen to do a two-year vocational training course. And it's true that, at that point, we stopped being school friends and started to act more like adults, that is, we began to go out independently. And I even went on holiday with her three years ago to Spain, our relationship really did start to get a bit stronger.

The relationship has now firmly taken root following a symbolic gesture that has rendered it timeless, quite detached from any activities:

She's a real friend, because she can count on me and I can count on her. Now she's making me a bit more part of her family in the sense that I'm godfather to her son. That's a bond that logically is going to last. It's an important form of recognition.

Thus, multiplexity and specialization can both, at different times, contribute to the specification of a relationship. We can further clarify their respective roles and contributions by examining these dynamics at the level of biographical time, in this case, the period of transition to adulthood. After all, the link between multiplexity and specialization evolves not only over the course of the relationship but also with age. In the Caen panel, 34.3 percent of the relationships were multiplex in the first wave; this proportion reached 57.7 percent in the second wave and 65.2 percent in the third wave but fell back to 53.5 percent in the fourth wave. If family and romantic relationships are put to one side, the tendency remains the same. If we take relationships that lasted over two waves of the survey and examine how the degree of multiplexity evolved, it is clear that they became more multiplex over time. They were specialized when the partners met and became more multiplex over time. However, this tendency weakened from wave to wave. The differential between the dynamics of multiplexity and specialization weakened over the course of the transition to adulthood. The tendency to specialization strengthened. In the years following their departure from high school, the young people had a clear tendency to diversify the contexts and activities in which they were involved with the same people, whereas several years later they tended to specialize their relationships to at least

---

[5] *Baccalauréat* in the French system.

the same extent by doing fewer different things with each person. Thus, 56 percent of partners increased their number of shared activities between waves 1 and 2, 23 percent between waves 2 and 3, and just 9 percent between waves 3 and 4.

Referring to contexts, in high school, relationships often remained confined within the context of the school. If they were not musicians or involved in sport, these young people had no shared activities with a good proportion of their relationships. "In fact, all we do is hang out, we don't do anything special, we're just together," said Valentine in wave 1. Then, once they had left the high school that furnished them with a context in which they met "as a matter of course," they deliberately sought out their friends by increasing the occasions and contexts in which they met as the relationship became more intense. For them, making friends involved taking the other person to a wide range of activities and sharing an increasing number of different things. As a relationship intensifies, so the area of common ground increases. The number of shared activities in each relationship rose in waves 2 and 3. However, as they got older, the young people undertook fewer and fewer leisure activities. They shared an ever-diminishing range of activities with their friends. Thus, they reduced the activities they undertook together in order simply to see each other, to have dinner together, to talk and to exchange confidences. Furthermore, whereas the relationships that became more intense at the beginning of the period had more and more activities in common, at the end of the period they became more intense while sharing fewer and fewer activities. The share of relationships in which the partners saw each other only rarely (less than once a month) also rose in the last period. Thus, the way in which a relationship is strengthened and maintained also changes with age.

Taken in its entirety, the data reveal a very clear dynamic, and one that is undoubtedly specific to these years of transition from adolescence to adulthood. The young people began by associating predominantly with school friends, initially confining themselves to the school playground and then gradually increasing the number and frequency of the shared activities and contexts as the relationship becomes more intense. Later, this proliferation of contexts ceased and their relationships, whether new or old, became more specialized. When these relationships became more intense, the young people were more likely than previously to restrict the number of shared activities in order to concentrate on social activities or even to see each other only rarely and to communicate with each other at a distance.

INDIVIDUATION: SINGLING OUT ONE PERSON

The individuation dynamic involves separating one individual from a circle, "uncoupling" him from the context or activity in order to endow that individual with autonomy and focus on the quality of the interpersonal link or dyadic relationship. The person is then singled out as an individual in his own right. The seeds may be sown in the move toward multiplexity, as unexpected events are shared, or, for adults, in a rapid detachment of the relationship from its initial contexts, which links it to the dynamic examined above, to which it cannot, however, be reduced.

Let us return to the example in which Guy asked his colleague Sidonie whether she would like to come and listen to him in his choral concert. This seemingly anodyne event is, in fact, crucial to a sociologist. In going beyond the world of work, this relationship was extending the scope of its meanings: Guy was now wearing his "singer" hat in addition to that of "colleague." Furthermore, this extension of the relationship reduced the importance of his status as a colleague. As roles become more diversified, they lose their power to define. And gradually, as the number of shared contexts increases or as a crisis situation is shared, a colleague becomes a person, that is, someone unique who, for Sidonie, could not be reduced to any one hat or any one role. Thus, this plurality of contexts in which interaction takes place leads to the individuation of the relationship. By increasing the number of situations in which they interact, opening up new perspectives, and thus rendering the relationship less dependent on one particular context, the partners draw closer to what forms the basis of their individuality.

In the case of childhood friends, with whom people have shared many episodes in their lives, these changes succeed one another: the number of shared contexts initially increases before they begin to be less relevant as the importance attached to close personal relationships grows. Thus, Gaël recalled his meeting with Jérôme and the various phases of their relationship:

We were always in class together anyway. And then afterwards, all those student nights out . . . . We certainly drank a lot, but beyond that I noticed his sense of humor appealed to me. And last year, the geography department organized a field trip, we went to the Pyrénées Orientales, and there, the fact of spending every day with him, we liked the same things . . . . It was more from that time onwards that we started spending time together with our girlfriends, all four of us really making an evening of it, with Karine.

Beyond an initial shared context in school and university classes and lectures, student nights out added a further context. Gaël certainly made a distinction between the conviviality of these evenings out ("We sure did drink a lot") and the emergence of a much more personal criterion, linked to Jérôme rather than the group as a whole (his humor). Then, in another phase, the geography field trip took them away from the university and immersed them in another space, thereby disrupting their daily routines and roles while at the same time providing them with an opportunity to live and work together. Experiencing life together in this way brought our two friends even closer together. They discovered they "liked the same things," which encouraged them to share their worlds even more by introducing their girlfriends to each other, thereby initiating a trend toward additional connections to which we will return later. Similarly, during a trip to Morocco, Gaël noticed that he was moving out of his role as one of his other friend Abdouk's hotel guests:

Gradually he saw that it was no longer a question simply of a hotel and a guest but that we were on the same wavelength, he brought us into his family, we ate with his family. He no longer saw us as tourists and we no longer saw him simply someone from the hotel.

This move toward individuation uncouples a relationship from its environment: the partner becomes detached from the context and his or her accustomed role, the relationship moves outside the circle and becomes focused on one individual, who is singled out by virtue of his or her personal qualities. In some cases, the partner will be introduced to others, as happened with Karine and Abdouk's family.

Our analysis of the Caen panel identified all the sets of relationships involving more than three people (including Ego) who "do things together." Thus, each Alter could be associated with one or more social circles or with none. This is one of the indicators that enables us to see to what extent a dyad was decoupled from any social circles or, conversely, deeply embedded in one or more circles. Forty-nine percent of the relationships existed outside of a circle, while 45.1 percent were embedded in a single circle and 5.9 percent in several circles. Most mere acquaintanceships had no connection with a circle, while buddies tended to be linked to a single circle and real friends and individuals were described as "important" to several circles. Outside of a circle, alongside mere acquaintances, we also find the oldest ties, such as childhood friends with whom these young people had maintained a one-to-one relationship even after the original contexts (school, neighborhood, childhood leisure activities, etc.) had disappeared. Thus, the individuation of relationships was associated as much with the fact of not being embedded in a circle as with the fact of being involved in several. While the majority of the most important relationships were embedded in several circles, very old childhood friends not linked to any circle at all constituted a notable specific case.

EMBEDDEDNESS: BECOMING PART OF A CIRCLE

The process of embedding a relationship involves integrating it into a social circle, thereby incorporating it into a group, into collective activities, and into a set of shared concerns and challenges. It is important to make a distinction between this dynamic of inclusion and the "original" embeddedness of a relationship that remains in the group in which it first became established. This original embeddedness, which is characteristic of groups of young people, indissociably links relationships to contexts. In particular, most high school relationships remain embedded in the world in which they originated. However, what interests us most here is the embedding dynamic through which a dyadic relationship becomes integrated into a group in which a number of individuals engage in shared activities. Thus, Gaël involved a high share of the people he met in his musical activities. His childhood friend Gilles, for example, was introduced to his new friends and included in his music group:

Previously we saw each other mainly on a one-to-one basis because Gilles was originally just my friend and now, as I hang out with Fabien and Jérôme he's become a friend of theirs as well. All four of us spend time together and then we rehearse together. Fabien bass, Jérôme guitar, Gilles percussion, and I sing or play guitar, it just depends. At the beginning, I was the center of the group really. But we've got to know each other and now we have shared tastes and so we're all together in the group.

These dynamics should also be examined as they evolve over time, combining relational and biographical dimensions. Such examination reveals that new ties tended to be located within a single circle in the second wave (48.9 percent) but in waves 3 and 4 were more likely to exist outside circles (52.2 percent and 50.6 percent). Thus, for the youngest at the time of the first waves of the survey, new relationships tended to be established within a circle. As they got older, they uncoupled their new friends from the initial context much more quickly in order to see them outside of any circle. Those ties maintained from one survey wave to another were subsequently more likely to be located within several circles. Thus, the longer a relationship was maintained, the more likely it was to become embedded in several circles; but the older survey respondents got, the more likely their relationships were to be decoupled from circles right from the outset.

Furthermore, examination of the motivating forces driving the relationships, identified as we saw above by the answers to the question "What brings you together?," confirms that, as a relationship becomes uncoupled from its original contexts, so it becomes more intense. The more it becomes detached from its context, the more it depends on its own qualities and on the bond between the two people concerned and the more it is experienced as a strong tie. These motivating forces evolve as the relationship is sustained over time: the older the ties are, the more the share of contextual motivating forces declines and the more the share of motivating forces rooted in the tie itself increases. Thus, as a relationship endures over time, less importance is attached to shared activities, the common network, mutual assistance, and the characteristics of the Alter, and greater priority is given to the pleasure of being together, to the affective dimension and, of course, to the shared past. There is a tendency from wave to wave of the survey for the share of "contextual" motivating forces to decline. In the first wave, their share was 44 percent, in the second wave it was 38 percent and in the third and fourth waves it fell to 27 percent and 22 percent respectively. Thus, it would appear that the shift away from the contextual motivating forces toward the substance of the relationship itself is linked not only to the relationship's own internal temporality but also to advancing age. At the outset, the relationship is situated within a context; over time, it becomes detached from that context and (more quickly with age) it becomes focused on the quality of the relationship itself. This tendency to become detached from the original contexts becomes stronger with age.

Thus, what emerges from our analysis of the Caen panel survey is a tendency for new relationships to be rooted less and less in contexts as our respondents got older. With increasing age, these new relationships were increasingly more focused in their initial stages on factors directly linked to the interpersonal dimension. Over time, all the relationships became more strongly focused on the tie itself than on a particular context. Thus, as time passed and the young people become adults, individuation took precedence over embeddedness.

DISSOCIATING TIES FROM THE ORIGINAL CONTEXT: TOWARD "ONE-TO-ONE" RELATIONSHIPS

Another of these dynamics concerns the links between relationships within a network rather than their embeddedness in a circle, even though the two are sometimes linked: when we introduce our friends to each other, they are sometimes included in a circle, but not always. They may simply constitute an additional relational connection, but one not surrounded and sustained by collective activities or shared references. On the other hand, connections may disappear and members of Ego's network may stop seeing each other and dissociate themselves from each other while continuing to keep company with Ego. To introduce one's friends to each other or, conversely, to see them separately without bringing them together is to choose between two very different modes of sociability that affect the network's overall structuring.

The dissociative dynamic involves separating friends whom one used to see together. Gaël experienced this process with his friend Alexandre:

At the start, he was a friend of Jérôme's, one of my high school friends. And then, gradually, one thing led to another and after a few nights out we realized we get on well and we started hanging out together without necessarily being with the whole gang. I think it's more that we had things in common, quite simply. We enjoyed each other's company. In the beginning, when you don't know the people, you need to be in a group in order to get to know each other. Afterwards, we used to call each other and then began to hang out together without the others.

In this case, the dissociative dynamic was closely linked to the individuation dynamic. However, as we shall see, they can also diverge and vary over time.

In the first three waves of the survey, a question about strong ties was asked: "Have you ever arranged for the two of you to see each other just by yourselves?" The responses showed that this was the case for 61 percent of the strong ties (excluding family and romantic relationships). The connection between this question and that of circles requires further examination. The people most likely to see each other on a one-to-one basis were those belonging to several circles. Those who belonged to just one circle were more likely never to see each other alone, possibly because they were rather "imprisoned" in the circle. It would seem that membership of several circles gives a relationship greater autonomy and facilitates its individuation. This further confirms the hypothesis of a connection between the proliferation of shared activities and the individuation of relationships: the more the partners keep company with each other in different contexts and circles, the more the other is perceived as a person in his or her own right and not simply as someone playing a role. Thus, in this initial process of dissociation, relationships become detached from the original group and continue on a one-to-one basis.

The girls in the Caen panel were slightly more likely than the boys to see their friends "face to face" only and the youngest individuals were slightly more likely to do so than the oldest. Members of the highest and inter-mediate social categories, as well as holders of the baccalaureate, had a slightly greater tendency than the others to enter into dyadic relationships. Eighty-one per cent of "real friends" saw each other face to face, compared with 54 percent of buddies and 33 percent of mere acquaintances. The likelihood of two people seeing each other on a one-to-one basis also rose very steadily with the duration of the relationship. At the same time, however, these strong ties and real friends were also the ones that were most closely connected to other members of the network, making them the most central members. Consequently, they were more likely both to be "alone together" and to keep company with many others. Some of the oldest ones, on the other hand, remained totally isolated, such as childhood friends who had survived the disappearance of the group and no longer saw anyone but Ego on a one-to-one basis. Their closeness remained rooted in a shared past and would undoubtedly be out of step with Ego's more recent associates.

It is true that this tendency toward dissociation has certain similarities with the tendency toward individuation described earlier. In both cases, the dyadic dimension is given priority over the collective as the relationship is detached from its contexts. In view of this, significant and intense relation-ships are often more closely connected to other relationships, whereas they are relatively detached from circles. Thus, a distinction has to be made between embeddedness in circles and the interconnectedness of Alters with each other in networks. In circles, the context acts as an all-embracing environment in which the relationships are immediately more intertwined, multiplex. and based on shared activities (the "group"). In the intercon-nections, on the other hand, it is the relationships themselves that take precedence, with the characteristics and factors that bring together an Ego and an Alter in an "individuated" relationship. In circles, the transitivity is "contextual" and fundamental; in connections between members of a network, on the other hand, it is "relational" and constructed. It is to this latter aspect that we now turn.

ONLY CONNECT: THE DYNAMIC OF NETWORK CONSTRUCTION

We saw above that 25.7 percent of the meeting modes in the Toulouse survey and 31.2 percent in the Caen survey were products of the dynamic of network extension and strengthening; in other words, Ego got to know these people through third-party intermediaries. In return, Ego also introduced some of his friends to others. The triangle between Ego, Alter 1, and Alter 2 may be "closed" on the initiative of one of the Alters who introduces the other to Ego or by Ego introducing one Alter to the other. The perspective adopted here is that of Ego. This act is not an innocuous one: in introducing one person to another, Ego is evaluating these two Alters and deciding that they are compatible; however, he is also assuming that his relationship with both will not be adversely affected by the introductions. After all, these two Alters, who each have a more or less precise idea of who Ego is, will subsequently be able to compare these images of him, pool their information, and exchange their opinions on his behavior. Thus, Ego is putting the coherence of his personal "facets" at risk. If one of the Alters is a drinking pal and the other a very serious work colleague, Ego will have to manage the reconciliation of these two different identities. Introducing spouses or partners is just one example of these sometimes-awkward situations. Even though "centered" networks show us that Ego's partner is the most central figure, the one with whom the other relationships are most widely shared, this cannot always be taken for granted. Extensive areas of a network are sometimes not covered by this sharing, as was the case for Kévin, who liked to see his friends without his partner, and for Vérène, who reserved some of her holiday time to spend with her friends without her partner.

Bringing together friends previously unknown to each other may reveal or exacerbate differences, as it did for Viviane, who became aware of Pierre's social background by introducing him to Géraldine and Angélique:

They didn't really hit it off, because it's not really the same world. When all's said and done, Géraldine and Angélique don't come from the same background. It's true that where Pierre comes from, his father is very serious, they're very . . . not snobbish exactly, but still . . .. Whereas Géraldine comes from more of a working-class background, so it's not the same world. My background is similar to Angélique and Géraldine's, working-class, we can't do everything we'd like to.

On the other hand, sport brought her closer to Pierre. Thus, with Géraldine and Angélique she emphasized her working-class background, while with Pierre it was the sporty Viviane that came to the fore. However, having all been introduced to each other, they had not found enough points in common for the relationship to become firmly established. Thus, in some cases the "third link" does not take root, or fails to do so securely, and the triad functions like an inadequately closed triangle, as in the case of Colette, who ultimately turned this weak connection between her friends to her own advantage:

They must have known each other for ten years, but without really knowing each other. They know each other as friends of Colette in fact. From time to time I moan about Laure to Thifaine and then I moan about Thifaine to Laure.

Sometimes, conversely, this third tie is stronger; the friends introduced to each other may really hit it off and their relationship eventually becomes more important than their respective relationships with Ego, sometimes to the latter's great disappointment.

The closure of a triangle through a process of constructed transitivity may give rise to a "snowball" effect, with other people gradually becoming connected to each other, as Léa described:

It was through Wilfrid that I got to know Manu and Antoine, Antoine knew David, Manu is Charrette's brother and shares an apartment with Stéphane, and Laurent and Chantal were with me in my sophomore year and Isabelle knew Chantal, in fact everybody knew everybody, but it was all a question of connections. . .

For young people, this connectivity quickly leads to the formation of a group and in some cases a person can be connected to a whole set of people in one fell swoop. The relationship then becomes embedded in a circle.

However, although "triadic closure" is regarded by some structuralists as a virtually automatic tendency in the case of strong ties,[6] it proves to be much more uncertain in the dynamic of "real-life" relationships. Thus, for the Caen panel, calculation of the ratio of the proportion of three-edged triangles (transitivity completed) to that of one- or two-edged triangles (transitivity not completed) shows there was no clear increase in this constructed transitivity over time. There are, after all, many other biographical and relational factors that intervene to disrupt this tendency toward triadic closure. If this tendency is indeed confirmed, it will undoubtedly be over a very long period, whereas these young people's relationships were changing too quickly.

What happens over time to this tendency to connect or disconnect one's relationships? Measurement of network density and the centrality of ties over the various waves of the survey can help us identify changes in these dynamics. As they got older, from wave to wave of the survey, the young people in the Caen panel tended to have slightly denser networks (0.30 between age 17 and 20, 0.26 between age 26 and 33). More

---

[6] Granovetter even speaks of the "forbidden triad" when referring to triangles with just two edges in the case of strong ties. Establishment of the third relationship is for him structurally inevitable. M. S. Granovetter, "The Strength of Weak Ties," *The American Journal of Sociology* 78 (1973), 1360–1380; M. S. Granovetter, "The Strength of Weak Ties: A Network Theory Revisited," *Sociological Theory* (1983), 201–233.

Table 4.1 *Evolution of relative centrality over time*

Situation	% of high centrality second wave	% of high centrality third wave	% of high centrality fourth wave
Maintained	27.4[a]	25.0	19.2
New	15.1	12.7	17.0

[a] In the second wave, of the ties maintained since the first wave, 27.4 percent were in the high centrality category.

specifically, this density increased very slightly at the beginning and then steadily declined. The average values for the relative centrality[7] of the strong ties also declined from one wave to the next, falling from 0.29 to 0.22. In the case of friendships (excluding family and partners), the share of isolated relationships (degree centrality is zero) rose over time, from 20.7 to 28.95 of relationships, whereas the share of high degree centrality relationships declined steadily, from 28.8 percent of relationships to 22.3 percent). Thus, the Alters became less and less interconnected. Over the course of this life stage, the tendency was for relationships to become more scattered, more disconnected from each other. Our respondents tended to see their friends alone or two at a time rather than in larger groups and their friends were less likely to know each other.

In general terms, new ties were less central (in terms of this relative centrality) than relationships maintained since the previous wave. Thus, renewal of a network contributed to its dispersal. The ties that had been maintained from one wave to the next were more connected to other relationships than new ties, which tended to remain isolated (Table 4.1).

However, this tendency became less pronounced over time, with the gap narrowing very significantly. This means that, as they got older, the young people were less and less likely to centralize their established relationships and to leave their new relationships isolated. Maintained ties were less markedly central, while new relationships were slightly more central from the outset than in the previous periods; the individuals in question were more likely to be introduced to others without waiting for a number of years.

Over the precise periods that the relationships (excluding family and partners) were observed, the tendency among a slender majority of the

---

[7] This is the number of connections an Alter has with other Alters in the network in relation to the number of possible connections in that network.

Table 4.2 *Evolution of centrality from wave to wave of the survey (%)*[a]

Relative centrality	wave 1–wave 2	wave 2–wave 3	wave 3–wave 4
Increase	49.4	36.7	34.6
Reduction	47.4	60.0	58.8
Constant	3.2	3.3	6.6
Total	100	100	100
Total number[b]	247	330	379

[a] For example, centrality increased between wave 1 and wave 2 for 49.4 percent of the ties present in both waves.
[b] Some of the Alters retained from one wave to another do not appear in these centrality calculations since they are weak ties, for which this information was not collected.

Alters who were mentioned in waves 1 and 2 was for centrality to increase: the Alters become a little more connected to others. For the Alters present in waves 2 and 3, the main trend was in the opposite direction, toward a decrease in centrality: they became less and less connected to others. The same applies to the Alters present in waves 3 and 4 (Table 4.2).

Thus, what was being observed was a reversal of the initial trend: while the young people initially developed their relationships by connecting them slightly more with their other friends, which also explains the slight increase in network density in the first period, they tended to separate them more as they got older. Among the youngest respondents, a relationship that was maintained became more connected; as they moved into adulthood, such relationships became less connected. Thus, even though the most important and long-lasting relationships became increasingly connected with other Alters over the course of the relationship, it remains the case that, as they entered adulthood, the young people gradually developed a tendency increasingly to separate their friends from each other.

IMPENDING ADULTHOOD BRINGS A CHANGE IN THE WAY RELATIONSHIPS ARE FORMED

Thus, relational dynamics evolve along three main axes: multiplexity/specialization, individuation/embeddedness, and connection/dissociation. These dynamics are at work over the course of a relationship, causing it to evolve as it becomes established and takes root. They also evolve over biographical time, as young people get older and change the ways in which they conduct and sustain relationships.

In order to summarize these results, we can return to the diagrammatic representation of the transition dynamics between contexts, networks, and relationships presented in Chapter 3, Figure 3.1). The relational dynamics that prove to be dominant in these young people's modes of sociability are now represented by the large black arrows in Figures 4.1 and 4.2. A distinction has been made between two biographical periods, namely the end of high school (transition from first to second wave) in the first diagram (Figure 4.1) and, in the second diagram (Figure 4.2), the entry into adulthood (transition from third to fourth wave). These diagrams are analytical: in real-life situations, networks and circles are usually more closely intertwined. Our aim here is to identify the corners of the diagram that are the principal reference points for relationships. The arrows indicate the ways in which relationships' modes of reference typically evolve.

When they were in high school (Figure 4.1), the young people mainly met each other in that context. What counted above all was being "there together," without necessarily engaging in activities or keeping company with each other outside of school. This context disappeared after the

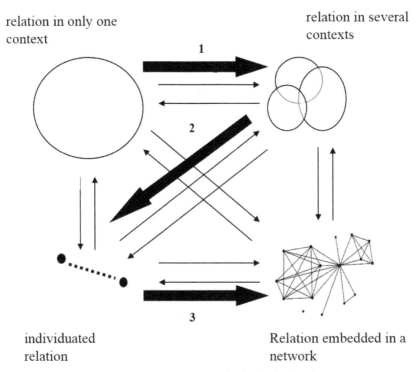

relation in only one context

relation in several contexts

individuated relation

Relation embedded in a network

Fig. 4.1 First survey waves (end of high school)

baccalaureate and many of these relationships were lost, although some were maintained as those involved frequented different contexts and shared an increasing number of activities, thereby gradually putting their relationships on a firmer footing (arrow no. 1). This multiplicity of contexts was a factor in the individuation of relationships: the more diverse the contexts in which a relationship was situated became, the less importance was attached to the original context so that the relationship gradually detached itself from its reference circles and became autonomous (arrow no. 2). Finally, the newly autonomous relationships were sometimes introduced to others, thereby forging new links between the Alters (arrow no. 3) and slightly increasing the network's overall density and the centrality of the most important relationships.

Some years later, the mode of sociability had changed (Figure 4.2). While relationships continued to originate in contexts, they now became detached and individuated much more quickly (arrow no. 1), without any prior need to increase the number of shared activities. Those relationships that had been multiplex became specialized by reducing the reference circles and cutting the range of shared activities in order to concentrate

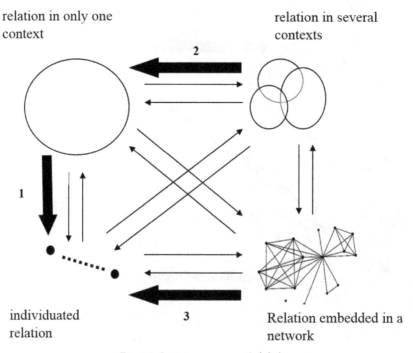

relation in only one
context

relation in several
contexts

individuated
relation

Relation embedded in a
network

Fig. 4.2 Last survey waves (adults)

solely on social activities, particularly meals together (arrow no. 2). Finally, relationships became increasingly separate from each other, with friends being seen on a one-to-one basis or, at most, with their partner (arrow no. 3). Ultimately, everything converged toward the individuation and autonomization of relationships, which were now constructed and consolidated very rapidly in a dyadic dimension based on the substance of the relationship itself rather than on context, activities, or groups.

Fleur gave us a clear explanation of this change:

> Before, there was the group, and now, I have friends but there's no group: I see people, and often that'll be just one person alone or maybe two or three, but there shouldn't be a lot of people. And I think the group is finished with … I've been in touch with Ludovic a bit because he's someone who's been able to stay in contact with me because we have a certain affinity, things in common. So meeting people individually, that's OK, but as a group …. Before, we used to do things together, and now I have the impression it was all a bit superficial, with hindsight at least. I tell myself yes, it's true, we used to party together, we used to tell each other things when we were together talking, but did we get to know what people were really like? Did we really know them, I'm not sure, and I don't just want to do things with people, I want to get to know them properly.

*

*   *

A later survey wave in 2015 with part of the same Caen panel showed that this process of individuation of relationships was confirmed when respondents were in their forties. The three axes on which the relational dynamics are situated and which we have identified empirically, namely the multiplexity/specialization, the individuation/embeddedness, and the connection/dissociation axes, might be entry points for comparisons and generalizations to different populations and life stages.

To summarize evolutions in this youthful period, it can be said that as they finish high school, young people's relationships tend to become established in the first instance through an accumulation of shared activities. This increase in multiplexity, which may also arise out of a specific difficulty or crisis, leads to the individuation of relationships: at the same time as the contexts proliferate, their hold weakens and the motivating force of a relationship becomes more personal. Once relationships have become detached from the original contexts and individuated, they can be connected to others in the network. When they advance into adulthood, young people change the way in which they form relationships.

They follow a different path. They are much quicker to detach dyadic relationships from the initial context and to do so without necessarily passing through the stage of accumulating shared activities and circles. Most relationships become specialized and also increasingly dissociated from each other. This process of specialization and dissociation goes hand in hand with a more general tendency toward the intensification of sociability: people have fewer relationships, but they are stronger than during their high school days, when they hung out in groups and engaged in a wide variety of leisure activities.

The analysis of relational dynamics is concerned with the emergence of relationships and with the connections that are established between them and with the other levels of the social world. Understanding how individuals become social beings is of course an important object of investigation in sociology. Here we have been able to observe the emergence of a change in the ways in which individuals connect with others at a stage in their lives when the adult mode of socialization is at stake. This original result can serve to confirm the value of analyzing individual trajectories, relationship histories, network configurations, and their links to social contexts in conjunction with each other.

5

Relationships That End, Relationships
That Endure

Any study of the dynamics of relationships should consider the question of their end. Whether it happens gradually or suddenly, this is a frequent occurrence. For sociologists, investigation of what causes certain relationships to disappear is certainly as instructive as any inquiry into the factors determining their course, and the two are of course linked. However, studies addressing this issue are very rare.[1] In examining the factors that cause relationships to end, we will at the same time be inquiring into those that encourage them to persist. Network structure is itself changed by these disappearances and, conversely, it plays a part in ensuring the solidity of relationships.

THE REASONS GIVEN WHEN RELATIONSHIPS END

One of the innovations in the Toulouse survey compared with the Californian survey on which it is based was the introduction of questions on defunct relationships. Such relationships were touched on in the following way: "Are there any individuals who were important to you two years ago and with whom you no longer have any relationship?" For the first three individuals named, the interviewers asked the same questions as those for the relationships in the subsample, as well as a question on the reasons for the "disappearance" of each of these relationships. A total of 180 interviewees (45 percent) cited at least one "disappeared" relationship, which produced 249 relationships in all. This proportion was similar across the various occupational categories; it was a little higher among holders of

---

[1] See, for example, B. Wellman, R. Y. Wong, D. Tindall, N. Nazer, "A Decade of Network Change: Turnover, Persistence and Stability in Personal Communities," *Social Networks* 19 (1997), 27–50.

Table 5.1 *Reasons given by interviewees to explain the end of relationships (Toulouse survey)*

Reason for the end of the relationship	%
Breakdown of relationship	17.7[a]
Death, disappearance	25.7
Relocation	26.5
Don't know ("That's life," etc.)	30.1
Total (249 relationships)	100

[a] For example, in 17.7 percent of cases, the Toulouse interviewees attributed the end of the relationship to a relational breakdown.

the baccalaureate (53 percent) and qualifications requiring two years' post-baccalaureate education (55 percent) than among those who stopped before the baccalaureate (36 percent) or continued in higher education for four years after the baccalaureate (45 percent). The older the interviewees were, the less likely they were to mention defunct relationships: 65 percent of the 18–25 year-olds cited at least one, compared with 48 percent of 26–45 year-olds, 36 percent of 46–65 year-olds and just 34 percent of those aged over 65. The process of relationship renewal had slowed down with age. On average, those who mentioned defunct relationships mentioned more relationships in all.

Why did these relationships come to an end? There are many reasons why a relationship might become defunct (Table 5.1). Analysis shows that breakdowns for purely relational reasons accounted for a little less than one-fifth of the defunct relationships. A quarter of them were due quite simply to the death of the person mentioned. Another quarter were attributable to relocation. This leaves the "don't knows," which account for 30 percent of the defunct relationships and can be interpreted as context effects (disappearance of the collective contexts in which the relationships were actualized) or simply as an imperceptible "drifting apart" (relationships not maintained).

The Caen panel provides a closeup picture only of the period of entry into adulthood. However, the method here is also different. In this survey, which was repeated every three years, interviewees' networks were reconstructed in each wave using exactly the same procedure. By comparing the lists of names mentioned with those mentioned three years previously, the investigators were able to identify the defunct relationships. They then went back to the interviewees, showing them the lists and asking them to state the reasons for the disappearances. The longitudinal nature of the

survey made it possible to identify these defunct relationships more systematically. After all, there is a terrible tendency to forget people one no
longer sees. With the longitudinal method, the investigators were able to
keep track of all the people mentioned previously and remind interviewees
about them. It was also the case that some relationships were mentioned in
the first wave, not mentioned in the second wave and then mentioned
again in the third wave. Such relationships can be regarded as "dormant"
in the second wave and as having been subsequently reactivated.[2] Some
relationships even "disappeared" twice, namely those mentioned in the
first wave, not mentioned in the second wave, mentioned again in the third
wave and not mentioned in the fourth wave. We were interested in the
reasons on each occasion.

Out of a total of 10,804 relationships mentioned over the four waves of
the survey, 39.4 percent had disappeared at one point or another, 82 percent of which were non-family relationships (if Ego's family relationships
are excluded, then the total share of defunct relationships rises to 47.1
percent). The reasons for the disappearances were divided into seven
categories on the basis of the interviews. No information was gathered
for 19.4 percent of relationships (often family, since some interviewers did
not always ask about the reasons for the disappearance in the case of family
relationships). Consequently, Ego's family, which in any event "disappears" less and "reappears" more, is left to one side. This leaves a total of
3,097 relationships that are not Ego's family members and for whose
disappearance reasons were given (Table 5.2).

Over and above any method effects, the differences between the results
of the Caen and Toulouse surveys are attributable to the characteristics of
the Caen youth panel. Thus, it is logical that the share of deaths is –
happily – low. Similarly, geographic distance, which is often regarded as
temporary during this phase of the life course, becomes less important,
particularly since it is sometimes "absorbed" by the category relating to the
disappearance of contexts (which were attached to a place) or by that
relating to social distance when the two come into play simultaneously.

---

[2] It may be wondered whether there was a possible "survey effect" at work here, whereby the
mere fact of reminding interviewees of relationships proved likely to reawaken certain
dormant ties. This effect could not be avoided. However, we think it unlikely that it
persisted over the three years that elapsed between each wave of the survey. Rather, it was
immediately after the interviews that thinking harder about their networks might have
prompted interviewees to take steps in respect of their relationships that they might not
otherwise have taken. From the third wave of the survey onward, interviewees were
explicitly questioned about this.

Table 5.2 *Reasons given by Caen interviewees to explain non-mention of relationships, excluding Ego's family*

Reasons for non-mention	%
Context disappeared	35.4[a]
Lost contact	26.6
Network effect	15.3
Social distance	9.1
Falling out	7.4
Geographic distance	5.5
Death	0.7
Total	100
Number of respondents	3,097

[a] For example, 35.4 percent of respondents attributed the disappearance of the relationships they no longer mentioned to the disappearance of the context.

Ultimately, it is as if, by "zooming in" on a population of young people, we had managed to examine in greater detail the "breakdown" category in the Toulouse survey, thereby equipping ourselves with the means to evaluate the effects of contexts, networks, and social differentiation in greater detail.

Disappearance of Context and Loss of Contact

The disappearance of the context in which the relationship developed is the most frequently identified reason. This applies in particular to high-school friendships, which typically do not last once those involved have completed their secondary education. This was the case for Alban:

We were all at the same high school, we used to see each other several times a week. I went on to do a two-year technical diploma, the others went their separate ways, so we no longer saw each other. Even Maryline and Béatrice, we must have met up once or twice in September, like you always try to meet up after the summer holidays, but well, it just happened naturally.

Similarly, relationships that had been confined to a workplace, to a voluntary association, a leisure activity, or a neighborhood tended not to be sustained when those involved left the milieu.

The second most frequently cited reason is summarized here as "loss of contact." This means either that the relationship was not evidently broken off but just withered away gradually for no particularly obvious reason or that the individuals in question were not mentioned but could have been in a pinch.[3] In some cases, they left without leaving their contact details, so there was no way of getting in touch with them[4]. The young people sometimes said they used to bump into each other, say hello, and exchange news but without "seeking each other out," as Alexis said:

I run across Alexandra from time to time but that's because we see each other without seeking each other out. We see each other, that's nice, but we could just as well manage without. I think there's a change too. If you lose touch with each other, things become more distant and you go your separate ways.

Sometimes these relationships had been reactivated and then mentioned in the following wave. This is what Emeline said as she recounted how, quite by chance, she had met up again with her friend Virginie:

She changed schools. We didn't see each other for a very, very long time. In junior high school, we were as thick as thieves, but you get older, you develop, you go your own separate ways, I just accepted it. We met up again quite by chance a year ago. I'd just come back from holiday and bumped into her in a supermarket. Oh my goodness, we just fell into each other's arms. We had so much to say to each other, we spent hours in a bar. We caught up with everything we'd been doing all those years. And so we were off again. And what's more we had all the more things in common. She'd just started at a business school. I'd just finished preparing for the entrance examinations for a *grande école*. We were both obsessed by competitive exams! It was really funny . . . .. So we see very little of each other but really I don't think now I'd have any difficulty in getting back in touch with her.

Thus, such "dormant" relationships can be reawakened, new connections discovered, and old friendships reinvigorated.

The Network Effect and Chain Reactions

Next comes what we term a "network effect," which means that if such and such a person is not mentioned, it is usually because another person who acted as intermediary has himself disappeared. Thus, people often stop seeing a partner's family and friends following a separation, since it was the partner who "made the connection." If this network effect plays such a significant role in the Caen panel, it is undoubtedly linked to the fact that, among young people, groups of friends are often adopted (and abandoned)

---

[3] It should be noted that, if the interviewee stated at this point that he had forgotten to mention someone with whom he was still in contact, someone he still met intentionally, this Alter was reintroduced into the network and was not included among the lost relationships.

[4] On the effects of Facebook on this issue, see Chapter 12.

all together and at the same time; such groups disappear when the central element, the leader or "bridge," disappears. As we have seen, young people's relationships are more contextual and tend not to become individuated until later. This was the case for Alban, for example:

I've stopped seeing all the people who were with Cyril, practically, because we always used to hang out at Cyril's place. So as soon as I stopped going to Cyril's place, I no longer saw any of these people. And as for the others, Fabien, Annabelle, etc., we used to go skating together, but they were mainly Anthony's friends. And as soon as I stopped seeing Anthony, I didn't see them any more either. As soon as I stop seeing someone I also stop seeing all the other people he's connected to as well.

The network effect was also alluded to when incompatibilities had prevented relationships from continuing, as when someone found themselves dragged into a dispute or was forced by a third party to "decide whose side you're on." This is what happened to Fleur:

Sandrine is someone who appreciates me, she would have perhaps been very happy for us to see each other but I wasn't too keen on the relationships she had with some others. I didn't want to meet up with her friends, with whom I had nothing at all in common. There's perhaps also the fact that I had got close to Caroline and Caroline had got back together again with the brother of one of Sandrine's best friends, which may also have led to a bit of cooling of relations because there was no love lost between the two brothers. So against my better judgment I got dragged into all that business.

Moving in together as a couple can also give rise to tensions that lead to the abandonment of certain relationships, as was the case for Thibaut:

What happened with Manuela was that, before, she used to be my best friend. No doubt about it. And then all the ructions, it was because she and my wife just didn't get on at all, so I had to make a choice. I chose my wife.

Introducing friends to a spouse and managing relations within a couple does, after all, constitute a crucial test for a relationship. Here too, the future of a relationship depends more on its embeddedness in circles and on a series of interconnections than on interpersonal affinities and is determined more at the level of the network than at that of the dyad.

Social Distance: A Gulf Opens Up

Next on the list of reasons why relationships end is the notion of social distance, which encompasses a range of different situations. However, the central idea is that people grow apart because their lives have diverged in terms of social status. Many young people who get to know each other in the relatively homogenous environment of high school subsequently take divergent paths: some go on to higher education, others start work immediately on finishing high school, some are upwardly mobile, others are not, some get married and have children soon afterwards, others do not. These increasing differentiations make it more difficult to have shared activities, tastes, and affinities. And, more subjectively, a certain "class feeling" may also gradually emerge and open up a gap, as Léa experienced with her friend Nadège:

When I'd finished my technical diploma course, all I heard was "Her ladyship is taking the entrance exams for an elite business school...," and then she started to tell me about her courses and to lecture me because my technical diploma wasn't worth anything, whereas she was at an elite business school . . . she drove me nuts! She said to me at Christmas, "You've no idea, there's loads of guys in my class, you should see the cars they drive . . .." That's all she had to say to me. Before, when we happened to hang out with people who had loads of money, we didn't give a damn about them, we didn't want to be like them, always putting other people down. I don't know, they've really put ideas into her head at that school of hers . . . I've really fallen out of favor!

Paul had also had experience of these social classifications:

Céline got married to a lawyer, so you see, just to give you a brief idea, her first daughter was called Victoria. Victoria, I ask you! The first time I went to their house, the little girl said to me: "My daddy's a lawyer!" So they're people who are sufficiently twisted in their own minds to tell their four-year-old daughter that being a lawyer is a worthy occupation. Right? So that's already something I really don't appreciate!

Thus, marriage, which triggers a new "construction of reality,"[5] plays a part in estranging certain friends by bringing about changes in people's behavior and social lives, as it did in Solange's case:

I knew Sandra before Laurent, in high school. And when I started going out with Laurent, I introduced him to her, we had some nights out together. It's true they didn't really hit if off because he said she was a bit scatty. She is a bit eccentric, in the way she dresses and in the way she behaves as well. She's got her head in the clouds. She makes me laugh, she's a bit of an escape for me, an opportunity to do something different. For Laurent, there are people he doesn't try to get to know.

---

[5] P. Berger, H. Kellner, "Marriage and the Construction of Reality: An Exercise in the Microsociology of Knowledge," *Diogenes* 12(46) (1964), 1–24; Cf. also E. Bott, *Family and Social Network: Roles, Norms and External Relationships in Ordinary Urban Families* (New York: Free Press, 1971 [1957]).

When he doesn't like someone, he doesn't like them, there's no way round it. And I'm getting a bit like that too.

Moving in together as a couple and the arrival of children contribute to the differentiation of lifestyles and can cause certain friends to be rejected. If the two parties to a relationship do not go through them at the same time, these transitions can be enough to cause some relationships to disappear. It may be, when the second person goes through them in their turn, that the relationship becomes a candidate for reactivation, as Serge described:

I don't see Élodie anymore, because she's got a boyfriend and she's always with him. Now I've got a girlfriend, perhaps it'll get sorted out. Let's say it wasn't easy, when I was on my own, to foist myself on them. Now, if I see her again, this time with Carine, if they all get on with each other, we may be able to do things together.

Once both Serge and Élodie had partners, it was possible that the relationship might be resumed.

Spatial Distance: An Elastic Factor

Spatial distance, which is the next factor on our list, would seem to be a more objective form of separation: it is not difficult to understand why having to travel hundreds or even thousands of miles in order to see each other might be a factor in the end of relationships. Or at least of some of them: there are certainly some relationships, which, from this point of view, should indeed have come to an end but which in fact survive, with the person who relocated continuing to occupy an important place and remaining in contact by email, telephone, Facebook, or even, still today, by post. On the other hand, for some people (particularly those from working-class backgrounds), moving just two or three miles away can be enough to make some friends "inaccessible." It turns out, in fact, that the question of spatial distance is very often associated with various forms of social distance. For simplicity's sake, some people attribute the disappearance of a relationship to spatial distance whereas this is not the only reason, and other differences, in the life cycle for example, are also relevant and sometimes closely linked. This was the case, for example, when Suzie spoke of her relationship with Stéphanie:

I was still living with my parents. She left her parent's house three years ago now. So the fact that we were no longer living side by side, that she had gone to Caen, it wasn't easy. Before, I just hopped over and there I was, but she moved to live with her boyfriend and then afterwards, a year later, I met Fabrice, and after another year, we did the same thing. It's the distance that was the problem. I'd say it declined because I still had a year of school to do when she had already left. She did the beautician course and finished a year before me. So it began to decline because she was working and I was still at school. We saw less of each other because she no longer went with me to school. Because she was working and I was still at school. She was able to go out in the evenings, but I couldn't because I had my homework to do. Same at the weekend. And then she left the village.

Here, spatial distance, identified as the primary cause, was preceded by time and accompanied by other factors that also contributed to the relationship's decline. Suzie remained in education whereas Stéphanie was working, then Suzie continued to live with her parents while Stéphanie left home to live with her boyfriend, a factor that also came into play alongside the fact that she had left her village (which is only three miles or so from Caen).

Furthermore, the influence of spatial distance is closely linked to the strength of the relationship. It is an obstacle primarily for weak relationships or those that are already fading away, whereas it is not enough to break down strong relationships. Indeed, it may even further strengthen strong ties and help to sort out real friends from the rest. Nevertheless, it remains the case that, even when associated with other factors, the spatial dimension does affect relationships. We will return later to these questions of spatial and social distance.

Conflict: A Cause That Is Not So Intrinsic

Conflict, which arises out of the very heart of a relationship (even though it is fueled by other factors, of course), is ultimately fairly uncommon. The causes of disputes prove to be quite varied: jealousy, unfortunate and hurtful words, failure to fulfill the duties of friendship that gives rise to bitter disappointment, professional rivalries, love affairs, etc. Many of our interviewees gave vent to disappointment caused by discovering that a person was self-interested, profiteering, a sponger, or selfish. This was the case, for example, for Mélanie, who had supported Aurélie when she was in need but now resented her for having preferred other friends to her, and Jérémie, who resented Yves because he only called him when he had a favor to ask him. This behavior seemed to them to contradict their notion of friendship, and the severing of relations was painful.

In the workplace, disputes tend to take the form of resentment following a failure, tensions with superiors, competition for jobs, and feelings of injustice. Such incidents are also encountered in voluntary and community associations, as Thomas described:

War was declared. Music is like football, you're always getting at each other: "Well well, you're playing that," "I'm playing this, and better than you" .... In fact, Yohann is the only son of Guy, who is the conductor of the brass band, I was giving percussion lessons, Yohann's girlfriend arrived, she played percussion, and he wanted to give her my job, well that didn't happen, certainly not.

Some of these disputes come about through a sequence of network effects: out of solidarity, someone supports a friend who has been hurt by another with whom the first individual therefore also ceases relations. Thus, Emeline chose to support one friend against another:

I tried to break off contact with Céline, because she had had occasion to work with Isabelle, among others, and it went very, very badly. There was no affinity between them at all. Céline played a few nasty tricks on Isabelle. I only got one side of the story, I only heard Isabelle's take on it all, but I trust her absolutely and I decided that Céline was no longer someone I wanted to have anything to do with.

People are frequently enjoined to choose sides. This type of chain reaction is also typical of family disputes, a very thorny topic, into which young people sometimes find themselves dragged despite themselves.[6] More generally, incompatibilities of mood, jealousy, and the marking out of areas of influence between spouse and friends, or between friends, are the cause of many disputes and relationship breakdowns. In some cases, the hurt arises because expectations are not fulfilled, because the friend does not put an equal amount of effort into the relationship, or because he shares his relationships too much. Célia, for example, was offended by and indeed became jealous of Virginie's other relationships:

I really had a very strong friendship with Virginie; we spoke on the phone, she came to my house, I went to hers at the weekend, we shared everything ... and then we managed to fall out. There was Nadine, in the beginning we used to see her a little bit, she was nice but I wasn't too keen on her and so there came a point where they started doing lots of things together. Virginie began to go off the rails a bit with those girls, to do things I didn't like and so one day we had to stop talking to each other completely, we explained everything to each other in writing and since then I've never been able to discuss anything like that again.

---

[6] D. Le Gall used the Caen survey to examine this question: D. Le Gall, "Family Conflicts in France through the Eyes of Teenagers," in R. Klein (ed.) *Multidisciplinary Perspectives on Family Violence in Europe* (London: Routledge, 1998), pp. 79–109.

The breakdown of a love affair is not always really conflictive but is generally fraught and painful and also arises out of the very heart of a relationship. As we shall see, it frequently leads to the restructuring of an entire network. These questions of family conflicts and the breakdown of love affairs are very complex topics, on which we cannot dwell here, however.

Of course, a relationship can also end because the person in question dies. While this is not a frequent occurrence in the age range of our survey population, friends do die, whether as a result of accident or, more rarely, illness or suicide. In some cases, this constitutes a genuine trauma, as it did for Elodie, whose best friend Jack committed suicide. The consequences were serious on various levels: for the structure of her network, which lost a central figure, for her boyfriend, who failed to understand what was going on, causing her to break off the relationship, and for her education, with Elodie leaving the business school where she had been studying and going to join her parents in the United States. This suicide raised many questions for Elodie and led to some profound changes in her life. Young people's relationship to death could be a subject in its own right, but it is not the focus of this book. It is an age at which death is not envisaged at all, and when grandparents or friends die, the shock can be very great indeed.

The reasons for the ending of a relationship are more intertwined than this typology suggests. There is more likely to be a bundle of interconnected factors at work than a single cause. In the interviews, various explanations were advanced over the course of the conversations and the various factors that emerged had all affected each other. One could see reasons being put forward one after the other and then becoming linked: relocation, moving in with a partner, career decisions, differences in lifestyles, etc. were all interacting with each other. One factor may conceal another, but their power lies above all in their coexistence and (de)synchronization.

Who Loses Which Relationships and Why?

The reasons for losing relationships are to be found in the social space and the characteristics of the relationship in question, mainly age and the length of time it has existed. In the Caen survey, which, it should be remembered, focused on a young population, it was the youngest respondents (up to high-school leaving age) from working-class backgrounds who were the most likely to lose relationships because they stopped spending time in the context. The fact of having "lost touch with each other" was also more frequently cited by those from working-class backgrounds, but later in their lives, after the age of twenty-five. Network effects were more frequently cited by the youngest respondents from the higher social classes. The impacts of social and spatial distance were more pronounced among the higher social classes and between the ages of twenty-one and twenty-five: it was at this point, at the beginning of their working life, that these differentiations became more firmly entrenched. Finally, disputes were more frequently mentioned after the age of twenty-six and by respondents from working-class backgrounds. There was no difference between the behavior of men and women in these regards. In the Toulouse survey, which covered a much wider range of ages but on the basis of less detailed data, "fatalistic" reasons ("don't know, that's life"), which may be likened to contextual factors or simply loss of contact, become increasingly common with age, as well as the death of friends, of course. Conversely, relationship breakdowns and other disputes decline very markedly with age, while reasons linked to spatial distance decline more gradually. Thus, relationships break down for contextual reasons, because of disputes, or because of geographic distance among young people, in particular, whereas in the older age groups they fade away without the reasons being clearly identified or simply disappear because one of the partners dies (Table 5.3).

Moreover, the more recently established relationships were proportionately the ones most frequently lost; for young people, the causes were largely contextual. Typically, there was an unstable set of weak ties, particularly around the high-school years. Relationships of medium length were a little more susceptible to the impact of geographic and social distance but were also more typically strong ties. Once deaths are set aside, the longer the relationships had lasted, the less likely they were to end because of a relationship breakdown (particularly after they had existed for

Table 5.3 *The reasons why relationships end, by age (Toulouse survey) (%)*

Age group	Death	Breakdown	Distance	Don't know (that's life)	Total
18–25	7.3	36.6[a]	34.1	22.0	100
26–45	23.1	20.1	28.4	28.4	100
46–65	31.5	3.7	25.9	38.9	100
Over 65	65.0			35.0	100
Total	25.7	17.7	26.5 (66)	30.1	100

[a] For example, in the 18–25 age group, 36.6 percent of the relationships that end do so because of a breakdown, according to interviewees.

more than ten years) and the more the causes became undifferentiated ("that's life" or "lost touch"). Those who had "disappeared" were usually isolated individuals not connected with other people in the network; the relationships in question had begun at school, at university, or as a result of involvement in associations of various kinds, and ended because of geographic distance or simply because the partners had "lost touch" with each other. Turnover in personal networks is very clearly linked to changes in life contexts.[7]

All this confirms that relationships are constantly changing over the course of an individual's life and that this recomposition takes place a little more quickly during the periods of transition between the various phases of the life course (adolescence and youth, starting a family, retirement). In these transitional periods, affiliations to various groups (fellow students, work colleagues, family, etc.) are reconfigured, which is reflected in changes in individuals' relational environments and also in the ways in which they evolve. In the younger age groups, context effects play a major role. Thus, at the beginning of adulthood, social distinctions, geographic distance, network effects, and conflictive break-downs begin to play their parts; it is during this period that adult roles take shape and social identities separate out. Later in life, relationships tend to fade away gradually without any identified cause or obvious breakdown.

The same individual usually experiences various causes of relationship breakdown in his own network: he loses some friends by giving up a particular leisure activity, others by moving to a different town, and yet others following a dispute or indirectly when a group breaks up. However, some people seem more likely than others to experience certain forms of breakdown. Amélie, for example, had a tendency to fall out with everybody and both her friendships and her family relationships were studded with numerous disputes. Joël, who was still single, distanced himself gradually from all his friends who had set up home with their partners. Diane observed that all her friends were leaving her village to live in the city and bemoaned the fact that she was "stuck" there. In the wake of her divorce, Solange saw her network suddenly reduced in size as her ex-husband's family decamped, together with many of her own friends who, as Catholics, disapproved of the divorce. Thus, the reasons why relationships

---

[7] M. L. Small, D. P. Vontrese, P. McMahan, "How Stable Is the Core Discussion Network?," *Social Networks* 40 (2015), 90–102.

end are a product of configurations in which sociographic and demographic factors and personal situation play a part, as well as cultural "dispositions" and more or less predictable biographical events. These considerations can also help us identify what, conversely, makes relationships endure.

THE FACTORS THAT MAKE FOR LASTING RELATIONSHIPS

Systematic comparison of those relationships that last with those that disappear enables us to identify the factors that help to make relationships last or, conversely, jeopardize their durability. The Caen longitudinal survey is particularly well suited to this type of comparison. Over the four waves of the survey, various scenarios might emerge. Relationships might appear in the first wave and still be cited throughout the survey or they might disappear in waves 2–4. They might appear later, if Ego and Alter did not meet until wave 3 or 4. The time span of each relationship can be constructed over the nine years covered by the four waves of the survey. For that purpose, the relationships were divided into four temporal categories:[8] the "perennials" are the Alters that remained present from the point at which they first appeared onward; the "disappeared" are those who, at one point or another, stopped being mentioned "once and for all"; the "ephemerals" appeared in just one wave of the survey and then disappeared; the "returners" appeared, disappeared, and returned. No fewer than 44.2 percent of all the relationships were maintained over all four waves of the survey, making the "perennials" the largest category. Returners accounted for 7.1 percent of the total. Slightly less than one-third (31.9 percent) disappeared at one point or another, while 16.8 percent made a fleeting appearance. However, in the end, we grouped the "returners" and the "perennials" together: the returners remained dormant for a while but were reactivated by a chance meeting in the street, a birthday, or a contextual reconnection. Family and romantic relationships were significantly longer lasting. To a certain extent, family ties are longer lasting because they are constructed as such. They may go unmentioned at a certain point, but they are always "there" in the background (Table 5.4).

What are the characteristics of the individuals and relationships that influence the time span of the ties, that is, their propensity to disappear or to endure over the course of the survey? The specific effects of a number of

---

[8] We excluded those Alters who were mentioned for the first time in the last wave of the survey. This leaves a total of 9,627 relationships.

Table 5.4 *Temporal categories for relationships over the four waves of the Caen panel survey by type of relationship (%)*

Temporal category	Relationship				
	Non-family	Family	Partner's family (in-laws)	Partner	Total
Perennial	34.0[a]	79.4	71.5	82.6	51.3
Disappeared	41.4	17.9	15.5	13.0	31.9
Ephemeral	24.6	2.7	13.0	4.3	16.8
Total	100	100	100	100	100
Number of relationships	5,628	2,769	709	161	9,267

[a] For example, 34 percent of non-family relationships are classified as perennial.

variables can be measured by means of a logistic regression on this time span. Only non-family and non-romantic relationships are considered here, a total of 5,628 relationships. Neither Ego's gender nor the fact that Ego and Alter are of the same gender is significant. Social background is not significant if it is isolated from educational stream, which in fact doubles its impact. This plays a part in the sense that those leaving high school with the baccalaureate in economics and social sciences were less inclined to have relationships that disappeared or were ephemeral and were thus better at maintaining them. The youngest age groups had a very strong tendency to have relationships that disappeared rather than endured. This reflects the impact of leaving school and the subsequent loss of contact with large numbers of classmates during this period of transition. This effect was also evident among the 21–25 year-olds, albeit to a lesser extent, and was undoubtedly due to the time spent in higher education, which did nothing to stabilize relationships. For those in higher education, moreover, relationships were more transient. Those in employment were less likely to lose their relationships. Specialized relationships were more likely to disappear than multiplex ones. Thus, the fact of cutting across a number of different contexts and sharing a range of activities and roles was associated with stable relationships. Other studies have shown that the most "peripheral" and least multiplex relationships in a network are the ones most likely to disappear.[9] Finally, recently established

[9] See, in particular, R. L. Kahn, T. C. Antonucci, "Convoys over the Life Course: Attachment, Roles and Social support," in P. B. Baltes and O. Brim (eds.) *Life-Span Development and Behavior* (New York: Academic Press, 1980), pp. 253–286; D. L. Morgan, M. B. Neal, P. Carder, "The Stability of Core and Peripheral Networks over Time," *Social Networks* 19

relationships were much more ephemeral than others and were also more likely to disappear. Thus, the fact of having endured for a long time was clearly correlated with durability. This is not necessarily a tautology, since the ties that had been established longest were also the most solid. Thus, friendships formed in childhood were more likely to endure (48.6 percent) than to disappear (44.9 percent); friendships formed during high school, between the ages of 16 and 19, were much more likely to disappear (59.9 percent), while those formed at university or in the early stages of the working life (between the ages of 20 and 30) were above all ephemeral (42 percent to 49 percent). This being so, the limitations of the Caen survey do deprive us of a certain degree of distance. However, the fact that the longest established relationships were also in general the most stable ones has also been observed in other studies, which have identified this "core" of long-established ties around which a group of more transient relationships gravitates. Moreover, the friends one sees rarely may also be enduring relationships: this applies particularly to childhood friends who have moved a long way away but with whom one remains in touch. After all, 57.5 percent of the people seen just once or twice a year were enduring relationships.

For Antoine, for example, the long history of his relationship with Manu has, in his view, helped to make it virtually everlasting, come what may:

The older you get, the more selective you become, that's clear. And then the relationships you retain are stronger . . .. We're aware there's a past, a history that connects us and when we see each other, we get on very well. And I think that Manu, now, whatever happens, unless there's really a massive, massive bust-up, I think that even if we don't see each other for two years, when we do eventually meet up, it'll be as if we'd seen each other just the day before.

He makes a clear distinction between this relationship and his present, more transient ones

I put the people I see into two categories. There are people I mix with because they're the ones I'm working with at the moment, they're temporary relationships, casual friendships. It's work that connects us. They're people I'm going to lose touch with, that's clear. And then there are others, I'm at the age now where you invest more in some relationships because you're able to judge them with a little more distance.

(1996), 9–25; I. K. Klein, T. van Tilburg, "Broken Ties: Reciprocity and Other Factors Affecting the Termination of Older Adults' Relationships," *Social Networks* 21 (1999), 131–146.

Whether a relationship endures or disappears may also be linked to the extent of its connection with other individuals in the network. It is, after all, more difficult to drop a friend who also mixes with one's other friends. This hypothesis is verified by measuring the degree centrality of the tie (only strong ties were measured): in the Caen panel, durability clearly increased with Alter's degree centrality. Zero or low centrality increased Alter's risk of disappearance; transient relationships were more characteristic of isolated Alters, that is those not connected to any other Alter. It can be concluded, therefore, that the fact of being connected to others protects a relationship, making it more durable. The fact that Ego and Alter are connected to the same other people, that their networks overlap to a large extent, is a stabilizing factor.[10] Reciprocally, an enduring relationship may become more connected to others through a process of constructed transitivity, in which an Ego introduces Alter to other friends, as we saw in Chapter 4. By tracking each Alter's history, it can be shown that those who disappeared between two waves of the survey were more likely to be in the zero or low centrality category than those who were retained between the same two waves. Furthermore, the average of the relative centralities of the Alters[11] who disappeared between two waves of the survey is always lower than that of the Alters who remained present during the same period. Thus, the relationships that endured from one wave to the next were more central than those that disappeared. This result remains valid regardless of period. Thus, it can be confirmed that the fact of being connected with others reduces an Alter's risk of disappearing. However, some childhood friendships are exceptions to this rule, since the depth and duration of the relationship have made them "inalienable," even though the only connection is with Ego (Table 5.5).

Is spatial distance a factor in the ending of relationships? As we have seen, it is mentioned fairly frequently as a cause. However, spatial distance does not prevent some ties from being perennial (see Table 5.6). In the Caen survey, after all, friends living in the same conurbation were more likely to be lost than perennial, whereas those who lived outside of the conurbation had a higher proportion of "perennials."

Between two waves of the Caen survey, the Alters living close to Ego were always more likely to be lost than retained, whereas those living in

---

[10] S. L. Feld, "Structural Embeddedness and Stability of Interpersonal Relations," *Social Networks* 19 (1997), 91–95.

[11] Here we are dealing with the number of connections an Alter has with other Alters in the network relative to the number of possible connections in the same network.

Table 5.5 *Time span of the relationships over the four waves of the Caen panel survey by Alter's degree centrality category (strong non-family and non-romantic ties only) (%)*

Centrality	Zero	Low	High	All centralities
Relationship				
Perennial	40.6[a]	44.2	53.3	46.3
Disappeared	31.9	35.6	30.3	33.7
Ephemeral	27.5	20.2	16.4	20.0
Total	100	100	100	100
Numbers	389	2,008	908	3,305

[a] For example, 40.6 percent of Alters whose degree centrality is categorized as zero had relationships classified as perennial.

Table 5.6 *Time span of the relationships over the four waves of the Caen panel survey by distance between Ego's and Alter's residences (non-family and non-romantic relationships) (%)*

	Same conurbation, less than nine miles	Outside of conurbation, greater than nine miles	
Perennial	31.5[a]	39.4	34.9
Disappeared	45.7	34.9	41.1
Ephemeral	22.7	25.8	24.0
Total	100	100	100
Numbers	3,084	2,314	5,398

[a] For example, 31.5 percent of relationships in which both partners live in the same conurbation or less than 9 miles away are perennial.

another region were likely to be retained than lost.[12] What we are observing here is undoubtedly a high-school effect: at the end of their general education, young people lose touch with many of their classmates who, by definition, used to live in the same area. Nevertheless, the later tendency to retain friends who live a long way away may be further reinforced by the tendency to individuate relationships that, with age, become less dependent on the immediate contexts. However, it can also be said, conversely, that the friendships in question overcame the subsequent geographical distance because they were strong ties. Or, to put it another way, since

[12] These degrees of geographic remoteness – 9 miles (15 km) and a different region – prove to be relevant for France. See also Chapter 8.

fewer weak ties survived the geographical separation, the distant relationships that did survive included a higher share of strong and therefore enduring ties. Thus, the link between the disappearance of friendships and spatial distance is a complex one and is heavily dependent on the strength of the tie and on age. For some young people, a distance of a few miles may constitute a very large gulf, particularly when they do not have access to a car. Noémie, for example, was simply unable to envisage having any relationships beyond the confines of her village. Social and cultural factors also play a part and influence what is regarded as a "tolerable distance" for all age groups. It remains the case that distance always puts relationships to the test.

*

*   *

These factors contributing to the various modes of relationship loss or survival reflect the effects of the dynamics identified above. During high school, relationships are very strongly embedded in contexts and activities. They become more elective and individuated when young people enter the world of work and learn to classify and choose their relationships. After all, the shift toward individuated ties plays a part in the disappearance of certain relationships, which, as long as they were based on activities and embedded in groups, held together by virtue of the group cohesion but did not have enough intrinsic strength to endure as interpersonal ties. Alice testifies to this transition:

I don't see Jacques anymore and I'm none the worse for it. We no longer live as a group, that's clear. The advantage of being in a group is that there are several of you and you can party together; the downside is that you sometimes have to hang out with people you're not particularly keen on. Now there are more individual relationships, so you only mix with the people you want to mix with. There's a sort of natural selection process at work – we're no longer obliged to hang out all together like before. So if I want to see just one person, I see just that one person. I've got back in touch with some people, that was my own initiative, which certainly shows that it's much more about personal choice now. Before, there were people who were more or less imposed on me, I'm thinking of Jacques, I never got on with that guy, it was awful, we couldn't stand each other. It's a good job we're no longer in touch. You shouldn't be afraid of that either. . .

Thus, in view of the changes in the very way of establishing relationships that occur at the point of entry into adult life, the disappearance of relationships "does not frighten" most of these young people. In the older age groups as well, family relationships are often seen as an advantageous "replacement" for friendships. It is nevertheless the case that networks shrink, become more concentrated, and perhaps offer fewer potential resources.

Although it is an unacknowledged subject in sociology that has scarcely been investigated at all in network analyses, the question of the ending of relationships speaks volumes about the factors that weaken or, conversely, strengthen the social bond. By shedding light on the processes leading not only to disaffiliation but also to the disintegration and evolution of certain forms of social cohesion, it reveals to us what is at work as relationships disappear. What are the factors that determine whether ties survive or fade away? What distances turn out to be significant, what gaps open up, for whom and when? Analysis of what makes relationships endure or come to an end uncovers their links with other dimensions of the social space that help to shore up, strengthen, or weaken those relationships. Social divisions, spatial distance, and dissimilarities as well as time spans, activities, and biographical transitions take on new resonances. It is true that the substance of a relationship, its history, its possibly conflictive nature, and its interconnections within the network may hasten or slow down its demise. Here too, however, context, life stage, and social environment usually exert their influence over the fate of relationships.

6

Networks and Their Dynamics

Networks are constantly evolving, reconfiguring, spreading out, or contracting. These changes are linked, in part, to changes in relationships, the two combining in system effects. The breakdown of a relationship has effects on other relationships and on the whole of a network. In particular, it can trigger a spate of further breakdowns or weaken other ties. A typical case is a marriage breakdown, which often causes each spouse to abandon a large part of the relationships associated with the other partner (spouse's friends, in-laws, etc.). Conversely, the overall shape of a network can have an impact on each of the relationships that make it up. However, network dynamics cannot be reduced simply to relational dynamics, to the addition or elimination of relationships. Some dynamics are generated by the interactions between those relationships or by the network's overall structure, which can evolve without there being any change in the number of its constituent relationships. It may become denser or more concentrated or, conversely, more dispersed or fragmented.

The dynamics of personal networks may be the result of multiple processes, some of which depend directly on the characteristics of the networks or relationships concerned, while others arise out of biographical events involving a significant renewal or reconfiguration of relationships. The ideal, of course, is to separate out and examine in conjunction with each other changes in the characteristics of ties, in the composition and regeneration of the network, in the evolution of some of its characteristics and in its structure, as well as in biographical developments and the events that occur over the life course. These dimensions are only seldom taken into account together in network analyses.[1] Of course, some may evolve

---

[1] This is what is particularly deplored by B. Wellman, O. Frank, V. Espinoza, S. Lundquist, C. Wilson, "Integrating Individual, Relational and Structural Analysis," *Social Networks*

while others may not. For example, a network's size or structure may remain stable although it is made up of different people. This being so, these dynamics are not always easy to disentangle, as we will see. However, if observers confine themselves to examining network structure, they may be led to believe that there is no more to discover. However, if the analysis is opened up in order to take the biographical dimension into consideration, they will see more interactions between what is attributable to the network's own dynamic and what is engendered by the context. In this chapter, we describe all the dynamics that can be observed, drawing mainly on the Caen longitudinal survey.

CHANGES IN SIZE AND COMPOSITION

There are small networks and large networks, networks that remain relatively stable and others that change a lot. In the Caen panel, network size varied considerably from one person to the next as well as from one moment to the next. The largest network comprised 130 names, the smallest just 6. Of the 75 individuals who were followed over at least 2 waves of the survey, 48 had networks that shrank between the first and last wave, 26 had networks that increased in size and 1 a network that remained the same size. However, there were many changes in the meantime. Networks expanded, then contracted, then expanded again and so on.

Figures 6.1 and 6.2 depict the evolution of all the networks constructed for the 60 individuals in the Caen panel who were present from the beginning to the end of the survey. Some explanation of how to interpret the diagrams is required. The first diagram (Figure 6.1) depicts the ties with individuals outside the family. The central axis represents the stock of relationships (strong and weak non-family ties) that existed at each wave of the survey. There were 1,625 at the first wave, 1,348 at the second, 1,345 at the third, and 1,392 at the fourth. Of the 1,625 observed at the first wave, 1,278 were no longer being mentioned at the second wave. At this second wave, 1,001 new relationships were mentioned, whereas they had not been previously, and 1,047 no longer existed, with the rest (347) carried over from the first wave. The other elements of the diagram are to be interpreted in the same way (Figure 6.1).

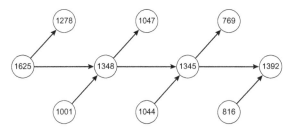

Fig. 6.1 Turnover of non-kin relationships

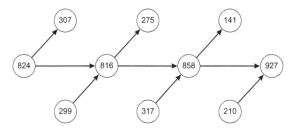

Fig. 6.2 Turnover of kin relationships

The second diagram (Figure 6.2) depicts the family relationships and can be interpreted in the same way. Worthy of note is the relatively large number of changes that took place in the networks in this second diagram, even though they all involved respondents' family members.

The stock of relationships mentioned in each wave of the survey did not vary enormously. It fluctuated between 1,300 and 1,600. Thus, if we were to limit ourselves to a one-off count, we might be tempted to say that the number of relationships mentioned remained stable over time. However, we have flow data for each wave, which show that the largest share of the relationships mentioned was replaced every three years.[2] In this particular phase of the life course, namely the entry into adulthood, relationships change more quickly and to a greater extent than in other phases. Fewer relationships disappeared in the fourth wave than in the third and fewer in the third than in the second. This may indicate overall stabilization. It is true of non-family as well as of family relationships.

By observing what happened to relationships between two waves, it becomes evident that the changes were much greater at the beginning of

---

[2] See A. Degenne, M.-O. Lebeaux, "The Dynamics of Personal Networks at the Time of Entry into Adult Life," *Social Networks* 27(4) (2005), 337–358. A similar finding on link renewal is made by a Dutch team based on a longitudinal survey (Mollenhorst et al. 2014).

Table 6.1 *Losses in non-family ties (excluding Ego's partner as well) from one wave of the Caen survey to the next (%)*

	Wave 1–2	Wave 2–3	Wave 3–4
Lost	79[a]	78	57
Retained	21	22	43
Total	100	100	100
Numbers	1,625	1,348	1,345

[a] For example, for the 60 young people who responded to all 4 waves of the survey, of the total of 1,625 non-family ties mentioned in the first wave, 79 percent had been lost (they were mentioned in the first wave but not in the second wave) and 21 percent had been retained (they were mentioned again in the second wave).

the survey than at the end. This development is even more evident if family and Ego's partner are excluded (Table 6.1).

As time passed, the number of lost ties fell, while more and more were retained. To a certain extent, therefore, the networks became stabilized over time. As the young people had just left high school, defunct relationships were very much in the majority, as well as in the following period between waves 2 and 3. Later on, between waves 3 and 4, the number of retained ties increased sharply. Thus, on becoming adults, the young people retained more of their relationships and lost fewer than in the period immediately following the end of their school careers.

Did this stabilization go hand in hand with changes in the intensity of ties? Now we include all the respondents, even if they did not participate in all the survey waves. The share of strong ties (either multiplex ties or those declared to be important) rose steadily from one wave of the survey to the next, from 52.4 percent of relationships in wave 1 to 62.1 percent in wave 2, 69.2 percent in wave 3, and 69.3 percent in wave 4. The general tendency, therefore, was for relationships to become more intense. However, regardless of the wave in question, new relationships tended to be weak ties, with the individuals concerned being described as buddies or just acquaintances, while the relationships that were retained were mainly strong ties described as real friends. The lost ties also tended to be contacts and were described as pals or acquaintances, except at the beginning of the survey period, when the term "friend" was also used to describe many of the lost ties. At the beginning of the survey period, as the young people were leaving high school, it was the young women who were establishing most of the new relationships. Subsequently, however, in waves and 3 and 4, they were overtaken by the men, with the women accounting for a higher

Table 6.2 *Network composition by wave of the Caen survey (%)*

Type of tie	1	2	3	4	Total
Non-family	67.6[a]	61.3	60.5	60.0	62.8
Ego's family	28.3	28.1	27.3	26.1	27.6
Ego's partner's family	2.9	9.0	10.3	11.6	7.9
Partner	1.2	1.6	2.0	2.2	1.7
Total	100	100	100	100	100
Number	3,450	2,597	2,438	2,319	10,804

[a] For example, in the first wave of the Caen survey, for all the respondents, 67.6 percent of relationships involved individuals from outside the family.

share of the lost ties. At the beginning of the survey period, the new ties were being established mainly by young people from the more advantaged family backgrounds who had taken the economic and social sciences baccalaureate; at the same stage, it was mainly young people from working-class backgrounds who had taken the vocational baccalaureate or had been on a work experience program who were abandoning relationships. However, this difference tended to become blurred over time. The most one can say is that, by waves 3 and 4, it was the young people from the more advantaged backgrounds who had taken the economic and social sciences baccalaureate who now accounted for the greater share of lost ties. Thus, this group started off by establishing more ties but ended up losing more; in their case, these losses were, as it were, delayed, probably because continuing in education enabled them to maintain a young person's mode of sociability for longer. Whether the ties were strong or weak, the share of non-family ties declined steadily, as did, to a lesser extent, that of family members. Only romantic relationships and, above all, the associated ties with partners' families saw their shares in all ties increase (Table 6.2).

At the beginning of the survey period, moreover, the new links mentioned at each wave were mainly non-family relationships and members of the partner's family. Further into the survey period, the partner's family tended to become regarded as family members and romantic relationships tended to be maintained from one wave to the next. Finally, at all stages of the survey, the lost ties were mainly non-family relationships.

These changes are certainly consistent with what we have seen of the evolution of relational practices during the entry into adult life, which is a period that combines considerable biographical changes with changes in

Table 6.3 *Average network densities (Toulouse survey)*

Respondent's age	Average density
18–25	0.48
26–45	0.40
46–65	0.52
65+	0.55
Total	0.46

modes of sociability. This all conspires to produce significant changes in network size and composition. The end of high school or university marks a major change in weak ties, a process that subsequently trails off as relationships become more intense and stable and family comes to occupy a more important place with the entry into adult life. However, other, more structural dynamics can also be examined in considerable detail.

CHANGES IN NETWORK STRUCTURE

One intrinsic process that affects network structure is its densification or, conversely, dispersal, when the ties that constitute the network become disconnected from each other. Several factors and dynamics can influence network density: the disappearance or appearance of certain central Alters, transitivity (when relationships are established between two individuals linked to the same third person, thereby closing the triangle), dissociation (when Ego moves from "group" to "dyadic" relationships), and so on. One indicator of this intrinsic dynamic is the evolution of network density with advancing age. In the Toulouse survey, density started by declining before the age of forty-five, after which point it increased significantly with age, at least until sixty-five (Table 6.3).

In the Caen survey, on the much-reduced scale of a population of young people only, average density fell overall (Table 6.4).[3]

Thus, the two surveys confirm that there is an initial tendency for networks to become more dispersed between the end of high school, when they are particularly dense (due to the presence of large numbers of family

---

[3] The difference between the averages for these two surveys is due to differences in survey procedures. In the Caen survey, density is calculated on the basis of connections between all the strong ties in a network, while in the Toulouse survey the basis for calculation is five of the people mentioned by Ego.

Table 6.4 *Average network densities by survey wave (Caen panel)*

Wave	Respondents' age	Average density
1	17–23	0.30
2	20–26	0.31
3	23–29	0.27
4	26–32	0.24
Total	–	0.28

members who are "naturally" interconnected, and highly interconnected friendship groups), and the beginning of adulthood, when the more selectively chosen friends are more likely to be seen singly or in pairs. This is followed by a tendency toward further densification after the age of forty-five as networks become more highly concentrated around a smaller number of more intensive relationships (in adulthood) and family (greater presence after age forty-five). Generally speaking, density increases as network size declines and the share of family ties rises, which schematically describes the overall tendency over the adult life course. However, closer examination reveals many subtle distinctions. In the Caen survey, for example, average density is higher for the girls (0.30) than for the boys (0.26). Moreover, it tends to be lower the higher up the social scale one goes: from 0.31 for young people from working-class backgrounds, it falls to 0.26 for those from the intermediate classes, and then again to 0.22 for those from the higher social classes. While these last measures relate only to the 287 networks identified in the Caen survey, they are, nevertheless, consistent with what is known about patterns of sociability in the various social classes.[4]

TYPICAL SEQUENCES IN THE EVOLUTION OF YOUNG PEOPLE'S NETWORKS

In order to take full advantage of the possibilities of a dynamic approach, let us now bring into play the various types of network identified in Chapter 2, namely the dense, centered, dissociated, and composite types. From one wave of the survey to the next, the network of a young person in the Caen panel may stay in the same category, that is, it may remain dense,

---

[4] See, in particular, the study by P. V. Marsden, "Core Discussion Networks of Americans," *American Sociological Review* 52(1) (1987), 122–131.

dissociated, etc. However, it may also change category, moving from the dense to the dissociated type if, for example, density declines sharply, or from the centered to the composite type if the Alter on whom the maximum centrality was concentrated disappears. Thus, it may undergo three transitions in the course of the survey: between waves 1 and 2, between waves 2 and 3, and between waves 3 and 4.

Relative Structural Stability

It will be noted, firstly, that certain types are more stable than others and thus less likely to undergo a transition toward another type. This is evident from the number of networks situated on the diagonal of the transition matrix (See Table 6.5). The three transition periods are combined here: if a network moved from the centered category to the dense category between waves 1 and 2, it will be combined with another network that underwent the same move but between waves 3 and 4.

The "dense" and "centered" categories were the most stable: more networks remained in these categories from one wave to the next than those in the other categories. This may mean that these networks had attained a certain "equilibrium," that is, that they changed configuration less than the others. The dissociated and composite networks[5] were less stable.

In some cases, a network decreased or increased in size but its general profile remained unchanged (dense, centered, dissociated, or composite). The relationships gained or lost did not alter the network's overall structure. Occasionally, a network had a considerable turnover, with most of the friends changing but the profile remaining the same. However, this distinction between turnover in a network and its structural properties is seldom explained in network analyses, which generally focus on one or the other aspect. Nevertheless, the fact that a similar overall profile can be maintained with members who have changed in the meantime is an important finding, which clearly shows that some biographical transitions have less influence than others on the structure of an individual's network, which turns out to be more stable than its composition.[6] Our survey shows, for example, that some young people who had dense networks made new

---

[5] These types combine the centrality of one Alter and the presence of very dense as well as isolated friendship groups.

[6] As D. L. Morgan, M. B. Neal, P. Carder also note in "The Stability of Core and Peripheral Networks over Time," *Social Networks* 19 (1996), 9–25.

Table 6.5 *Transitions between network types*

| | | \multicolumn{5}{c}{Final category} | | | | |
		Dense	Centered	Dissociated	Composite	Total
	Dense	32[a]	17	10	10	69
Initial	Centered	12	20	5	8	45
category	Dissociated	8	10	17	7	42
	Composite	6	9	15	14	44
	Total	58	56	47	39	200

[a] For example, 32 networks that were classed as dense in one wave of the survey were classed as dense in the next wave. The color of each square is proportionate to the difference between the value observed and the value that would be obtained if there were no correlation between the initial category and the final category. Thus, it emphasizes the scale of the moves from one category to another.

friends from within groups that were already interconnected or were more likely to mention family members. Others who already had centered networks adopted their partners' friends, who were therefore already connected to the central individual, while yet others whose networks were already dissociated made friends who remained isolated from each other. In some cases, active measures were taken to adapt the new relationships to the type of network. Thus, in the case of the dense networks, they might not already have been linked together in a group but were very quickly introduced to the old friends or to the family. In the case of the centered networks, they might not have been friends of Ego's partner but were quickly introduced to him or her. In the dissociated networks, the new Alters might have been left isolated like the other friends, while in the composite networks the new relationships were treated in a variety of different ways.

In some cases, finally, the dominant characteristic of the network type became more pronounced from one wave of the survey to the next. Density increased yet further, for example, when friends disappeared, leaving just the family group and the individuals associated with it, or when friends who used to be seen separately were abandoned. And dissociation could be further reinforced by the breakup of a group or the appearance on the scene of new isolated friends, the two phenomena sometimes going hand in hand.

However, it is time to shift our gaze away from this diagonal of networks that do not change type despite changes in size or in their constituent relationships, toward those that do change type. Of the 200 transitions from one wave of the survey to the next, no fewer than 117 led to a change in the type of network structure. The most common type of change saw dense networks becoming centered networks (17). There were more dense networks among the initial categories (69) than among the final categories (58), whereas the opposite was the case for the centered and dissociated networks, which tended, consequently, to be final rather than initial categories. Altogether, 83 transitions remained within the same category, 36 saw a shift towards greater centralization, 35 led to dissociation, 33 saw the networks concerned becoming denser and 13 led to decentralization. Let us now examine each of these dynamics in greater detail.

Dissociation

The tendency for relationships to become dissociated from each other is the most pronounced trend in this period of entry into adult life. Overall, the average density of these young people's networks and the average centrality score for Alters declined over time. Several tendencies contributed to the reduction in network density, and did so in clearly identifiable sequences. The first of these sequences saw the disappearance of highly interconnected relationships, as when a large group of friends disappeared entirely, leaving only one or two people behind. The second was characterized by the dissociation of ongoing relationships, as when Alters who used to see each other ceased to do so or a friendship group broke up, leaving behind a few members whom Ego then saw individually. In the third and final sequence, relationships emerged that remained separate from each other, as when new friends were seen individually and not introduced to other friends.

The most radical transition is that involving a move away from the dense network category toward the dissociated type. However, other transitions, such as the shift from the composite category to the dissociated type or from the dense category to the composite type, are also driven principally by a significant reduction in density compared with the preceding situation, which indicates a process of dissociation. In some cases, the main factor contributing to the dispersal of a network was the disappearance of close-knit groups. When Rose, for example, left her family and the town of Caen to live in a hostel for young workers in Paris and took a civil service entrance examination, she lost a significant part of her network, which in wave 2 had been made up principally of neighbors and friends of her parents, who were strongly connected to her family.

By wave 3, all that remained was one female friend, Jeannette. Her new friends at the hostel and at her work in Paris had no connection at all with each other; they were discrete elements in her network and had not been introduced to her family. This also happened when a group that had coalesced around a leader split up, leading to a loss of the circle's "common motivation," even though Ego continued to see these friends individually from time to time. This was the experience of Patrick who, in wave 3, was no longer seeing his friend Yann and, as an indirect result, the group had disintegrated:

I lost Yann because of divergences with other people. He'd taken up with some people with whom I didn't get on at all and with whom Ismaël didn't get on either. After that, we saw less and less of each other; I hardly saw him at all myself, Ismaël continued to see him a bit and then in the end nobody saw him much at all. The group started to unravel and then just fizzled out.

Yann's disappearance partly explains the group's breakup, which can be observed on the left-hand side of the graph (Figures 6.3 and 6.4), but it was not the only cause. Ismaël, for example, remained central but nevertheless lost contact with Patrick's family and with Malik, and he had no connection with new friends such as Loïc, Jean-Benoît, or Vincent. In the meantime, Patrick's sociability had moved in the direction of greater

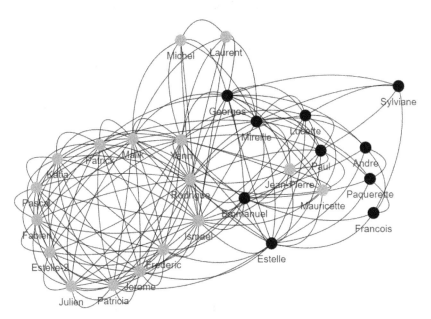

Fig. 6.3 The network of Patrick in the Caen panel (wave 2)

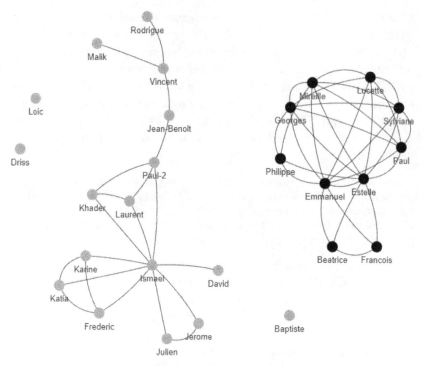

Fig. 6.4 The network of Patrick in the Caen panel (wave 3)

individualization, with new friends being seen separately, which further
reduced the density of his network, leading to its dissociation:

My new friends, some of them anyway, are more people I've chosen than friends of
friends, really people I met and with whom I decided to establish friendships.

Sometimes it is the addition of new ties, whether singly or in small
groups, that is the main factor in a reduction in overall density, even when
the other ties do not disappear. This was the case for Violette, for example,
who left to work in southeastern France but maintained contact with her
family and friends in Caen while at the same time adding other people she
met in her new home but whom she saw singly or in small groups of two or
three. This was sufficient to reduce the overall density of her network.
There are also cases in which some Alters remained in contact with Ego
but stopped seeing each other. In particular, there are a number of
examples in which childhood friends were initially connected with the
family, visited Ego at his or her parents' house, involved Ego's younger

brother in their activities, and also associated with his or her cousin. However, they lost contact with the family when Ego left home or simply put a little more distance between his friends and his family.

These sequences frequently cumulate: at the same time, a network might experience the loss of tight-knit groups, the emergence of isolated relationships, and the ending of links between the Alters. For some networks, the change was a radical one: a person might lose an entire group of friends and meet new ones who were completely isolated from each other. They were young people who had moved a long way away from Caen or who had radically changed their lifestyle. Some had changed occupation, such as Patrice, who stopped being a carpenter in order to study industrial design. Others, such as Colette or Sylvain, had set up home with a partner who had children and, as a result of this "accelerated" family transition, made a more radical break with their single lifestyle than others. Thus, those caught up in this process of dissociation included young people who had undergone very significant biographical events and changes, who had simultaneously changed their friends, lost many and met many others, and usually changed their lifestyles and ways of establishing ties. This brings us back to the relational dynamic described earlier, in which a mode of sociability based on embeddedness gives way to one based on individualization, with connected relationships being replaced by relationships dissociated from each other.

Densification

Conversely, a network may become increasingly dense over time as connections between the Alters proliferate. Here too, the process consists of a number of different sequences. A large set of connections might be added to the network, for example, when Ego joins a new group of friends that is already connected or when he mentions more members of his family, which increases the density of a block. A new Alter may appear, who is introduced to many others, thereby becoming highly connected, as in the case of Ego's partner. Or the Alters who were present but previously isolated from each other may become linked to each other through a process of transitivity. Here, Ego has decided to introduce them to each other and thus to bring these dispersed friendships together. And finally, isolated Alters may disappear, which increases network density by giving greater weight to those who remain connected.

The most radical change here is the shift from the "dissociated" category to the "dense" category, although the move from "composite" to "dense" is

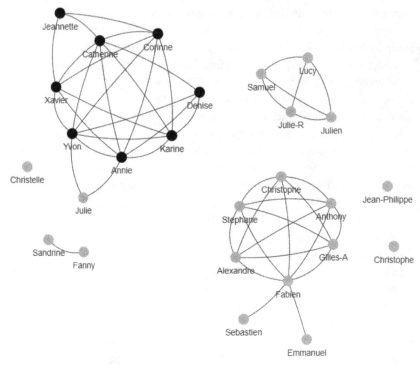

Fig. 6.5 The network of Jean in the Caen panel (wave 2)

similar. The evolution of Jean's network between the second and third waves of the survey included all of these sequences, the end result of which was a denser network (Figures 6.5 and 6.6).

In the third wave of the survey, Jean mentioned more family members, linked them to his partner Stéphanie, had met a new group of friends who were all linked to each other, and was no longer in touch with a number of friends who had been isolated. He had even introduced all his group of old friends to his new friend Faouzi, whom he met on holiday on the Ile d'Oléron and who was living in Paris. Thus, through diverse but often complementary sequences, some networks become denser rapidly. Moving in with a partner may influence this process, as when that partner becomes connected with the family, when there is considerable contact with the family-in-law, members of which are sometimes introduced to Ego's family, and when the couple spends time with friends together. It is very common for the family to be "reactivated" when young persons start their own family. If the other Alters are relatively unconnected with each other

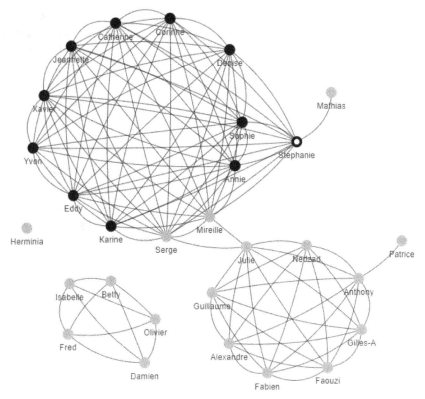

Fig. 6.6 The network of Jean in the Caen panel (wave 3)

and most of the interconnections are concentrated on Ego's partner, then the network tends toward the centered type.

Centralization

Here too, a number of sequences may combine to shift a network toward greater centralization, a process that results in most of the interconnections being centered around one of the Alters. A new Alter may bring with him a group of friends or, in the case of Ego's partner, his own family, with whom he is already connected. Or an Alter may become central to a network by being introduced to more and more other members of the network through a process of transitivity. In other cases, groups disappear or disintegrate, thereby reducing general network density and giving greater relative weight to the centrality of one particular Alter. Finally, Alters who were not connected to the central Alter may disappear.

The most radical change is when a network moves from the dissociated to the centered category. In most cases, it is setting up home with a partner that links together and restructures a network previously made up of small groups and isolated individuals into a set of relationships centered around Ego's partner and shorn of the friends associated with Ego's life as a singleton. Friends not shared by the new couple are abandoned, while the others are connected with Ego's partner, who occupies a central position. However, the partner may also remain very peripheral, as was the case with Léa, who balked at introducing him to her friends because he was older than her. It was also the case with Serge, who had introduced his new partner only to his brother and sister. The clearest examples of centralization are those in which setting up home together is combined with migration, as in the case of Nicolas, who had left Caen for Spain, causing his network to disperse, and then went to live in Italy with Véronica, with whom he built up an entire new network. It is also the case with Violette, who had gone to live in Toulon but then went to Paris to rejoin Stéphane (Figures 6.7 and 6.8).

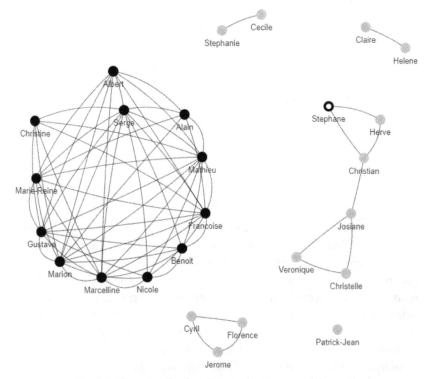

Fig. 6.7 The network of Violette in the Caen panel (wave 2)

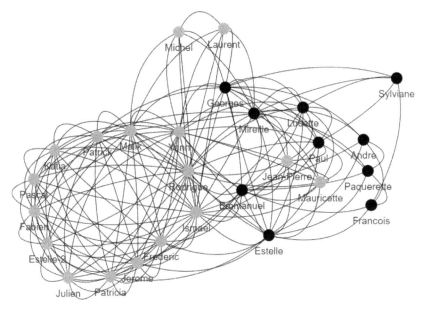

Fig. 6.8 The network of Violette in the Caen panel (wave 3)

At this point, Violette mentioned fewer members of her own family but now included her family-in-law in her network and introduced Stéphane to Cécile and Hélène, two of her school friends from Caen, as well as to two of her female friends from Toulon. Thus, it was Stéphane who served as the link between parts of the network rooted in different places and different periods of Violette's life.

The network often closes in around the young couple who, in the early stages of their relationship, no longer see anyone apart from family members and their closest friends, even though they may reactivate their ties with the others at a later stage. Thus, Louisa, Suzie, and others concentrated their networks around their partners, close family members, and one or two friends, only opening it up again when the first child was born. In other cases, conversely, a network increases in size when a couple start living together, as it did for Nina, who mentioned her family more as she felt herself become more "family-oriented" and introduced her partner to her friends. In some cases, the network increases in size largely through the addition of the family-in-law and friends of Ego's partner, who are, by definition, more closely connected to him/her and thus place him/her at the center of the network.

When a dense network changes to become a centered network, Ego's partner moves into a central position rather by default. Overall network density declines, its constituent ties having trodden the familiar path toward dissociation, but the remaining interconnections then become concentrated around the partner. The network decreases in size. This was the case for Antoine, for example, who between waves 1 and 2 lost his friends Carole and Arnaud, who were very closely connected with others, including his family, and also lost a group of five school friends. He cut the connections between his remaining friends and his family. As a result, his partner Sabrina, without having been introduced to anyone, found herself the only "bridge" between family and friends and the Alter with the highest centrality score in the network, particularly since her own family had now been incorporated into the network. In this scenario, the network's centrality was constructed on the basis of a decline in the other factors contributing to its density, as Ego's partner was herself becoming connected to an increasing number of people. Network density sometimes shifts without really changing its overall value across the network as a whole, simply moving from groups of Ego's friends to new groups of the couple's friends or to the family. Thus, certain networks, like those of Vérène, Katia, and Corinne, retained the same overall density and very gradually became centralized, with a few isolated Alters simply being replaced by a number of new ones connected to Ego's partner.

It is sometimes also the case, as it was with Gilles and Joël, that it is not Ego's partner but a childhood friend around whom the network's maximum centrality is concentrated because he or she is not only connected to the family but is also introduced to new friends as a matter of course:

Yann, Joël tells us, is a hell of a lot more sociable, he's really much better liked, they all ask me for news of Yann. He's always so enthusiastic and warm. He's so sociable, he brings people together.

Thus, some more charismatic friends, or those who share more activities with Ego and are able to join various social circles with him, come to occupy particularly central positions . . . in singletons' networks.

Decentralization

Even though this process is less common among these young people, a centered network does sometimes become dissociated, composite, or dense. Here too, various sequences play a part in this process of decentralization: Alters connected to the central Alter may disappear; some Alters become disconnected from the central Alter; the Alters may forge more connections among themselves or new groups may emerge, leading to a reduction in the relative weight of the central Alter, who then finds himself "submerged" in a density that has become more distributed.

The most obvious example of such a process is, of course, a couple that separates, causing the centralizing element to disappear, and indeed this is very often the case. In Nina's case, the network had become centered around her partner Sidicki, but their separation in the third wave of the survey subsequently led to her network moving into the dissociated category (Figures 6.9 and 6.10).

Some new friends were introduced to certain old ones, such as Sylvain and Bob to Fabien and Géraldine, Paolo and Serge to Karine, and Sandrine to Peggy; others were seen separately, in small groups or singly. The Alter with whom Ego had shared the entire network was no longer there.

In other cases, it is on entry into the labor market that the greatest change occurs, as a network of friends that used to be centered on a childhood friend "explodes," as it did for Mélanie in wave 2. She had acquired a new group of friends at work and was no longer in touch with old friends, such as Stéphanie, the childhood friend who was the most

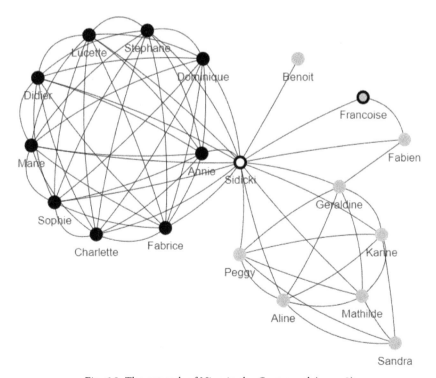

Fig. 6.9 The network of Nina in the Caen panel (wave 2)

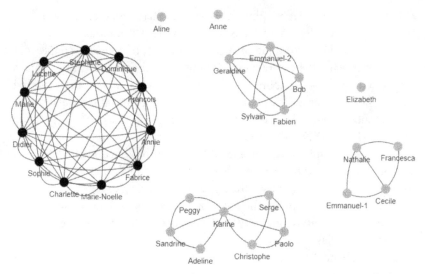

Fig. 6.10 The network of Nina in the Caen panel (wave 3)

central figure in her network but had been introduced to only one of the new friends. Her network had been radically changed and dissociated.

Sometimes, Ego's partner is still present but sees less and less of Ego's friends, as in Antoine's case. His network, which in waves 2 and 3 was centered around Sabrina, became composite in wave 4. Antoine was now sharing fewer of his activities and friends with Sabrina. Some ties had even been broken, such as those that had previously linked Sabrina with some of Antoine's friends. The process at work here was one of transitivity in reverse. It has to be said that Antoine and Sabrina's marriage had been through a difficult period; they had separated for a while and when they got back together again, they decided their relationship should be less intensely close:

The problem was that, previously, we never left the house separately. Our relationship was very close. Perhaps that was what eventually pulled us apart. Now, she has her own friends, they go out together. And she also has a job, so she's more able to do what she wants in her free time. I also have my own friends. This was one of the rules we agreed on when we got back together again. We said to each other: "Be careful! Now, if we want to do things separately in our spare time, that mustn't hold us back!"

The effects of these new resolutions on Antoine's network can be readily observed, as they can in the case of Viviane, who had gone through a similar process of uncoupling her world from that of Emmanuel after living together for several years. This decentralization may also occur when a friend who had been very central becomes less so, as in the previously mentioned case of Joël who, in wave 4, lost contact with a whole group of friends linked to Yann.

Some networks move from the centered to the dense category. These also include cases of marital breakdown, but here the family tends to come back into play strongly, regrouping around Ego. This is what happened when Aude returned to her parents and mentioned more of the highly interconnected members of her family than when she was living with Sébastien.

However, another sequence may also play a part in this transition from centered to dense network. Rather than connections being taken away from the central individual, some are added to the other Alters, thereby "submerging" the centrality in a general density. This is the case, for example, when Ego meets a large and highly interconnected group of friends that overshadows Ego's partner's centrality, even though this remains strong. This is what happened to Victor, Yves, and Luc, for whom their partners' centrality became virtually insignificant compared with these multiple interconnections. In the cases of Thomas and Etienne, it was the ties with their families and families-in-law, as well as those between the two families, that particularly increased. When his child was born, Gaël saw his family and family-in-law become increasingly directly connected with each other but also got to know a new group of friends and combined some new and some very old friends to form another large group. While his partner's centrality was still evident, it was surpassed by the overall centrality of the network as a whole.

In the case of transitions from any type of network to the composite type, everything depends on the starting situation. When a network moves from the dense to the composite type, the dominant dynamic is dispersion. When it moves from the dissociated to the composite type, the principal dynamic at work is densification or centralization, when the move is from centered to composite, the most influential dynamic is decentralization, and so on. These sequences have already been described; this composite type is associated with versions of them that are both attenuated and combined with other elements.

*

*   *

Although we make no claim to exhaustiveness, the dynamics and their effects on network structure outlined here, which are particularly perceptible as young people enter adulthood, a time when many things are happening on both the biographical and relational levels, offer us some "living" images of the evolution of personal networks. More purely structuralist studies undoubtedly consider a much broader range of precise and original indicators. We have preferred to give our investigation of these changes in network structure a more personal and social form and leave them rooted in the "real lives" of the social actors. This emphasis on individual and relational histories, as well as on the qualitative data that explain these changes, provide a basis throughout this book for our efforts to identify structural effects and link them to extrinsic events. At the end of this section, it seems to us very difficult indeed to separate "pure," that is, intrinsic structural effects from "extrinsic" effects caused by social situation, getting to know or separating from a partner, moving abroad, increased involvement with family, and so on.

We have identified four main processes that are at work. The process of dissociation, which is most frequent during the transition to adult life, combines with the individualization dynamic that underpins the shift away from a group-based mode of sociability to one based on dyadic relationships. It comes into play especially in the most intense phases of change in personal circumstances, such as the transition from education to work. The densification process manifests itself when highly connected groups are introduced (family-in-law when couples move in together, the family that is "rediscovered" when a child is born, a group of friends who hung out together at university, etc.) or when certain Alters are introduced to each other. The centralization process is associated primarily with a couple setting up home together, when Ego's partner arrives with his or her own family, is introduced to Ego's family and to most of his friends, and from then on occupies a particularly central position in the network. This process is even more pronounced when a person relocates. Finally, the reverse process of decentralization is set in motion particularly when a marriage breaks down or even when spouses simply "distance" themselves a little from each other and take to spending more time with their own friends.

Our analysis has revealed effects linked to the characteristics of Alter or to the nature of his or her relationship with Ego at least as much as structural effects such as transitivity. The sudden emergence of typically central Alters, such as a partner, for example, whose particular position is linked to the role he or she plays in Ego's life and to the norm associated with that role, which demands, among other things, that he or she becomes connected to Ego's family, plays a major part in these developments. As a result, it becomes very difficult to ignore these biographical events in any attempt to understand the structural effects. If one attempts, for example, to measure the extent to which the triangles, which, for some network analysts, "automatically" tend to connect B and C if they are both linked to A, actually do become closed, it is evident that in reality such closure is not widespread. Only by taking into account the fact that B and C live hundreds of miles apart, that one has children while the other does not, or that they do not play the same kind of music can this observation be further interpreted. A can put up with their differences by seeing them separately; he may even adapt to their diversity, with each one finding his or her own place in his network. However, C will undoubtedly not strike up a close friendship with B. Thus, it is only by examining individual Alters' cases that we can understand why certain triangles do not close. They may even open up again, having once been closed, as in the case of Julien, for whom the process of transitivity went into reverse because of the strength of the tie between his friends Samuel and Aurélien:

They were always round at each other's place and that shifted the relationship towards Samuel and Aurélien, it was no longer the three of us, just the two of them. And then afterwards, Aurélien and Samuel got together a jazz group, which meant that from then onwards I saw them less and less often. Then they established a new circle of friends and in the end Aurélien disappeared from view behind Samuel, that is, there was now an intermediary. If I wanted to see Aurélien or get news of him, I had to go through Samuel. Little by little I ended up having no direct relationship with Aurélien.

The fact that his two friends had become embedded in a new circle strengthened their mutual tie and weakened that between Julien and Aurélien, with Samuel now acting as an intermediary between them. Thus, from the perspective we have adopted here, the dynamic of the relational environment does not lie entirely in network structure and in "pure" structural effects. Rather it is driven by the changes in relationships explored above (more or less intense, multiplex embedded, individualized, etc.), by the links between them within networks and circles (more or less dissociated or connected, decoupled or embedded, etc.), and by the transitions and events of Ego's biographical trajectory, which influence the composition and configuration of his or her network. Some changes do not affect the structure itself but rather the size, composition, or renewal of the network. Others affect the structure by triggering processes consisting of a number of sequences, some of which we have summarized here.

The study of relational dynamics avoids locking itself into a single dimension, focusing rather on revealing the actual links between individual, biographical, dyadic, contextual, and structural data. In so doing, it sheds light on the relational dynamics that insert themselves between the effects of social frameworks (which are the principal object of macro-level sociology) and the effects of individual actions (which are the principal object of micro-level sociology). Rather than calling it "meso-level" sociology, we prefer to describe it as the sociology of relational dynamics, which puts the emphasis on both its object and its problematic. For example, the fact of knowing that the dominant structural tendency in young people's networks is for relationships to become dissociated from each other when they enter into adult life establishes a link between several macro- and micro-sociological levels: the modes of socialization specific to the French educational system of the 1990s, based on a radical separation of the world of education from that of work, the conditions under which the education-to-work transition takes place, the cultural norms governing "coupledom" and the sharing of relationships, individual decisions to separate one's friends, relationships with one's family, widening interpersonal divergences, etc. By identifying the relational dynamics, light is shed on the significance of social norms and frameworks in the activities of actual individuals rather than abstract beings, who are connected to each other by specific ties that constitute relational environments of varying degrees of homogeneity and cohesion.

7

As the Years Go By

Individuals' life trajectories are punctuated by phases that are socially constructed and framed (childhood, youth, old age) and by partially instituted phases of accelerated change (entry into adult life, setting up home with a partner, transition into retirement), as well as by more discrete events. Some are experienced by most people of the same age (school leaving examinations, retirement, etc.). Others happen to many people but at different ages (moving house, divorce, bereavement, health problems, unemployment); yet others are out of the ordinary, rare, unforeseeable (birth of a sick child, accidents, chance encounters). Thus, there is a temporality that advances steadily, while others proceed more intensely and more slowly; there are also more sudden and unforeseeable interruptions. All processes are made up of sequences in which are combined various elements, contexts, temporalities, driving forces, and, occasionally, forks or turning points. The evolution of relationships and networks over the life course proceeds within these multiple temporalities and is influenced by these various types of events. Some transitions are known to be more favorable than others to the partial renewal of an individual's relational environment (entry into adult life, divorce, moving home, transition into retirement). However, there are few systematic studies on a scale that enables us to compare the dynamic of personal networks on the basis of various social characteristics (level of education, occupation, family situation, etc.), taking into account the various types of temporalities and events.[1] Nevertheless, it is important to separate out the effects of age, of biographical transitions, and other less foreseeable events.

---

[1] As is noted with regret by B. Wellman, R. Yuk-lin Wong, D. Tindall, N. Nazer, "A Decade of Network Change: Turnover, Persistence and Stability in Personal Communities," *Social Networks* 19 (1997), 27–50.

MAJOR CHANGES OVER THE LIFE COURSE

Relationships are constantly being reconstituted throughout the life course. At certain junctures, particularly the periods of transition between the various phases of the life course – adolescence and youth, starting a family, retirement – the process of reconstitution proceeds a little more rapidly.

The contexts in which relationships are created differ from one stage of the life course to the next. Relationships with one's family obviously develop in childhood, as do those established in school, those established at university are entered into during one's "youth," and so on. Since we have at our disposal data on the duration of the relationships listed by respondents in the Toulouse survey, it is possible to calculate the age these individuals were when they first met the person in question. The shares of the various periods of the life course in the process of relationship formation are summarized in Table 7.1.

Relationships established in childhood (family, for the most part) began to decline as a share of total relationships once respondents had passed the age of 25. Their share then remained stable before falling gradually after the age of 65. Relationships formed in adolescence, which played an important role until the age of 25, subsequently faded away, to be replaced by relationships established during the working life, which continued to account for the highest share of relationships among the over-65s. Thus, the "stock" of relationships was being constantly renewed, with a stable base of long-standing relationships. This stock of long-standing

Table 7.1 *Respondents' age at first meeting by age bracket (Toulouse survey) (%)*

Respondent's age	18–25	26–45	46–65	65+	Total
Respondent's age at first meeting with the individuals mentioned					
0–15	46.8	29.3	27.0[a]	19.0	30.2
16–18	19.7	5.3	1.6	2.6	6.2
19–25	33.5	26.5	10.1	7.8	21.6
26–35		31.2	21.3	14.4	22.6
36–45		7.7	26.8	11.8	11.6
46–55			12.0	19.6	4.9
56–65			1.1	15.7	1.9
65+				9.2	0.9
Total	100	100	100	100	100

[a] For example, respondents aged between 46 and 65 established 27 percent of their relationships when they were under 15. The shaded cells represent impossible situations.

Table 7.2 *Duration of relationships by respondents' age (Toulouse survey) (%)*

Respondents' age	18–25	26–45	46–65	65+	Total
Duration of relationships					
0–5 years	68.1	33.6	16.2[a]	14.2	31.9
6–10 years	23.1	30.5	16.6	9.4	23.9
11–20 years	6.9	24.9	31.1	21.3	23.7
More than 20 years	1.9	10.9	36.1	55.1	20.6
Total	100	100	100	100	100

[a] For example, respondents aged between 46 and 65 had been involved in 16.2 percent of their relationships for less than 5 years and in 36.1 percent of their relationships for more than 20 years.

relationships increased over the life course, although there was always room for change, with the share of relationships established for less than five years stabilizing at around one-sixth or one-seventh of the total (Table 7.2).

Let us turn now to the contexts of first meeting for the various age brackets. For the under-25s, Figure 7.1 clearly depicts the relatively swift transition between the "inherited" family context (parents and siblings, essentially), which constituted the overwhelming majority of relationships before the age of 15, and the emergence of other, more consciously "constructed" relationships in other contexts (neighborhood, school, etc.).

In the succeeding age brackets (26–45 and 46–65, which appear together in Figure 7.2 because their profiles are similar), "constructed" relationships (community associations, neighbors, colleagues, sociability, etc.) account for much higher shares, since the early years of the working life are a period of intense relationship formation.

Finally, among those aged 65 and over, relationships within the family first established after adulthood (children for the most part) accounted for an increasingly large share, as did relationships rooted in the neighborhood. The organized contexts encompass two different groups of relationships: those that were retained from the 19 to 35 phase, which tended to have been established at university and at work, and the most recent ones established between the ages of 46 and 65, which tended to have been established within the community. It would seem that community activity gradually replaced university and work as the context in which relationships were formed. Relationships established through a spouse or through friends (i.e., through sociability) tended to be formed in two phases, at the beginning of the working life (19–35 age bracket) and at the end (46–65 age bracket); the middle period tended to be rather arid in

As the Years Go By

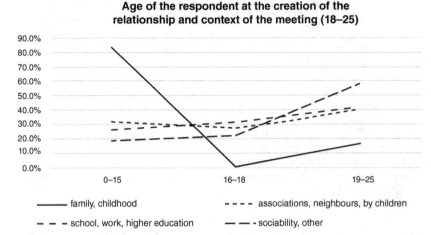

Fig. 7.1 Age of the respondent at the creation of the relationship and context of the meeting (25 and under)

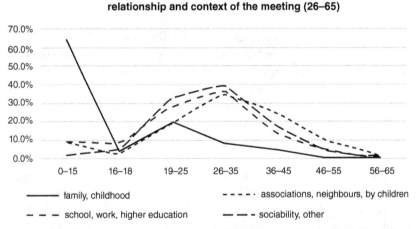

Fig. 7.2 Age of the respondent at the creation of the relation and context of the meeting (26–65)

this respect, not because it produced fewer relationships but because they proved to be less durable than those established earlier. This is a finding already obtained for the younger age groups: the most durable relationships are the oldest ones and the relationships mentioned at any one time are a mixture of old, long-lasting relationships, and recent ones.

This overview of the various phases of the life course reveals how the contexts in which relationships are created succeed one another. First comes the family that is "inherited" at birth or in childhood. Adolescence sees the emergence of relationships linked to school and sociability. Higher education and then work bring cohorts of new relationships as well as the establishment of a new family (spouse, children, family-in-law). However, constructed relationships turn out to be less durable than family relationships and they change over the course of the working life. The changes take place in phases depending on the circles to which people become affiliated. Thus, university and work are replaced by associative activities as the context in which relationships develop. Relationships rooted in sociability seem to change more continuously, but their durability declines with age, which means that at the end of the life course the relationships that are left are mainly those established during one's youth and the most recent ones. At retirement age and beyond, fewer new relationships are formed and those that do develop are linked mainly to associative activities, sociability, and neighborhood.

This question can also be approached through an analysis of the evolution of network size over the life course based on a calculation of the average number of relationships by age bracket. In the Toulouse survey, the evolution of the number of relationships does not follow a regular trend, with network size steadily increasing or, conversely, declining. This result differs somewhat from those of the "Contacts" survey (INED and INSEE), on the basis of which Héran[2] concluded that the volume of discussions started to decline after age 40. In the Toulouse survey, it is only after age 75 that a steady decline in the number of relationships is observed, and even then the decline is pronounced only among those who completed only primary or secondary education. This difference is undoubtedly due to the difference between the name generators; this indicates that contacts decline with age more rapidly than relationships likely to provide resources.

Network composition in the Toulouse survey, as measured by the designation of relationships by respondent's age (Table 7.3), also proved to be relatively stable, expect after the age of 65, when the effects of the disappearance of work-based relationships began to make themselves felt. The share of friends and acquaintances also declined with age. On the

---

[2] F. Héran, "La sociabilité, une pratique Culturelle," *Économie et statistique* 216 (1988), 3–22.

Table 7.3 *Network size and composition by age (Toulouse survey, all relationships)*

Respondent's age	18–25[a]	26–45	46–65	65+	Total
Designation of relationship					
Average number of relationships, of which:	26	28	29	22	27
Family (%)	31	38	43	51	40
Colleagues (%)	13	7	7	1	7
Neighbors (%)	1	3	5	6	4
Community/associations (%)	2	3	4	10	4
Friends (%)	48	41	35	24	38
Acquaintances (%)	12	9	7	7	9
Others (%)	3	5	6	1	5
Total (%) (multiple responses)	100	100	100	100	100

[a] For example, respondents aged between 18 and 25 mentioned on average 26 people, 31 percent of whom belonged to their families and 13 percent of whom were colleagues.

other hand, family, neighbors and community activities played an increasingly prominent role.

Do a network's relational contents tend to be distributed in the same way over time?[3] In the Toulouse survey, again taking age as an indicator of passing time, a significant decline in the average multiplexity of relationships can be observed. On this basis, personal networks would tend, from the start of adulthood onward, to include increasing numbers of specialized relationships, as we have already seen incidentally. This tendency may indicate that ties undergo a form of diversification in terms of relational contents. The greater their range is, the more difficult it is for a single relationship to contain them all, except for the most intensive ties, of course. Age is always a difficult item of information to interpret, since it combines a number of different aspects, including historical context, advancing age, life cycle, and so on. As we have seen, the social milieus frequented, family situation, and social engagement are at least as likely to explain the evolution of relationships as an interpretation based simply on ageing. Nevertheless, all the indicators certainly seem to point in the direction of a relative diversification of relationships over the life course.

[3] This question has been addressed in numerous studies by social psychologists, in particular. See specifically those by Steve Duck, *Friends, for Life: The Psychology of Personal Relationships* (London: Harvester Wheatsheaf, 1991).

Narrowing the focus down on to the period of entry into adult life, we will now enter these other, less linear temporalities within which biographical transitions as well as less predictable events occur.

BIOGRAPHICAL TRANSITIONS

Biographical transitions interfere with personal networks. This is particularly true of changes directly linked to the relational dimension (formation or breakdown of a romantic relationship, for example). The impact of biographical events on a personal network depends on the nature of those events (the domain of activity concerned), the strength of the ties that might be affected by the change, and the structure of the network. This impact may affect the number of relationships within the network and the level of turnover, as well as the ways in which ties are forged and friends seen.

Of the 287 young persons' networks in the Caen panel (all waves of the survey combined), average network size was smaller for those living with their parents (37.7 relationships), greater for those living alone (38.4) or with friends (40) and greater still for those living with a partner (40.8). However, it fell for those with children (34.2), all the more if they were single parents (33). The more life is centered around the family, the smaller the network becomes. As far as the employment situation is concerned, the highest averages were found among those young people who were combining study and work, generally through work-based training programs (45 relationships). Students came next (43). Those in employment had a lower average number of relationships (37); those in precarious employment had an even lower average number (32), while the lowest figure was observed among young people who were unemployed or economically inactive, among whom there was an even greater reduction to just 25 relationships on average.

In order to examine the impact of these transitions in greater detail and, above all, to reconstruct their dynamic character, we can measure the upward and downward shifts in size in the same network from one wave to the next.[4] Of the 200 transitions between one wave of the survey and the next, 52.5 percent led to a reduction in the number of relationships, 46.5 percent to an increase and the remaining 1 percent to no change. The reductions in size were proportionately greater at the beginning of the

---

[4] C. Bidart, D. Lavenu, "Evolutions of Personal Networks and Life Events," *Social Networks* 27(4) (2005), 359–376.

period, between waves 1 and 2 (66.2 percent), compared with 43.9 percent between waves 2 and 3 and 45 percent between waves 3 and 4. Once again, the effect of the loss of relationships formed in high school makes itself felt, leading to a significant reduction in network size at the very beginning of this period.

The entry into adult life is punctuated by a number of "first time" events (first job, first stable job, first time living with a partner, first child, and so on). It is true that more and more of young people's biographical transitions are becoming reversible: they return to the parental home after having left, they experience periods of unemployment after finding work, marriages break down, etc.[5] While bearing this possible reversibility in mind, we will nevertheless identify the segments that include these first-time events, since they mark significant moments in the life course. Within the 200 segments between waves of the survey, respondents sometimes experienced biographical transitions: entry into employment, moving out of the parental home, setting up home with a partner, and sometimes they did not.[6] It is thus possible to compare these segments. In general terms, more networks diminished in size than increased within each interval. However, the greatest differences between decrease and increase are observed at the time of the first job, then on the birth of the first child, on moving out of the parental home and the first move outside the local area and, finally, on moving in with a partner. Thus, the transitions into employment and parenthood are more strongly associated than the others with a decrease in network size. These transition effects on network size in the Caen panel are mitigated: the differences are not enormous and the effects of these transitions vary from case to case. In fact, other factors such as social background, for example, turn out to be relatively significant: more young people from working-class backgrounds saw their networks reduce in size, while a higher share of those that increased in size were found among young people from the higher social classes (Table 7.4).

---

[5] Cf., in particular, O. Galland, *Boundless Youth: Studies in the Transition to Adulthood*, (Oxford: The Bardwell Press, 2007); A. Furlong, F. Cartmel, *Young People and Social Change: New Perspectives* (Buckingham: Open University Press, 2007).

[6] It should be noted that, except for the first wave of the survey, which took place just before a "threshold," namely the taking of the baccalaureate, all the other waves were completely random in terms of synchronization with biographical events. They simply took place every three years. Within these three-year periods, much could have happened or very little, depending on the individual cases.

Table 7.4 *Share of changes in network size by social background and gender between two waves of the Caen panel survey (%)*

	Social background			Gender		
	Upper	Intermediate	Working-class	Boys	Girls	Total
Decrease	40.6[a]	51.7	56.5	48.4	56.2	52.5
Increase	56.3	46.7	43.5	49.5	43.8	46.5
No change	3.1	1.7	0	2.1	0	1.0
Total	100	100	100	100	100	100

[a] For example, 40.6 percent of the networks of respondents from the upper social classes decreased in size between two waves of the survey.

The girls were more likely to see their networks decrease in size, while the boys were more likely to see an increase. Thus, "sensitivity" to the transitions and their effects on network size is differentiated.

Of the 1,649 non-family relationships that disappeared between waves 1 and 2, 58.4 percent were relationships of young people who had found their first jobs in the same period. The same trend can be found for this transition in all waves of the survey. Thus, obtaining the first job is associated with the disappearance of a majority of relationships. Conversely, a greater proportion of new ties were formed by young people who had just left the parental home for the first time, except for the "late leavers" in the last wave of the survey, who had more lost ties. Thus, age may also have an effect on sensitivity to this event. This is valid whether or not family ties are included.

The effects of setting up home with a partner also vary with age. The youngest couples in the panel lost many of their non-family ties, which were partially compensated for by new family ties (they gained a family-in-law but also named more people from their own families). On the other hand, for couples who set up home together at a later stage, particularly in the last wave of the survey, the lost ties were not offset by a gain in family ties. Thus, couples who got together later lost more ties than those who got together at an earlier stage in their lives.

Young people who had just had their first child lost ties in the first wave of the survey but subsequently (in waves 3 and 4) the new parents retained more ties and also acquired new non-family ties. Thus, those who had children at an early stage of their lives tended to lose ties, while those who delayed having children until a later stage of their lives tended to retain more of their ties.

Finally, in waves 2 and 3, the first move to another area was associated with an increase in ties, whether family is taken into account or not. On the other hand, if this move took place later, in the fourth wave, it tended to be associated with an increased share of lost ties. Here too, there is an age effect that causes the effect of the transition to vary. The fact of experiencing at an earlier or later stage alters its impact on the evolution of ties.

The dynamics of network structure as identified earlier are also sensitive to these biographical transitions. The most significant transition is the birth of the first child, which has the effect of making networks more dense. Couple formation is also associated with densification, as well as with centralization. Conversely, obtaining a job causes networks to become more dissociated (Table 7.5).[7]

A number of pictures have now snapped into focus: the transition into employment is accompanied by a reduction in the number of relationships, the loss of many ties, and the relative dissociation of personal networks. Couple formation is associated with a slight decrease in network size, in which non-family ties, in particular, are lost; networks tighten around family ties, increasing density and centralization. The birth of the first child is associated with a decrease in network size, particularly when the child arrives at an early stage of the life course, and with an increase in network density. Geographic distance goes hand in hand with an increase in network size as a result of new ties when the move takes place at an early stage (and as a student) but is associated more with losses when it takes place at a later stage (and as a worker); it leads to two contradictory tendencies, one toward densification, the other toward dissociation, depending on the cases in question. These general tendencies associated with biographical transitions require further qualification, with regard not only to the young persons' social positions but also to the age at which they are experienced. These effects are not always the same either, depending on whether we are dealing with family relationships or friendships. Thus, in analyzing these generally predictable and relatively standardized transitions, which propel young people into adulthood, we have by no means uncovered everything there is to say about the evolution of personal networks at these stages of the life course. Other factors and other events are involved that cause the impacts of these transitions to vary.

---

[7] The only event that is very significant statistically is the "first child." The first job and couple formation are weakly significant and the others are not significant at all in the statistical sense. They are mentioned here as tendencies, which, identified by more systematic counting, confirm the links glimpsed in Chapter 6.

Table 7.5 *Evolution of network structure and biographical transitions (Caen panel) (%)*

Network Transition	Dissociation	Densification	Centralization	Decentralization	No change	Total
First job	22 [a]	15.3	8.5	6.8	47.5	100
without	15.6	17	22	6.4	39	100
First stable job	20	12	14	6	48	100
without	16.7	18	19.3	6.7	39.3	100
First leaving parental home	16.9	20.3	15.3	6.8	40.7	100
without	17.7	14.9	19.1	6.4	41.8	100
First living with partner	13.2	26.4	20.8	5.7	34	100
without	19	12.9	17	6.8	44.2	100
First child	0	36	4	16	44	100
without	20	13.7	20	5.1	41.1	100
First move away	20	20	5,7	8,6	45,7	100
without	17	15.8	20.6	6.1	40.6	100
Total	17.5	16.5	18	6.5	41.5	100
No. of transitions	35	33	36	13	83	200

[a] For example, 22 percent of the networks underwent a process of dissociation after the respondent had taken his or her first job.

SOME STORIES OF ORDINARY TRANSITIONS TO ADULT LIFE

In order to analyze the effects of transitions on relationships and networks in greater detail, we will now examine, using a more qualitative approach, a number of examples of progression across these "ordinary" thresholds toward adult life.

The Education-to-Work Transition

The transition from education to work has a very powerful impact on network size, since large contingents of peers, of class mates, disappear as they leave this structuring and unified environment. Work-based relationships are not formed in anything like the same way and are much smaller in number.[8] Workers' networks are also less dense and their relationships more dispersed than in the networks of the economically inactive, the unemployed, or students. Agnès is a typical example of the changes associated with the transition into work. When she left school, she went on to higher education and her network initially expanded as she made new friends, but it decreased subsequently. Agnès had mentioned 117 ties in the first wave of the survey, of which 106 were non-family relationships, and 131 in the second wave, of which 119 were non-family. However, of these 119 ties, only 16 were left over the from the first wave, the remaining 103 being all new. She was living alone in Paris at the time and having a number of romantic relationships, most of them brief and episodic. Her network was made up for the most part of recent contacts established in her new life, friends on the same course and friends of friends. Three years later, in the third wave, she had a permanent job in advertising and was still living in Paris in a shared apartment. Her (non-family) network had contracted from 119 to 64 ties. Of these 64 friendships, 11 were left from the first wave, forming a stabilized core, and 19 from wave 2; 34 were new ties mentioned in the third wave for the first time. Thus, Agnès's network continued to evolve, albeit less radically; in particular, there were fewer new ties (34 compared with 103 in the second wave). She was forming new relationships at a much slower pace and her network was evolving around a stabilized hard core of ties.

Agnès recounted the story of these abandoned and newly formed relationships in the third wave of the survey:

[8] C. Bidart, A. Pellissier, "Copains d'école, copains de travail. Evolution des modes de sociabilité d'une cohorte de jeunes," *Réseaux* 20(115) (2002), 17–49.

Sophie, Joël, Rémi, Yasmina, Thierry were all doing the same vocational course as me. I left that course, everyone went their separate ways . . .. It's the same with the people I know from university, they're scattered all over the place . . .. I think it's the fact that they stayed at university. I got myself a job and a big gap opened up between us. They're no longer the people I spend time with now, they're all married with children, they've gone their own ways . . . I think most of them met girls I didn't really have anything in common with. They adopted a lifestyle that wasn't mine.

The social distances had widened further. On becoming an adult, Agnès was increasingly concerned to separate kindred spirits from the rest. A distinction also emerged between three groups of relationships: a stabilized core of childhood and high school friends that remained unaffected by the changes in her life and network, a larger but less stable group of university friends, which provided large numbers of ties in the second wave that had largely disappeared by the third wave and, finally, the more homogeneous ties that were current at the time of the final wave, fewer in number than in the previous waves and many of them linked to work.

However, just as for some young people the education-to-work transition constitutes a shock and causes their networks to contract severely, so for others, who find the transition more difficult, their eventual success in finding a job is a breath of fresh air, opening up new prospects for relationships. Katia, who in the first wave was on a work experience program, returned to education and by the second wave had obtained a post-graduate certificate. She subsequently worked in a residential care home for young people. For her, this job was an enormous opportunity, a happy outcome after a very difficult childhood, and one in which she had invested very heavily:

This job is so important to me, I can't allow myself to make any mistakes, I really can't let my mind wander at work . . .. Perhaps I've changed as well and I can now sympathize with people more as well. As for my relationships, you'll see that a lot of them are connected with work. I'm more willing to make friends, I'm more open to that, perhaps I find it less scary now.

It is clear from these two examples that the impact of the transition into employment also depends on the starting point of the whole process, whether it constitutes a more or less secure continuation of university life or a way out of a situation characterized by distress and precariousness.

Moving In Together

Setting up home with a partner has several types of implication, some of which concern relationships very directly. Firstly, a spouse or partner never comes alone, since they bring with them their own friends and family.

Secondly, life as a couple sometimes means withdrawing from relationships the two had formed in their "single days." Finally, the new partner and existing friends and acquaintances may not always be compatible. Various authors have concluded from survey data that it is setting up home with a partner that has the greatest impact on the evolution of networks and also that there are different types of couples when it comes to sharing partners' networks.[9] The most significant threshold in the entire, sometimes lengthy process, from the first meeting to starting a family, is generally moving in together. Here too, the effects on the Caen panel were varied. In some cases, network size increased, in others it fell. This depended in part on the family's share in the network (it usually helps to increase network size), on whether the family-in-law was adopted by Ego, who might or might not mention it as part of his or her network, and on whether Ego accepted his or her partner's friends and cited them as their own ties. In some cases, a network increased in size as a result of these additions. In others, conversely, the network shrank as the young couple withdrew into their own little cocoon, with only the people closest to them being mentioned. Thus, for Emeline: "When Frédéric and I look lovingly into each other's eyes, we say: 'Oh my goodness! We've got each other and that's enough!'" And indeed, her network shrank from 78 to 38 ties after she started living with Frédéric.

Suzie's case also shows that her network began to shrink from the point at which she met Fabrice (Figures 7.3 and 7.4).Suzie even dropped her own family to some extent in order to "adopt" her family-in-law.

In the third wave, Suzie left her parents' home in order to live with Fabrice (Figure 7.5). From this point onward, the couple very clearly withdrew into their own "cocoon."

Network structure also evolved in different ways. In some cases, Ego introduced all his/her friends to his/her partner, who in turn introduced all his/her friends to Ego, which triggered a strong process of centralization within the network. In other cases, the two sets of relationships remained

---

[9] See, in particular, E. Bott, *Family and Social Network: Roles, Norms and External Relationships in Ordinary Urban Families* (New York: Free Press, 1971 [1957]); M. A. Castrén, F. Maillochon, "Who Chooses the Wedding Guests, the Couple or the Family? Individual Preferences and Relational Constraints in France and Finland," *European Societies* 11(3) (2009), 369–389; M. Kalmijn, "Shared Friendship Networks and the Life Course: An Analysis of Survey Data on Married and Cohabiting Couples," *Social Networks* 25 (2003), 231–249; R. M. Milardo, "Friendship Networks in Developing Relationships: Converging and Diverging Social Environments," *Social Psychology Quarterly* 45(3) (1982), 162–172; B. Wellman, O. Frank, V. Espinoza, S. Lundquist, C. Wilson, "Integrating Individual, Relational and Structural analysis," *Social Networks* 13 (1991) 223–249.

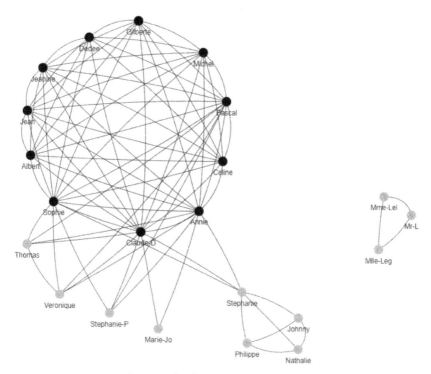

Fig. 7.3 The network of Suzie in the Caen panel (wave 1)

relatively separate from each other, with each partner seeing his or her friends separately. As a result, the network remained dissociated or composite. This second option might follow an initial centralization phase when, after a preliminary period of convergence, Ego and partner decided to distance themselves a little from each other and undertake leisure activities and see their friends separately, as we saw happened to Antoine and Viviane in Chapter 6.

There were also couples who did not share their friends or even their families. In some cases, they had met only recently and things had moved very quickly. This applied to Thibaut, for example, whose partner Karine fell pregnant after a few months and did not "know many people." To make things worse, relations with their families, both of which were reconstituted, were fairly difficult. Samuel too was having some very serious disputes with his family and kept his partner away from these tensions. And Colette's relationships with her divorced parents were not exactly easy, all the more so since she had started living with a man who

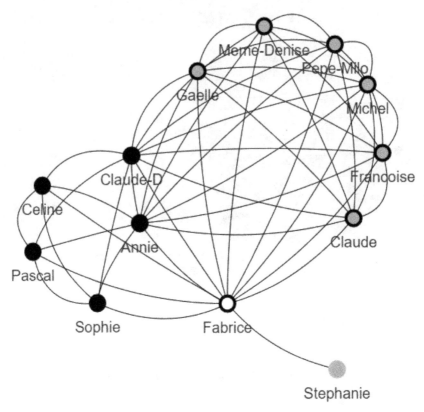

Fig. 7.4 The network of Suzie in the Caen panel (wave 2)

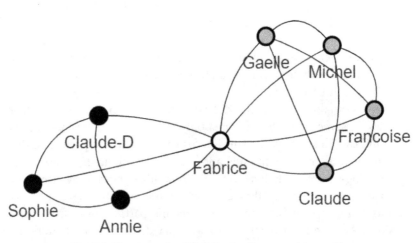

Fig. 7.5 The network of Suzie in the Caen panel (wave 3)

already had children of his own. For Julien also this transition had been difficult:

All the same, there were quite a lot of difficulties to be sorted out, because Aurélie was leaving a relationship from which she already had a little girl, breaking up with her ex had been difficult, so at a certain point we perhaps became rather closed in on ourselves to try to protect Chloé as much as possible, as a result we lost contact rather with groups of our friends and others. Things change so quickly, almost overnight you move from being single to being a family man, without any intermediate stage.

In other cases, there was a slight degree of centralization because of an important activity that left Ego's partner sidelined, as with Gaël and his music and Kévin and his boxing.

Thus, the centralization of a network around a couple is the dominant but not universal dynamic. Setting up home with a partner is a process that exerts a very powerful influence on the future of relationships and of personal networks. However, it is itself influenced by other aspects of the couple's history, both as individuals and as a couple. Consequently, its effects vary considerably, depending on a number of factors. These include the prior relationships with both families, whether or not the new partner has dependent children, possible tensions and conflicts, relocation, and whether or not one or other partner has serious commitments or is heavily involved in a particular activity, to say nothing of the changes the couple itself might undergo. It is sometimes the case that, after an initial period of considerable convergence, a couple's life space, leisure activities, and relational spheres start to diverge to some extent.

Birth of the First Child

The birth of the first child can also have a very significant impact on network size and structure. The most immediate explanation for this concerns the time required to care for a child, but such constraints are not the only consideration and this particular life event can give rise to many other changes in a person's social interactions. Thus, after the birth of his child, Gaël found himself dividing his world between what was important (his family and his four best friends) and "the bonus" (the others). Vérène also made the connection between family life and the transition toward relationships dissociated from each other:

You pare things right down, you don't have time to see thirty-six people. At a pinch, if all my friends knew each other, we could see them altogether, that would be possible. But ultimately we see all the couples we're friends with separately, and we really don't want to amalgamate them all. We have rather different relationships with each of them . . .. We've got rid of the people we used to see from time to time more as an obligation. And then with the baby, it's true there are times when we want it to be just us three together, just our little family.

Whether or not friends have children themselves is a significant selection criterion and reinforces network homogeneity, as Corinne testified:

Before, I liked to go clubbing or out to eat, but not anymore. Now, if it's really necessary, I prefer to buy a piece of furniture, something for the house, and I'd rather do without my nights out. As far as Pierre and Delphine are concerned, the important thing was the birth of Thomas. And seeing as how they already had a little baby, I think that brought us together. It was the same with Christine and Frédéric. There are some things you understand more clearly when you have a child.

However, it is sometimes the case that the birth of a child increases the degree of sociability, particularly with family members, as happened in Suzie's case. We saw above that her world became very closed in around her and her partner. In the fourth wave, however, she had a child and opened up again toward her family, as well as to her partner's friends who also had small children. Her network "rediscovered" her family and was reconstituted in pairs, which are also connected to Fabrice's sister Gaëlle and her husband Michel (Figure 7.6).

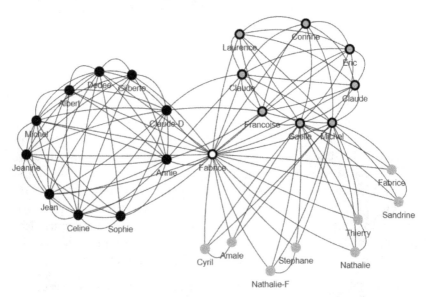

Fig. 7.6 The network of Suzie in the Caen panel (wave 4)

Thus, her network was extensively reconfigured when her first child was born. Her "partying friends" and "superficial acquaintances" were dropped in favor of family ties and good friends who were themselves also the parents of young children. Her network became more homogeneous.

SOME BIOGRAPHICAL EVENTS ARE LESS DUE TO THE LIFE CYCLE

Other biographical events are less typical of the transitions into adult life. They are less common and may also be experienced by individuals older than those in the Caen survey.

Geographical Mobility

Some of the young people in the Caen panel moved a long way from the town in Normandy. Elodie went to join her parents in Boston and François moved to Oslo. However, these two saw their networks increase in size in the second wave because of the number of new contacts they made at university and in the part-time jobs they did in their new homes. Thus, Elodie's network increased from twenty-six to thirty-two ties, while François saw his expand from thirty-one to thirty-nine ties. At university, even in a new country, young people make new friends easily, particularly if they come from the higher social classes. Other students who had not moved quite so far away also made friends very quickly, in Paris or in a region other than Normandy. However, for those young people who left Caen to find work elsewhere, the uprooting placed constraints on their networks. In some cases, they stagnated and in others they contracted sharply; in general, however, they began to build up again later. Thus, Joseph, for example, had left for Lyon in the second wave and his network at that time had shrunk from twenty-nine to twenty-one ties. His friendships from high school, his leisure activities and his village did not survive this move. In the third wave, Joseph was still in Lyon and had built up a sizeable network that now contained forty ties, significantly larger than his network in the first wave, from which he had retained only three friendships. His twenty-eight new ties were formed mainly at work and through leisure activities (football and *pétanque*, a type of bowls played in the South of France). The process of network reconstruction proved to be just a little longer than for students.

These migrants' networks generally went through a dissociation phase: they retained ties with friends who had remained in their home area but

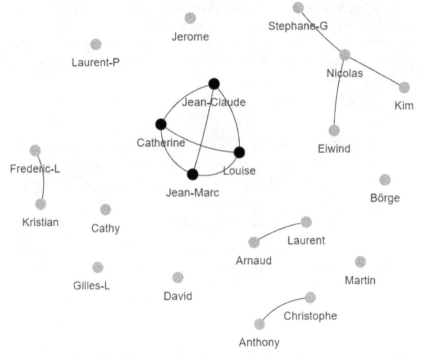

Fig. 7.7 The network of François in the Caen panel (wave 4) after six years of single life in Norway

found it difficult to introduce them to their new friends in the area to which they had moved. Thus, their networks tended to be made up of very small groups or isolated relationships. However, while a migrant who remained single, like François, who had gone to Norway in the second wave, had a network that remained dissociated, a migrant like Nicolas, who went as one half of a couple, had a centered network. Right from the outset, he met with all his new friends together with his partner (Figures 7.7 and 7.8).

Furthermore, experience of a number of moves and stays abroad produces a sort of "skill" that helps people to retain friends despite the distances. Since the second wave, Nicolas had lived in the United States, in Wales, in Spain and, finally, Italy. He succeeded not only in maintaining friendships in each country but also in bringing some of them together as well:

In fact, the friends who have remained are the friends I managed to keep in touch with despite moving around the world. Because in fact, I have one friend, Luc, who is still my friend despite the fact that I've left, I've already lived in four countries

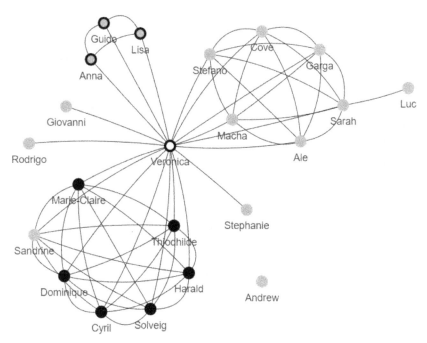

Fig. 7.8 The network of Nicolas in the Caen panel (wave 4) after two years of conjugal life in Spain

since we've known each other. Andrew is a friend I met in the United States and Giovanni is a friend I knew in Wales and am still in touch with despite roaming all over the world. For me, that's what real friends are. I think I'll be friends with them all my life.

The EU's Erasmus student exchange program lay behind some of these relationships, which, incidentally, often involved people from other countries[10] and in some cases continued long after the end of involvement in the scheme, particularly through the reunions organized with former participants. Here too, therefore, a number of factors influence the evolution of networks when people relocate to far-flung places.[11] Their effects often go beyond the specific impact of distance on network structure.

---

[10] A. de Federico, "La dinámica de las redes de amistad. La elección de amigos en el programa Erasmus," *REDES* 4(3) (2003), 1–44.

[11] J.-L. Molina, J. Lerner, S. Gómez Mestres, "Patrones de cambio de las redes personales de inmigrantes en Cataluña," *REDES* 15 (2008), 50–63; M. J. Lubbers, J.-L. Molina, J. Lerner, U. Brandes, J. Avila, C. Mc Carty, "Longitudinal Analysis of Personal Networks: The Case of Argentinean Migrants in Spain," *Social Networks* 32 (2010), 91–104.

Unemployment

As we have already seen, starting one's first job can lead to a reduction in network size. However, the unemployment and difficult life circumstances that sometimes accompany this transition may also trigger processes of disaffiliation and withdrawal from social circles, leading to a loss of relationships. For Marie, for example, finally getting a job marked the end of a period of hardship. Having obtained the vocational baccalaureate, she went to university but dropped out during her first year. In the second wave, she was doing a number of occasional unskilled menial jobs and was no longer very sure of how to make progress in her life. Her prevarications were also affecting her relationships. Her network had contracted from thirty-three to six ties. She commented coldly on this reduction:

That's just how things are. I perhaps miss Carine, but not the others. As time passes, you grow away from people. I'm happier being on my own. Anyway, I don't see anyone any more. (Don't you want to?) No. I'm not interested any more.

Marie's inertia and the decline in her social interactions could have been a cause for concern. Later, however, Marie had found a job and her network had expanded from six to fourteen relationships in the third wave. This job certainly made her change her tune:

I've changed because before, I didn't necessarily communicate with people. Now I really like talking to people, I like people telling me about their lives. This has something to do with my work environment, because that's where I learned to communicate. And then with the atmosphere there is there, we've never had any tensions between us.

More confident and more involved, Marie named four friends in her workplace.

Thibaut, for his part, had worked for several years as a petrol pump attendant in a supermarket. However, he was finding the job unbearable and he resigned after the third wave. He immediately lost contact with the friends he had there and he also stopped playing sport. His personal network was now concentrated around his family, his family-in-law, some neighbors, and a female friend of his wife. He particularly regretted no longer having any male friends, and the short-term nature of the job he had at the time did not help much:

It's a pity I'm not on a permanent contract in the job I have at the moment. In any case, it'll come to an end soon because, as far as the people I've got on well with are concerned, it would have been good to work there longer, I'm sure there are one or two I might perhaps really have been able to make friends with.

The problem is indeed that the difficulties associated with unemployment as such are further aggravated by precarity and the difficulty of making plans for the future. In the Caen panel, precarious and seasonal workers, together with economically inactive women, had by far the smallest networks; they tended to be limited to a few close family members (if disputes had not yet divided that particular circle), a few neighbors and one or two friends in the best of cases. At this point, unemployment ceases to be an event and becomes a constraint on individual's lives.

Professional Bifurcation

A new job generally brings people into contact with individuals hitherto unknown to them. Some of these contacts may develop into more significant relationships. Similarly, when one leaves a job, most of the relationships associated with that job are deactivated or broken off. As we have seen, the only ones that survive are those that have become sufficiently detached from the work context. In the topography of networks, work-based relationships generally remain "in their own corner," forming a separate group and not mixing with friends from other contexts. If, following a change of job, they are replaced by other colleagues, another group appears but the overall structure of the network is not affected. The same applies when this new job takes the form of a real bifurcation, a specific change that is both unforeseeable and marks a radical change of direction, affecting the other spheres of a person's life, usually irreversibly.[12]

This was the case, for example, when Jean suddenly left his occupation of salesman, exhausted by the constraints it placed on his life:

In fact, when I started out, I'd just graduated, I was convinced I could become a great salesman, that I could flog the Eiffel Tower and then sell it a second time to someone else. And then I realized things weren't that simple . . . . In fact, it was a crazy job, the pace was intolerable . . . . Because I was no longer in touch with

---

[12] M. Grossetti, "L'imprévisibilité dans les parcours sociaux," *Cahiers internationaux de sociologie*, Trajectoires sociales et bifurcations, 120 (2006), 5–28; M. Bessin, C. Bidart, M. Grossetti (eds.), *Bifurcations. Les sciences sociales face aux ruptures et à l'événement* (Paris: La découverte, 2010); C. Bidart, "What Does Time Imply? Contributions of Longitudinal Methods to the Analysis of the Life Course," *Time and Society* 22(2) (2013), 254–273; C. Bidart, M. E. Longo, A. Mendez, "Time and Process: An Operational Framework for Processual Analysis," *European Sociological Review* 29(4) (2013), 743–751.

anyone, I didn't have the time, I was working seven days a week. I aged terribly in a year ... I had to do something.

So Jean did do something: he went to live in Rodez (a small town in the center of France) with his partner.

I completely cut all ties with all the people I'd known before, I no longer wanted to have any relationship at all with them ... not even the few individuals I got on well with, who were more or less straightforward and genuine, I just lumped them all together. I really wanted to cut myself off from that period of my life and I changed my mobile number. A few people tried to get in touch with me but I never got back to them because I wanted it to stop and have no more contact with them.

So Jean even made the ultimate break with his past and changed his mobile number, making his change of direction even more irreversible. Although it does not always go quite so far, a change of direction or occupation or even a return to education in a different discipline, as Alban, Patrice, Julien, Fabienne, Rose, and Victor experienced, leads to a recomposition of the work-based component of personal networks but does not necessarily change their overall structure.

Furthermore, the work environment is also more likely to produce conflict situations and relationships break off there more suddenly and discordantly than in the other spheres of life (except for the romantic sphere). Thus, Paul, having set up his website design company with a group of friends, experienced the relationship difficulties that often accompany this sort of venture. He had fallen out with Julien, Bruno, and Mathieu but had just found some other partners with whom to embark on a new venture, this time setting up a web-based estate agency. However, his "hard core," the group of a dozen individuals he had known since school, remained unchanged and kept apart from his work, even though these friends had to accept the part his work played in Paul's life:

As far as my work was concerned, the people around me, my hard core, understood what I really wanted to do. That's important. And also what I was prepared to sacrifice, willing to do in order to get where I wanted to be. That's real friendship.

Alban was less fortunate and lost some of his friends when he left his sales job to train as a dentist, an old childhood dream:

They thought I was mad, they told me I'd never make it, so that put a bit of a damper on things and since I no longer have anything at all to do with the world of sales, they no longer phone me.

On the other hand, Alban had drawn much closer to his family, who were supporting him. Thus, a change of job or occupation leads to the severance of certain relationships and some degree of selective sorting among former colleagues, and also among certain circles of friends when the change of direction is a radical one. However, these events have little impact on overall network structure since work-based ties are usually kept separate from the others, forming a small group on their own.

Breaking Up with a Partner

Just like moving in with a partner, the breakdown of a romantic relationship has very marked effects on the whole network. However, these effects may differ considerably. In some cases, the network contracts considerably when a couple separate, in others it expands in size and in yet others it decentralizes as it is renewed. Solange's case is typical of the first situation, when she and Laurent separated. It has to be said that for Solange the divorce marked a boundary between "before" and "after" in general terms, including her relationships. The role of sociability in her separation from Laurent was, moreover, not insignificant:

After living together for eleven years, we realized we were friends rather than husband and wife and that we had never done anything on our own, just the two of us, there was always a third person in the pack, Mathias among others, and that ultimately we were living more as a group of three than as a couple. And then he changed jobs and was away the whole week, he came back on Fridays and then we spent the weekend with our pals and well, that was it. And then I had other friends I saw during the week, Emmanuel among others, and then, well, there wasn't much point in going on like that.

Shared friends, those who had always been with them, might not stay shared after the breakup:

Mathias was one of our best friends, so a shared friend, he was as much Laurent's friend as mine. He was my confidant at the time, so he found himself caught in the crossfire, and then made an obvious choice, he stayed friends with Laurent (Figures 7.9 and 7.10).

Among the few people who remained from "before" was Marianne, who had something in common with Solange: "Marianne and Julien are separated, so being divorced herself she understands the situation very well." Moreover, her new partner, Emmanuel, played a very active role in the evolution of Solange's network:

We've lost touch with each other rather now, also because Emmanuel wasn't overly keen on seeing the people Laurent and I hung out with, so it's true I naturally did some selective sorting .. ... And the people we choose to be friends with now, we

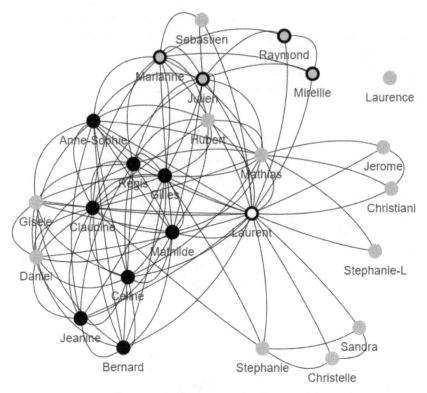

Fig. 7.9 The network of Solange in the Caen panel (wave 3)

choose them together, so the people we mix with now have to be accepted by the two of us.

Thus, the relationship that Solange rebuilt with Emmanuel was very different from the one she had formed with Laurent, and her network very clearly showed the effects of it as it contracted from forty-nine to twenty-one relationships.

Nina's case is very different. The graph of her network in Chapter 6 showed the process of dissociation triggered by separation. Nina was very happy with her rediscovered freedom and found herself going out more and undertaking more leisure activities than she had when living with her partner. Her network had contracted from twenty-four to twelve relationships but increased in the third wave to twenty-five relationships, despite the disappearance of friends shared with her former partner:

As time passes, I'm regaining my independence more and more. It was the breakup with Sidicki that led to me seeing my girlfriends more, whereas I used to see them

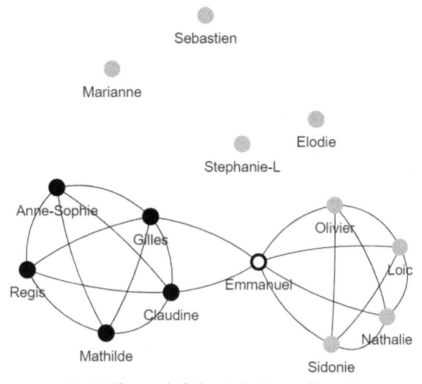

Fig. 7.10 The network of Solange in the Caen panel (wave 4)

less often. I wouldn't be seeing my group of friends in Caen if I was still with him, that's for sure. And I go out more. It's true that when you're in a group of girls, most of whom are single, you go out a lot. When you're on your own, you have more time for your girlfriends.

Thus, Nina, as a single and a student, returned for a time to a young person's mode of social behavior.

In other cases, like that of Clotilde, the main effect of the breakup was a process of decentralization. Like Solange, she lost most of the friends she had had in common with her partner, but she also met many new ones, particularly since she had returned to education and felt more self-confident:

I was very independent before getting together with Manu. And now I've become very independent again. It was becoming too stifling, I was no longer living for myself, I was living only for Lisa [her daughter]. I think that going to train as a special education teacher and becoming more self-confident as a result, I think that played a big part.

An individual's social and economic circumstances are crucial to what happens to people, particularly women, when a relationship breaks down. Various factors, such as having or not having a child, being a student, or working or being unemployed, make a huge difference that may overtake differences between men and women.[13] In general, there is an increase in contacts with people who, prior to the breakup, were not linked to the former partner.[14] This statement will have to be qualified depending on the other changes brought about by the breakup, particularly relocation, and it will evolve over time. As we have already seen, other factors, such as the partner's network, his or her attitude to their joint and separate friendships, as well as the stranglehold he or she might have on the couple's network, play a very important role in this regard. The part played by the family may also help to create significant differences, depending on the case in question.

Coming Out

Didier's network profile in the second wave was of the composite type, centered to some extent on his sister Ingrid, with several isolated relationships, a rather fragmented family and a small group of friends. His partner Mathilde, with whom he was not living, was linked to Ingrid and to Didier's mother (Figures 7.11 and 7.12).

In the third wave, this network was breaking up, even though the family had a greater presence and the small group of friends remained; Mathilde had disappeared. In the fourth wave, the network splintered into a large number of isolated microcomponents. Dissociation on this scale is quite exceptional and raises the question of why it happened. The presence of another partner called Sébastien may provide the beginnings of an explanation. Between the second and third waves of the survey, Didier had come out as gay. He realized that his network had changed considerably:

I see that lots of people have disappeared from my life. Even in my family, not many people know much about my present life. I think that's one of the main reasons. It's not a problem, but people aren't particularly well informed. And in fact if I can't talk to them about myself and my love life, because they're not well informed about things, that also prevents relationships from forming. Let's say

---

[13] L. A. Leslie, K. Grady, "Changes in Mothers' Social Networks and Social Support Following Divorce," *Journal of Marriage and the Family*, 47 (1985), 663–673.

[14] E. L. Terhell, M. I. Broese van Groenou, T. van Tilburg, "Network Contact Changes in Early and Later Post-Separation Years," *Social Networks* 29 (2007), 11–24.

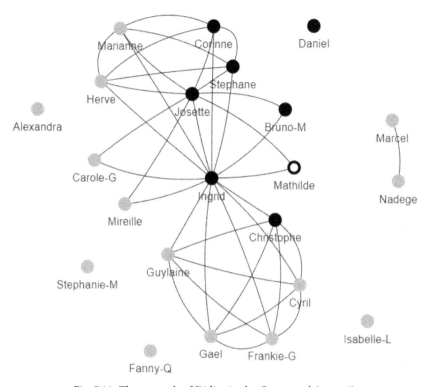

Fig. 7.11 The network of Didier in the Caen panel (wave 2)

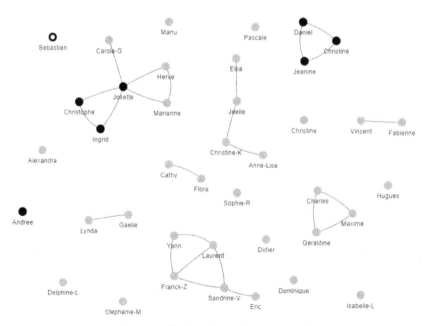

Fig. 7.12 The network of Didier in the Caen panel (wave 4)

I have no wish, nor any need, to tell the whole world about it. And there are some who don't want to hear about it. Ah well, I don't have so many close friends anyway.

Three years later, Didier's network had splintered still further through the addition of many weak ties whose superficiality he feared:

There are lots of people around me, and sometimes I have the feeling I'm drowning in all these relationships. Even though I share lots of things with these new friends, I still think some relationships are superficial.

For him, this type of relationship can be associated with the emotional vacuum created by his abrupt change of sexual orientation:

At that time, given it was a period of change, of personal searching and perhaps also emotional emptiness, I certainly wanted to fill the void with friendships come what may. I was forming relationships in order to avoid being lonely.

Didier had not yet introduced Sébastien to anyone:

It's still difficult. And there are still fights to be fought. It's five years now since I changed my sexual orientation. I'm comfortable with it, but it's true there are nevertheless still subjects that can be painful. Despite all that, even though there's been a lot of progress in terms of tolerance, there are still situations that bring us back to reality with a jolt.

Here too, it is not a question of reducing these unique individual stories to homogeneous sequences nor of standardizing the analysis of the effects on their relational environments. However, comparison of the network graphs with the life stories gives us a better understanding of the links that exist between relationships, and the ways in which they are structured and evolve, on the one hand, and more or less common life events, on the other. Other biographical events, such as accidents, illness, handicaps, the birth of a sick child, bereavement, and disputes at work or in the family – and obviously it is not possible to provide examples of all of these here – are also likely to give rise to changes in networks. It is also clear that the events described by the young people in the Caen panel by no means represent the full range of biographical events that concern older people.

*

*   *

Network dynamics are closely intertwined with life histories. Advancing age, biographical transitions, and important events have an impact on network size and renewal, as well as on structure and evolution. However, these factors linked to the life cycle are seldom the only ones at work; rather, it is whole sets of factors that give rise to complex and varied effects. Thus, differences in social circumstances play a key role in determining the effects of life events. They have an impact on the way in which individuals experience these events, both subjectively and objectively. Depending on the initial circumstances (leaving university or struggling for a long time), family history (coming from a divided or united family), partners' attitudes (having a jealous or more open-minded partner) and the "class cultures" that determine norms, the same transitions may cause a network to open up or close in on itself or to become more centralized or dispersed. Thus, social circumstances and earlier life stages give different meanings to life events and generate different effects.

Our observation of the way in which relational environments and networks react to events in individuals' lives while remaining sensitive to social frameworks, milieus, and norms shows the value of a sociology of relational dynamics. It is here undoubtedly that this intermediate level of analysis of social phenomena produces its most illuminating insights. It is, after all, through the processes of change affecting personal networks that the dynamics of their links to the social world over the life course are most clearly revealed.

PART III

NETWORKS AND SOCIAL WORLDS

8

Networks Have a Spatial Dimension

Where do those close to us or, more generally, the people with whom we maintain relationships live? Are we (spatially) close to those (emotionally) close to us? What effects have changes in the urban environment had on relationship structures? How does geographical mobility influence networks? The problem being posed in these questions is that of the spatial dimension of social networks or, to put it another way, of the link between "spatial" proximity and "relational" proximity. Sociologists tend spontaneously to emphasize the various forms of social proximity (such as similarities in origin, positions, resources, and so on), mention of which is usually accompanied by a denial or at least a downplaying of the importance of space. Network analysts, who are no exception in this regard, tend to present them as alternatives to territory.[1] Nevertheless, some authors (including Wellman) have carried out research showing that networks do have a spatial structure, that relationships are not, in other words, distributed randomly in space.

The main studies of social networks that incorporate the spatial dimension were carried out in the 1970s in response to the "community question," to use the expression coined by Barry Wellman, who conducted a survey of the personal networks of people living in the city of Toronto.[2] This question concerns the effects of urbanization on local communities (that is, in villages or urban neighborhoods), which were then regarded in the English-speaking world as the main framework within which the social

---

[1] See the article by B. Wellman and B. Leighton, "Networks, Neighborhoods, and Communities," *Urban Affairs Review* 14(3) (1979), 363–390.

[2] See the classic article by B. Wellman, "The Community Question: The Intimate Networks of East Yorkers," *The American Journal of Sociology* 84(5) (1979), 1201–1231, for a detailed presentation of this problematic.

bond was constituted and maintained. Ever since the beginning of the twentieth century, various authors, particularly from the Chicago School, had been examining the hypothesis that the mass society and urban growth lead to the loss of social ties and a situation of anonymity resulting in the development of anomic behaviors, which Wellman describes as the "lost community" hypothesis. Others refuted this hypothesis and sought to show that urbanization does not have any significant effect on neighborhood communities (the "preserved" community hypothesis). Drawing on the work of network analysts, Wellman advanced the idea that neighborhood communities are indeed in decline but are being replaced by "communities without proximity," that is, networks that do indeed generate solidarity but are more dispersed spatially and structured differently (the "emancipated" community hypothesis). Wellman's study and that by Fischer, whose method was adopted, in part, for the Toulouse survey, both validate this last hypothesis, albeit with certain nuances. Both surveys find that networks are as important in urban environments as in traditional "communities" but are structured differently. For example, they are of lower density.

The community question has a significant spatial aspect, since the communities in question are local communities. In Fischer's survey, 65 percent of the relationships were located within an hour's travel time from the respondent's place of residence. In Wellman's study, 75 percent of the relationships cited by his respondents in Toronto were located in the area in which they lived. As the "liberated" community argument suggests, these were not generally relationships in the immediate neighborhood. After all, only one-quarter of the individuals cited in Fischer's survey lived less than five minutes away from the respondent and barely one in ten of those in Wellman's survey were living in the same neighborhood as the person surveyed. Moreover, the move from neighborhood to city had little effect on the frequency of contact, whereas it fell rapidly when the distances were greater, which supports the idea that the relevant spatial level when talking of "local" relationships is undoubtedly the city and not the neighborhood.

WHERE DO OUR CLOSE FRIENDS AND RELATIVES LIVE?

These tendencies were valid for North America in the 1970s. What about Europe and France at the beginning of the twenty-first century? And what of the inhabitants of Toulouse and the villages and small towns in the Tarn

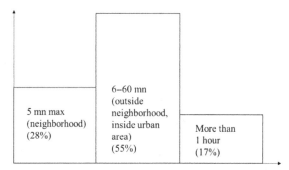

Fig. 8.1 Distance between respondents' places of residence and the places of residence of the named persons

who were questioned in 2001 as part of the survey on social solidarity and the young people in the Caen survey?

Very Local Networks

The values of five minutes and one hour's driving time were selected by Fischer as approximations for the local community and the conurbation. If we adopt the same categories, the relationships cited by those surveyed in Toulouse turn out to be more "local": 28 percent were between zero and five minutes away, 55 percent between six minutes and one hour, and 17 percent more than an hour away. Thus, 83 percent were less than one hour away, compared with the 66 percent observed by Fischer.[3] In the INSEE survey,[4] in which respondents were asked to name three friends, 76 percent of those named lived less than thirty miles away and 19 percent less than half a mile away, which is fairly similar. In the Caen survey, 18.5 percent of the individuals cited, excluding cohabitants, lived less than a mile away and 63.9 percent less than forty-five miles away (about an hour's journey), which is also very close to the other results. Thus, personal networks have a spatialized structure. The two "local" levels, namely the neighborhood (less than five minutes away) and the "city or administrative conurbation" (less than an hour's travel time) have a strong structuring effect on the spatial distribution of the individuals named (Figure 8.1).

---

[3] Nevertheless, for us, an hour's travel time denotes a somewhat larger area than the conurbation (at the time of the survey in 2001, the Toulouse conurbation had a population of 750,000, of whom about 400,000 lived in the city of Toulouse itself, while the city of San Francisco had a population of 650,000 at the time of Fischer's survey).

[4] Survey of Household Living Conditions in 1997 (*Enquête sur les conditions de vie des ménages en 1997*).

Strong Ties Withstand Distance Better

This structure varies with the types of relationships. As Table 8.1 shows, those emotionally closest to respondents were the least likely to be close geographically. This does not mean that people make long-distance friends but rather that strong ties withstand distance better than weak ties. In particular, long-standing ties were more likely to be distant ones (21 percent of relationships established for more than twenty years compared with 7 percent of those established for five years or less). Thus, we are dealing with three types of spaces in which relationships evolve. The proximity or nearness space (less than five minutes away) is what equates

Table 8.1 *Types of relationships and geographical proximity (Toulouse survey) (%)*

Travel time between respondent's home and that of the person named	five minutes maximum	from six to sixty minutes	more than one hour
Description of relationship at time of survey			
"family"	23[a]	51	26
"close relation"	23	56	21
"friend" without further qualification	20	66	13
"Colleague" without further qualification	27	64	9
"Acquaintances"	21	75	4
"Neighbors" without further qualification	96	4	0
Context of initial meeting			
Family	15	53	32
School	29	53	18
University	29	57	14
Work	22	66	12
Community associations	28	65	7
Through a friend	27	62	11
Neighbor	83	11	6
Total population (excluding cohabitants)	28	55	17

[a] For example, 23 percent of the individuals described as close friends or family lived less than 5 minutes' travel time away from the respondent.

to the notion of neighborhood. Beyond that, people were seldom regarded simply as neighbors. Individuals living between five minutes and one hour away were located within the urban space in which most ties of all kinds but particularly weak ties (colleagues and acquaintances) are situated. Beyond that, the "external" space, basically the country but in some cases abroad as well, was populated largely with strong ties (family, best friends). These results are consistent with those obtained by Fischer ("Do people feel emotionally closer to individuals with whom they have a relationship and who live close by or to those who are furthest away? For those we surveyed, it was the ones living furthest away").[5] This means that only "strong" relationships withstand distance.

In the Caen survey, the link between spatial distance and the duration of the relationship was less clear. The more recent relationships were more likely to be located in the same neighborhood, municipality, and conurbation, whereas in the other regions of France or abroad, relationships that had lasted more than ten years predominated, together with family. Similarly, more casual friends and acquaintances tended to be located in the same neighborhood or municipality, whereas closer friends and family were more likely to live in other regions.

This was confirmed by Rose who, despite having left Caen for Paris, had retained a very strong tie with her friend Séverine, whereas the less strong ties had disappeared from her network:

We still get on just as well. Whenever I go down to Caen, I go to see her, we set aside at least a day to spend with each other. We try to see each other as much as possible. The fact that I've left was a bit hard, but we said that if I had an apartment, she would absolutely have to come and live in Paris. She's my best friend, that's true, and I've known her now for thirteen years. I don't see any of the others at all actually. When I go down there, it's the weekend, so generally I only see my parents, my best friend, my family, but that's all.

Rose was delighted to be in Paris and had almost completely changed her network; nevertheless, her best friend was still Séverine, even several years after leaving. For Sidonie, leaving for Paris helped her sort her real friends from the rest:

I think it's now more organized geographically: there's really the friends from Caen, and work. I've really separated things out. Before, all my friends were mixed

---

[5] C. Fischer, *To Dwell among Friends: Personal Networks in Town and City* (Chicago: The University of Chicago Press, 1982), p. 173.

up together, but now I've got two separate groups of friends. Four years ago, the fact that we were all at high school together more or less forced us to hang out together, we didn't even ask ourselves whether we really wanted to see each other, whereas now there's the distance and work, so we know if we really want to see each other, we're not forced into it just out of sheer habit. I think I've really found my true friends. Having come to Paris, the distance means that if I really want to see someone, I telephone them.

For Joseph, now living in Lyon, it was actually the distance itself that had strengthened certain ties:

Relationships change because the distance means that, when we do meet up, we're more pleased to see each other. If I was still living in Caen, we'd meet up just out of habit. Because of the distance, we're very happy to meet up and we're able to talk with each other better. So our relationships have changed because of the distance. We've grown closer together.

Moreover, 27 percent of respondents living in the Toulouse conurbation mentioned at least one person living outside the urban area. This indicator of the geographical "dispersion" of a person's network varied with mobility, but even more so with level of education (it was particularly high among the economically active with two years' post-secondary education – 34 percent – and lower for those who left education before the baccalaureate – 19 percent), occupation (29 percent for managers and executives, 9 percent for agricultural workers, craft workers, and shopkeepers) and age (40 percent for the under-25s and 6 percent for the over-65s). The share of external ties rose with the total number of people mentioned and with the proportion of individuals described as colleagues among the names mentioned. It fell when the relational environment included a large number of neighbors and members of associations. In fact, individuals' networks were all the more local the more extensive they were, which was more likely for those who had completed post-secondary education. Thus, networks have a strong geographical structure, with high shares of "local" ties situated in the conurbation or, in rural areas, the canton (territorial subdivisions of the French Republic's 332 *arrondissements* and 101 *départements*).

Urban and Rural Networks

Rural areas today are far from being reliant solely on agriculture and are home to a diverse range of economic activities and populations – from "neo-rurals" to people working in nearby towns and cities but living in villages. This is why it is difficult to repeat the comparison Fischer conducted between "semi-rural" areas and the various "urban contexts."

Table 8.2 *Differences between rural and urban areas (Toulouse survey)*

Characteristic	Toulouse conurbation	Rural areas
Context in which relationships developed	More ties established: university, work, social life[a]	More ties mentioned: family, childhood, neighborhood[b]
Size of networks	Slightly fewer names mentioned	Slightly more names mentioned
Multifaceted nature of relationships	No difference	No difference
Density	Weaker over the conurbation as a whole but higher in city center	Higher
Same gender or age	Higher	Lower
Comparable education levels or occupations	No difference	No difference

[a] The difference is particularly significant for the more highly educated (four or more years' higher education).

[b] Once controlled by variance analysis for age, socio-occupational category, and educational level.

Table 8.2 summarizes the differences observed in the Toulouse survey between the 300 respondents in the Greater Toulouse urban area and the 99 from the various villages in the Tarn who also featured in our sample.

Once controlled for the most influential variables (age, socio-occupational category, and level of education), the contexts in which the relationships mentioned by respondents developed do differ somewhat from each other; in the rural areas, there were more relationships linked to family, childhood, or the immediate neighborhood, which is consistent with the standard findings. Similarly, the number of names mentioned was somewhat greater in rural areas than in all the urban areas. The difference was due principally to exchanges of services for domestic tasks, with inhabitants of rural areas citing on average twice as many names in this connection as urban dwellers (even when the analysis is limited to managers and executives with at least four years' higher education), most of them family members.

The differences between the two types of areas turn out to be more complex than might have been expected. For example, those surveyed in rural areas mentioned more names in connection with social activities (excursions, leisure activities, etc.), which are more readily associated with urban environments. As Fischer noted in the American survey, the average level of multiplexity does not vary significantly by geographical area, once age, educational level, socio-occupational category, and type of household have been taken into account. The difference in network density[6] between rural and urban areas was one of Fischer's most significant results. Density declined as an area became more densely populated, which Fischer explained by pointing to the greater opportunities for urban dwellers to be involved in groups that are unconnected with each other. In the French survey as well, network density turned out to be higher in the rural areas and weaker in some suburban areas, although it was higher in the city center. Thus, it did not decline along a rural-urban continuum but described a sort of U-shaped curve; according to this continuum, the city center was similar to the rural areas. In other words, the density of individuals' networks does not decline linearly when population density increases, as Fischer observed. However, this tendency needs to be confirmed in further research.

MOBILITY

The spatial structure of networks varies depending on individual's experience of mobility, because a high share of relationships do not withstand geographical distance. We have already seen that leaving high school, changing jobs, or moving in with a partner can have a considerable influence on network formation and transformation. All relationships arise out of a context and only a small proportion of them survive significant changes to that context. Individuals who have lived in different places in the course of their lives will have forged relationships that leave traces of their existence in their network. Thus, among the young people in the Caen panel, Agnès was able in the fourth wave, when she was living in Saint Malo, to name friends from the different places in which she had lived since the first wave: Caen, of course, where she still had five friends, Paris, and Levallois, as well as Granville, where she always spent her holidays and met up with her two groups of friends. She said of her friend Camille:

Three years ago, she was already someone who no longer lived in the same town as me, we didn't go to the same places on weekends. So it was a relationship that proceeded in fits and starts, with each of us getting regular news updates from the other. But it hasn't changed. When we do meet up, it is as if we'd left

---

[6] Network density is the ratio between the number of ties that exist between the Alters mentioned and the maximum number of possible ties between them (see Chapter 2).

each other just the day before. We lose sight of each other, we meet up again, but it doesn't change.

All the young people who had left Caen still had friends there, even though they had made new friends in their new regions, and they reactivated these ties at least once a year during visits to their families. However, it should be noted that this ability to make light of distance is strongly linked to social origin and level of education. In the Caen panel, it was among young people from working-class backgrounds that spatial distance was most frequently cited to explain the end of a relationship. Thus, in contrast to Agnès, many young people from working-class backgrounds were unable to envisage maintaining links with people who were no longer living close by. The same mile does not signify the same distance for the disadvantaged working classes as it does for the more advantaged and educated classes. It is necessary, therefore, to analyze mobility in order to understand the spatial logics at work in the dynamic dimension of networks. Let us now reverse the perspective and examine the various types of mobility in order to assess their impact on relationships and networks.

Mobility within the Country

Three types of mobility can be identified. The first is daily intra-urban mobility (travel from home to work, for example). The second is routine interurban mobility (regular travel to work in another town/city, for example). The final type is non-routine interurban mobility, which indicates a more radical change of place of residence. In the case of daily intra-urban travel, once place of residence is taken into account, modes of transport and travel times are not correlated with the number of relationships mentioned or with the density of individuals' networks. Thus, this form of mobility does not appear to have any effect on the structure of networks. On the other hand, the minimum travel time between the places of residence of those surveyed and those of their friends and relatives increases with the travel time between place of residence and place of work: the further one works from home, the more spatially extended one's network is. For economically active respondents living in the Greater Toulouse urban area, the travel time between them and their friends and relatives was approximately forty minutes on average for those who worked at home or took less than fifteen minutes to get to work, about an hour for those who took between fifteen minutes and one hour to travel to their place of work (without any differences between them) and more than two hours for those who took more than an hour to get to work. This equates to the three types of space identified previously, namely the neighborhood, the conurbation, and the external space (in most cases, the rest of the country, in some, abroad).

Answers to the following question asked in the Toulouse survey serve as an indicator of routine interurban mobility: "In the last two years, have you had to travel very regularly to a specific place outside the Greater Toulouse urban area?" The majority of respondents (72.8 percent) did not have to make such journeys, while 13.8 percent did so once a week and 13.4 percent once a month. Those who did travel regularly outside the Toulouse conurbation were mainly managers and executives (59 percent) and usually lived in the city center. Those who traveled at least once a month had significantly more relationships with people who lived more than an hour's journey away (19 percent, compared with 14 percent for those who were working but did not travel outside the urban area). Thus, routine interurban mobility certainly has an effect on the spatial spread of personal networks. Among their contacts living more than an hour from their homes, "mobile" respondents were slightly more likely than others to cite colleagues and, in particular, family members. Thus, work-related mobility is associated with a slightly greater degree of dispersion among the family members cited (particularly spouses in the case of geographically separated couples).

In order to evaluate non-routine interurban mobility, we have at our disposal the following data: respondents' place of birth, the place where they were living at age eighteen, the total number of towns/cities in which they had lived for at least a year, and the length of time they had been living in the region. Non-routine interurban mobility has no effect on the number of relationships mentioned (once the effects of educational level and socio-occupational category are taken into account). On the other hand, it is correlated with the proportion of individuals living more than an hour's journey from the respondent's residence. Those who were born in the southwest of France[7] and were living there at age eighteen named significantly fewer "outside" contacts, once differences in educational levels were taken into account. The length of time respondents had lived in their local environment (rural district or conurbation) also turns out to be significant. The longer they had lived there, the fewer "outside" contacts they mentioned, once differences in educational levels were taken into

---

[7] The regions at the time of the study. In 2016 the Midi-Pyrénées and Languedoc-Roussillon regions were merged.

account. Thus, the fact of having lived in different towns or regions leaves its mark on the spatial structure of individuals' networks. However, this is less significant than might have been expected. "Outside" contacts accounted for 40 percent of the relationships of the most mobile individuals (those having lived in four or more towns/cities in their lives) living in the city center (compared with 29 percent for the population as a whole).[8] This had no effect on density or the share of close friends and relatives.

The young people in the Caen panel who had just relocated did not necessarily see the size of their networks fall, and half of them actually saw it increase. The evolution of their personal networks depended a great deal on their social background and the circumstances of the move. Depending on whether they had left to continue their education or to work, alone or with a partner, the profile of the move changed completely, as we saw in Chapter 7. The most general change was that in average network density, which declined from 0.28 to 0.25. It was, after all, more difficult to make connections between old and new friends.

The individuals named and described as living a long way away often lived in towns or cities where respondents had lived, but they represented only a very small proportion of their networks and it was almost always strong ties that connected them with Ego. They were either family members, friends to whom Ego felt close, and some less-close friends but from whom the geographical separation was still recent. These results are consistent with those from a survey of 368 households that moved from one area of France to another between 1998 and 2000.[9] The authors show that people who relocate give priority to maintaining ties with family and close friends. They note that close friends, who tend to be limited in number (about five on average), differ from more casual friends through the specification of the relationship, whereas the latter are more difficult to dissociate from the context. When the context is local, a move away usually leads to its disappearance and the relationship has little chance of surviving. On the other hand, non-local contexts (colleagues in the same company operating at several locations) are less affected by geographical mobility and relationships are easier to maintain. They may even intensify if they involve colleagues in the new work environment. The telephone is

---

[8] All these proportions are calculated on the basis of respondents in the Greater Toulouse urban area who named at least four individuals in the subsample of relationships, none of whom was cohabiting with them.

[9] Cf. the article by P.-A. Mercier, C. de Gournay, Z. Smoreda, "Si loin, si proches: liens et communications à l'épreuve du déménagement," *Réseaux* 115 (2002), 121–150.

the favored means of maintaining contact with close friends and family who do not live nearby.

Thus, social networks are not without their spatial dimension, contrary to what is sometimes declared. They turn out to be sensitive to geographical proximity, even though the strongest ties and the most mobile individuals are better able than others to withstand the effects of distance. This does not necessarily mean that the "weak" ties of the past had disappeared but simply that they were not present in the types of exchanges that can be captured by the name generators used in our surveys. It might well be imagined that at least some of these relationships had become "dormant" and that they might have been reactivated in the event of a move on the part of one or other of the protagonists bringing them closer together again, even if only temporarily, or if one of them thought that the other could help him or her (to find a job, for example) or even if, in the event of a life-changing biographical event, one of them sought to reactivate old relationships. The results presented above relate for the most part to various forms of mobility within the same country. In the next section, we examine what happens when mobility takes the form of migration. Our data are of little relevance to such an investigation, but fortunately migration has been much studied by other researchers, particularly from the perspective of social networks.[10]

Moving Abroad

It is known that social networks play a crucial role in decisions to emigrate, in the choice of destination (with priority often being given to those where the would-be migrant already has direct or indirect contacts), in the implementation of plans to emigrate, and in the forms of integration into local contexts. Many studies have analyzed the composition of migrants' personal networks and distinctions are often made between ties with migrants from the same background, with other migrants, and with people from the host country.[11] Situations vary considerably, depending on the

---

[10] Cf., among others, the book edited by Alejandro Portes, *The Economic Sociology of Immigration: Essays on Networks, Ethnicity and Entrepreneurship* (New York: Russell Sage Foundation, 1995).

[11] Mention should be made here of the studies by Spanish researchers, among them those by J.-L. Molina, A. de Federico, and I. Maya Jariego, particularly those published in the journal REDES (http://revista-redes.rediris.es/). See also M. J. Lubbers, J. L. Molina, J. Lerner, U. Brandes, J. Avila, C. McCarty, "Longitudinal Analysis of Personal Networks: The Case of Argentinean Migrants in Spain," *Social Networks* 32 (2010), 91–104.

type of migration, the length of time since arrival in the country, the presence or absence of a community of migrants from the same country, etc. Compared with the situations described not so long ago by the Chicago sociologists who founded modern urban sociology, a significant change has taken place, linked to developments in long-distance transport and communications. Migrants today tend to remain much more closely in touch with their countries of origin, which they visit more regularly than did their counterparts in the first half of the last century or earlier periods. They also stay in touch through modern means of communication.

This twofold integration (which in some cases is even threefold, or well on the way to becoming truly cosmopolitan) is even more pronounced among temporary expatriates or students spending time abroad as part of their courses, such as the Erasmus students at Lille that Ainhoa de Federico studied[12] She analyses in detail the relationships these students maintained with each other and reveals the disconnection between the world of the Erasmus students and that of the local students, which she explains by significant differences in temporal availability and commitments. Cut off from the networks through which they were accustomed to conducting their day-to-day activities (eating, going out, playing sport, etc.), the Erasmus students differed from the local students, who were constrained by the various commitments arising out of their established networks, in having both time on their hands and a desire for interaction. We already saw in Chapter 7 the case of Nicolas, a former Erasmus student in the Caen panel, whose network still retained traces of the countries where he had resided.

Whether it is permanent or temporary, whether it takes place between wealthy countries or brings into play differences in wealth, migration both depends on networks and causes them to be extensively reconstituted. This reinforces the notion that personal networks are made up of both a core of lasting relationships that can withstand distance, particularly since its devastating effects are now mitigated by modern telecommunications and cheaper travel, and a more nebulous mass of less-strong local ties established in the course of day-to-day living. Thus, it is striking to note that the three young people in the Caen panel who had gone abroad all mentioned some of their oldest friends, even though they might no longer

---

[12] Cf., in particular, A. de Frederico, "Amitiés Européennes. Les réseaux transnationaux des étudiants Erasmus," *Informations Sociales* 147 (2008), 120–127. Erasmus is the name of a European Union student exchange program that funds students to study abroad within the EU.

meet up with them and new friends now occupied an important position in their networks. Nevertheless, Elodie, who had joined her parents in Boston and was living with them, and Nicolas, who was living with his partner in Spain, had retained fewer friendships than François, who was living alone in Norway and was perhaps a little more homesick. As has already been noted, expatriation or migration takes place today against the background of increasing opportunities for travel and the development of long-distance communications technologies. We will return in Chapter 12 to the issue of communication technologies.

ESTABLISHING A LOCAL NETWORK

The local element of personal networks remains significant, even for people who have moved around a lot. But how is it put together? And how quickly? In the Toulouse survey, from the third year of residence onward, the share of personal network members living more than an hour's car drive away became more or less the same as what it was for respondents who had lived in the city for a long time (Table 8.3).

The survey population in this case was representative of the region, with few international migrants. Might the results have been different with a population of highly mobile managers and executives? In order to verify this, we have at our disposal data from a survey conducted in 2007 as part of a European project[13] on 200 individuals in "creative" occupations, defined in this case to include both research and innovation as well as artistic and cultural activities. These respondents were asked to name three individuals who they themselves considered to be "creative." Of the total number of individuals named, 52 percent lived in the Greater Toulouse conurbation, 19 percent in the region outside the conurbation, and 29 percent outside the region (many of them in Paris or abroad). Comparison of this distribution with the length of time respondents had been living in the city shows that the results are fairly similar. For those who had been living there for two or more years, local ties had become predominant. It would seem, therefore, that for people who had "settled" in the city, at least temporarily, a stay on the order of two years was sufficient to acquire much the same share of local relationships as people who had been living there for much longer. Similarly, the young people in the Caen panel who had just moved reported more new ties than those who had not relocated.

---

[13] www.acre.socsci.uva.nl/.

Table 8.3 *Length of time living in city and geographic location of network members (Toulouse survey) (%)*

Distance between respondent's home and that of the person named			Total
Length of time living in city	Five minutes or less	From six to sixty minutes	More than one hour	

	Five minutes or less	From six to sixty minutes	More than one hour	Total
Two years or less	26.0[a]	49.4	24.6	100
From three to five years	31.7	57.7	10.6	100
More than five years	33.1	51.4	15.4	100
Total	31.2	52.0	16.8	100

[a] For example, 26 percent of the individuals named by a respondent who had arrived in the city less than two years previously lived less than five minutes from his/her residence.

Above all, however, examination of the overall structure of their networks shows that it changed little, even though a significant proportion of the ties had changed. For the most part, the network configuration of the young people who had moved a long way (outside of the *département*) did not change from one wave to the next, remaining just as dense, centered, or dissociated as it had been before they relocated. Those that did change usually saw a reduction in density, but the structure changed much less than after a marital or familial event. It can be assumed, therefore, that these young people built up new networks based on the same "model" and the same mode of sociability as in the region they had come from. After relocating, they would appear to have pursued fairly similar activities to those they had pursued previously, and as long as the move had not been accompanied by other events (moving in with a partner, entry into the labor market), it can be supposed that they became integrated into structurally fairly similar circles. This had the effect of renewing their networks but did not lead to any significant change in structure. This finding is consistent with the conclusions reached by Morgan, Neal, and Carder[14] who, in a longitudinal survey of recently widowed women, found that time had an effect on network renewal but not on structure[15] and concluded that this overall configuration was characterized by greater stability. The individuals who "had an effect on their lives" had changed but their

---

[14] D. L. Morgan, M. B. Neal, P. Carder, "The Stability of Core and Peripheral Networks over Time," *Social Networks* 19 (1996), 9–25.

[15] The first wave of the survey having been carried out after the husband's death, the effect of his death on network centralization is not observed.

network profile remained the same. It is important, therefore, to make a distinction between network composition and network structure.

In the case of the Toulouse survey, data are available on respondents' geographical origin. The most settled among them (those born in the region) had almost as many ties outside the region as the others. The managers and executives in this group traveled frequently, made intensive use of the various means of communication, and were therefore able to establish and maintain ties over long distances, even when they did not relocate permanently. This means that being settled is not incompatible with establishing and maintaining connections with external networks. Just as mobility does not produce networks that are particularly dispersed spatially, being settled does not mean that networks are solely local.

*

*   *

One initial observation that leaps out from this analysis is the strongly local (at the level of the city) nature of social relations. The overwhelming majority of respondents' relationships were located within a radius of one hour's car drive from their homes. Only strong ties seem to elude the influence of geographical space. The explanation for this high proportion of local ties is to be found in the process of establishing relationships in the contexts of daily life, which form the basis for renewing relational environments. We saw above that, throughout the life course, new ties are forged while others disappear, even though there is a core of relatively stable strong ties that endure despite the disappearance of these shared contexts. Our respondents' distant ties were usually strong ties, which seem to withstand the effects of distance better. As the "strength of the tie" metaphor suggests, strong ties are more difficult to unravel. However, in measuring the "strength" of a tie, the criteria of emotional intensity have to be separated out from those of frequency of exchange, which obviously require greater spatial proximity unless exchanges mediated through Information and Communication Technologies (ICT) are taken into account. This notwithstanding, these long-distance exchanges ultimately prove to be not as different from face-to-face exchanges as might have been imagined, as will be examined in greater detail in Chapter 12.

Thus, individual's environments can be divided into three groups of relationships: strong ties, which are dispersed to varying degrees depending on individuals' mobility patterns; weak social ties, characterized by reciprocal services, which are essentially local; and finally "dormant" weak ties, which may be reactivated in certain situations and are likely to be less local. To settle in a town or city is to reconstitute one's relational environment, and, in particular, that group of weak- or medium-strength ties that form the bulk of the lists obtained in response to the name generators, such as those that relate to excursions, leisure activities, or discussions at work. And to live in a place is to take part in different activities and local groups (work, leisure activities, voluntary associations, etc.) that generate relationships and are not dispersed to any great extent in space. It is because routine activities cannot be too dispersed that personal networks are so strongly local. Even after a move to a distant place, they are often reconstructed on the basis of the same model, with the same overall structure as before. Moreover, the spatial structure of networks could be used as a criterion to define what constitutes a town or a local space, one that would perhaps be as relevant as any other. The boundary of a local space would then be drawn at the point where active weak ties become more scarce. The core of strong ties remains more stable and even though renewal takes place rapidly, networks are often reconstituted with the same overall profile, regardless of trajectories and geographical mobility. This "persistence" of certain ties and of the overall configuration of relational environments, even when individuals are uprooted, shows that personal networks have real "consistency" and do not simply reflect or echo what happens to individuals. While it is true that networks react to life events and are sensitive to social divisions and environments, they also have their own dynamics and analysis of them reveals some novel realities. In the following chapters, we investigate in rather greater detail this epistemological "tension" between the autonomy of this object and its rootedness in the major social divisions.

9

Soft Segregation

How do we choose the people with whom we spend time? The familiar proverb has it that "birds of a feather flock together." But what happens in reality? In what respects, firstly, do "birds of a feather" resemble each other? After all, two individuals may resemble each other in age, but not in gender, occupation, or leisure activities. We must then take into account those effects of social structure that encourage certain similarities and dissimilarities. For example, people working in the same occupation are very likely to have the same level of education and qualification. Families, on the other hand, will "by definition" include people of different ages (grandparents, parents, children, etc.) and both sexes, and levels of education and qualification may well vary more. These more or less pronounced similarities, these affinities of all sorts, are also indicators of the structure of society as a whole, which may be relatively homogeneous or, on the contrary, tend to splinter into different social worlds, whether they be based on differences in social category, community of origin, or any other principle of similarity. If cross-mating is rare, this indicates that a wide gap separates the two membership groups in question. For example, the "princes" group can be seen to be strictly separated from the "shepherdesses" group by measuring the scarcity of marriage between them; this statistical rarity is surely the origin of the numerous fairy tales depicting just such unions! The detailed mechanics of how social relations are constructed, which we are trying to understand in this book, are an important element in the social structuring process.

The question of spousal choice, and the observation that spouses tend to come from similar backgrounds, has in fact been extensively investigated through the theme of "homogamy." By analogy with homogamy (marriage between individuals who are, in some culturally important way, similar to each other), the term "homophily" (bonding with the same) was coined in order to reflect the notion that people have all the more opportunities to meet up with each other the more points they have in common. Thus, all social relations may be characterized by various forms of similarity or dissimilarity ("homophily" and "heterophily" in the language of network analysts). A person's friends and acquaintances are seldom distributed across the whole of the social space. This gives rise to a form of segmentation that is all the stronger the "softer" it is, that is, originating not in community politics or confrontations but in the everyday interplay of encounters and affinities.

These questions have been the object of a very large number of studies on which we will draw in this chapter in order to supplement our own analyses. We shall examine similarities in friendships and relational environments more broadly.

SOCIAL SIMILARITIES AND RELATIONSHIPS

Endogamy, which is the tendency to marry within the same social milieu, is a key topic for the social sciences.[1] This tendency arises out of society's organizing principles, the structure of the contexts in which people meet, and the process whereby social ties are constructed. The question of homogamy is only one aspect of a broader question concerning social relations as a whole.

Indeed, homophily is an interesting indicator of a more macrosocial characteristic, namely social segregation. To what extent are social milieus coherent and inward looking or, on the contrary, not very homogeneous and shot through with relational chains linking them to each other? Is the overall social network of a given population made up of separate clusters that interact with each other only through the intermediary of legal or material arrangements or does it comprise fluid, heterogeneous networks, such that the notions of milieu, social category, or community no longer have any meaning? Clearly, in investigating homophily, we are broaching one of the central questions in the social sciences, namely, analysis of the social bond and the cohesion of the social world, as well as its segmentation and its evolution. Thus, when Fischer, working in the San Francisco region, observed that homophily was stronger in urban than in rural milieus, this may be interpreted as an indication that urban society is more segregated than rural society (young people have less contact with older

---

[1] M. H. D. van Leeuwen, I. Maas, "Endogamy and Social Class in History: An Overview," *International Review for Social History* 50 (2005), 1–23.

people, graduates are less likely to spend time with those with little education, and so on).

What causes people to spend time with each other? In a literature review,[2] Miller McPherson, Lynn Smith-Lovin, and James Cook conclude that the homophily principle structures ties of all kinds, including marriage, friendship, work, advice, support, information transfer, exchange, shared participation, and all other types of relationships. Personal networks tend to be homogeneous with regard to many sociodemographic and behavioral characteristics. Homophily limits and segments social worlds. Racial or ethnic homophily is the form that creates the strongest divisions.

The literature is remarkably consistent, regardless of the relationships and the aspects of similarity in question. Personal networks are character-ized by homogeneity because the relational principles at work in their construction encourage a certain degree of similarity.[3] The most frequently mentioned causes include location, which is perhaps the main cause (we tend to choose those to whom we are close in spatial terms, which may in turn favor other forms of homogeneity as a result of residential segmenta-tion); the effects of education, work, and organizations; equivalence of position; cognitive processes, and the selective breaking-up of ties. Pairs of individuals who resemble each other in numerous ways (apart from gender) are much more likely to know each other than those who differ from each other. Another specialist in networks, Noah Mark[4] contrasts two models: homophily and distancing. The homophily principle is, as we have already seen, the one given expression in the proverb "birds of a feather flock together." Individuals who resemble each other in terms of age, education, ethnic origin, occupation, social status, or other variables are more likely to be friends, associates, or spouses than individuals who differ from each other. In the distancing model, on the other hand, it is supposed that people make cultural choices in order to set themselves apart from others.[5] It is not too difficult to construct an explanation by combining the

---

[2] J. Miller McPherson, L. Smith-Lovin, J. M. Cook, "Birds of a Feather: Homophily in Social Networks," *Annual Review of Sociology* 27 (2001), 415–444.

[3] A team of Dutch researchers has shown the importance of contexts in building homophilic relationships: G. Mollenhorst, B. Völker, H. Flap, "Social Contexts and Personal Relation-ships: The Effect of Meeting Opportunities on Similarity for Relationships of Different Strength," *Social Networks* 30, (2008), 60–68.

[4] N. Mark, "Culture and Competition: Homophily and Distancing Explanation for Cultural niches," *American Sociological Review* 68(3) (2003), 319–345.

[5] Which is reminiscent of the processes described by Bourdieu in *La distinction* (Paris: Editions de Minuit, 1979).

two models, the main issue at stake in such differentiation practices being social position in different contexts. Thus, individuals have to distinguish themselves quite clearly from those with whom they do not wish to be confused and more subtly from those whom they wish to retain in their relational environment, that is, those who are the same as themselves or who have a more favorable social position.

If we adopt a dynamic perspective, two processes that may contribute to homophily can be identified. One is selection, by which we separate out those people who are like us from the others, who are less likely to be chosen or are more easily abandoned. The other is influence, which modifies our behavior by making us adopt that of our partners. The selection principle has been more extensively investigated in sociology than that of influence, if only because the study of selection brings into play some of the standard sociological indicators, such as social origin, occupational category, and gender, that change little over the life course. However, some recent studies carried out by the Dutch mathematician and sociologist Tom Snijders and his team have sought to model the impact of these two dynamics on the evolution of networks,[6] with reference to characteristics that are more susceptible to modification (being a smoker or a non-smoker). The combination of these two dynamics is confirmed in the Caen survey, as is demonstrated by the example of Patrick, who both identified those individuals who shared the "values" associated with rap and initiated the few acquaintances of his who were not already persuaded into them; the end result was a network that, from the point of view of this cultural preference, was very homogeneous:

It's not necessarily because they listen to rap that we get on well, it's mainly because there are shared values and perhaps it's those shared values that bring people together around rap. Because they discover things that they experience in their lives, situations, qualities that they appreciate and which are found in rap. I think that's more how it happens: "Ah, he listens to rap so I'm going to see if I can somehow become friends with him." And we get on well. I even know some people who didn't listen to rap, but I got to know them and then they started listening to rap and began to appreciate it, they found certain things in it.

The analysis in the rest of this chapter will focus on selection, with influence being examined in Chapter 10.

---

[6] L. Mercken, T. Snijders, C. Steglich, E. Vartiainen, H. de Vries, "Dynamics of Adolescent Friendship Networks and Smoking Behavior," *Social Networks* 32 (2010), 72–81.

Similarity in Age

In the Toulouse survey, the average age difference between respondents and the people they named was 11 years, but the median gap was 7 years (in 50 percent of cases, the gap was less than 7 years) and in 43 percent of cases it was 5 years or less. Age homophily is one of the sources for the notion of generation: many of our relationships are concentrated within a range of $\pm$ 10 years. The propensity to choose friends of a similar age is not universal, however. Women have a lesser propensity to age homophily than men, since they are more likely to sustain intergenerational ties within the family. More generally, personal networks tend to become more diversified in terms of age as people get older and relatives account for an increasing share of the Alters in their networks. Since family members are necessarily more heterogeneous in both age and sex than more freely chosen relationships, they cause the proportion of relationships with people of different ages, in particular, to rise. Age homophily with people regarded as friends increases with educational level, which is not the case for the other types of relationship.

It is young people who are most assiduous in maintaining relationships with people of the same age as themselves. Before the age of 24, for example, 70 percent of best friends are also under 24. This share goes into decline thereafter; between the ages of 40 and 50, 47 percent of best friends are in the same age group. The proportion starts to climb a little again after the age of 60. This predominance is explained in part by the fact that young people are usually embedded in contexts in which they necessarily associate with each other: school, university, national military service (formerly, nowadays non-military national service), entry cohorts into certain professions, etc. all construct forms of age segregation that do not change with advancing age.

In the Caen panel, the share of same-age relationships (71.1 percent) was also very high, which confirms young people's propensity to spend their time with others of the same age. Strong ties were built up with young people of the same age to an even greater extent than weak ties (75.7 percent of strong ties excluding family and romantic relationships were between young people with less than 5 years' age difference between them, compared with 64.8 percent of weak ties). The longitudinal data enable us to trace the evolution of this homophily over the course of the transition to adult life. The data clearly show that the percentage of same-age relationships (age difference 5 years or less) declined as the young people grew up, left high school and university and found themselves in more heterogeneous environments in terms of age (Table 9.1).

Table 9.1 *Age difference by Ego's age for all ties excluding family (family ties being more often of different ages) and romantic relationships (more often of the same age) in the Caen panel, all waves combined (%)*

	Ego's age			Average
Age difference	17–20	21–25	26–33	
>5 years	24.1[a]	29.8	31.4	28.9
<5 years	75.9	70.2	68.6	71.1
Total	100	100	100	
Total number	1,663	2,880	2,246	6,789

[a] For example, for a respondent aged between 17 and 20, 24.1 percent of non-family ties have an age gap of more than 5 years with Ego.

As they entered adulthood and the "high school effect" weakened for them, they became more likely to spend time with people of a different age. The highest share of same-age relationships was found among relationships established when the young people were aged between 16 and 19 (81 percent). Once again, the high-school context reveals its highly specific nature and turns out to be very different from the one that awaited the young people as soon as they had finished their education, namely, that of the workplace. Emeline was clearly very aware of the difference:

What was important was the changeover from student life to that of an employee. I no longer spend my days on a university bench with people just like me. I've absolutely left the easy pace of student life behind, I'm now a wage-slave, work, work, work, same old routine day in day out. Before that, I used to laze around a bit on a bench in the lecture theater. So obviously, the mere fact of spending your days with people in a lecture theater, you're all doing the same thing, so it wasn't difficult to find things to talk about.

Apart from the change of pace, many other acts of structuration await these young people in the workplace: no more hanging out just with people of their own age, since their new work colleagues are much more varied in age. This is exactly what leads young people to embark on a selection process in this respect. In particular, this "periodization" of homophily means that the relationships with people of a similar age are also the most long-standing ones. The ties established at a young age, when peers dominate personal networks, are the most homogeneous in age. Thus, those friendships that are maintained subsequently constitute an homophilous "core," made up of individuals who often achieve best friend status, within a network that overall has become more mixed in terms of age.[7] Again, according to Claude Fischer, the age gap between partners depends more on the age of the relationship (and hence on the time and circumstances of the first meeting) than on any other factors. Childhood and school friends, who are in any case the oldest ones, are obviously more likely to be of the same age than friends from work or the neighborhood whom one got to know later.

Marital status and position in the life cycle are also subject to a tendency toward homophily. Married people tend to spend time with other marrieds, while single or divorced people prefer to meet up with other singles or divorced individuals, parents prefer other parents, and so on. This was the case for Gaël who got close to Olivier:

> Frankly, there's something else, which is that Olivier had been a father for eight months now and we have that in common. Whereas Romain is going through a bit of a period of rebuilding, both professionally and romantically, and in those cases I'm the first to steer a bit clear of some people, if you see what I mean.

Similarly, the age of one's children is a very strong factor in the homogeneity of personal networks. People choose friends who have children of the same age as theirs to a much greater degree than they would if the distribution was purely random. Conversely, not being "in phase" in this respect can push friends apart, demonstrating the power of this not always so soft "segregation." Joël, a seasonal worker in the restaurant business, had remained single. In each wave of the survey, he noted the disappearance of a good number of his friends; in the majority of cases, he attributed the loss to the fact that their lives as couples and his bachelor existence were out of step with each other:

> At the age I am now, there are some who are moving in with their partners and more and more who are having children, all that . . .. So they have their family lives, their family commitments. So no more free time, no more hanging out like we used to, no more going places with the friends we had in common, all because of these changes. I haven't changed very much myself but because they're living with their partners and all that, their situations have changed, so inevitably their characters, their ambitions, everything's changed, their centers of interest and all that, inevitably. The partying side has been put aside, if you see what I mean. I haven't changed much because my situation hasn't changed much, I'm still doing the seasonal work. So inevitably I'm not really very settled anywhere. Time is

---

[7] L. M. Verbrugge, "The Structure of Adult Friendship Choices," *Social Forces* 56 (1977), 576–597.

passing. And for some people, things are taking their normal course! Well, my life is taking a less "normal" course, well a different one anyway, that's for sure.

It can happen that, having moved apart for a time, friends come back together again when the second finally crosses the threshold as well, as Serge hoped would happen with Elodie:

Now I'm living with my girlfriend, perhaps that will happen. Let's say it wasn't easy, when I was single, to worm my way into their life as a couple. That's not really my thing. Whereas now, if I see her again and it works out with Carine, if they hit it off together, it's possible we could start doing things together.

Gaël took up with his friend Jérôme again in the same way:

We stopped seeing each other because it was the same thing, we no longer had too much in common. But now, we do see each other again, because he's got a job, I find that better, he's had a girlfriend for quite a bit now. It's not that I'm making any value judgments, not at all, but I get on with him better, we've got more things to do together.

Thus, similarities in age and position in the life cycle are both very subtle and very powerful.

Similarity of Socio-Occupational Category

Homophily of social level has been much investigated.[8] It is also pronounced, but less so than homophily of age. Thus, 55 percent of friendships and 50 percent of intimate relationships are established with people of the same social status, which reveals a tendency toward homophily, since a random distribution would have produced much lower figures, namely, 35 percent and 30 percent respectively.[9]

Homophily is particularly characteristic of the categories at the extremes of the social scale, namely, manual workers and members of the higher social classes. The intermediate categories are considerably more eclectic. It should be noted that they undoubtedly constitute a "bridge" between the other categories and that their social mobility helps to reinforce this

---

[8] Cf. P. Blau, J. E. Schwartz, *Crosscutting Social Circles: Testing a Macrostructural Theory of Intergroup Relations* (Orlando: Academic Press, 1984).

[9] For more details of this type of calculation, see A. Ferrand, L. Mounier, A. Degenne, "The Diversity of Personal Networks in France: Social Stratification and Relational Structures," in B. Wellman (ed.) *Networks in the Global Village: Life in Contemporary Communities* (Boulder: Westview Press, 1999), pp. 185–224.

position effect.[10] We may also be dealing with an edge effect. The categories at either end of the social scale have only a limited range of choices at their disposal: those at the bottom can only choose friends of a higher status, while those at the top can only choose friends of a lower status. Because of this restriction, they tend to increase the relative share of friends of the same status of themselves. Thus, the "Interpersonal Contacts" (*"Contacts entre les personnes"*) survey reveals that half of the best friends of members of the liberal professions and senior managers are in similar professions; slightly more than half of the friends of manual workers are also manual workers. The best friends of white-collar workers, on the other hand, are more evenly distributed: 30 percent are manual workers, 23 percent white-collar workers, and 21 percent members of the intermediate professions.

Account also needs to be taken of the relative openness/closedness of the milieus in which people move, that is, of the degree of social diversity to which they are exposed in their daily lives. Work environments act as filters: in the course of the socialization process, people learn to sort out the partners who are acceptable from those who are not. Even before that, when young people at school are in principle all "equal," processes of homophily can be observed at work from lower secondary school onward, particularly with regard to educational streams. In the workplace, divisions become much more pronounced: workers are distributed on the basis of their work tasks, it is true, but also by skill level, sphere of activity, position in the hierarchy, wage level, etc. Some have the power to give orders and organize work.

In the Toulouse survey, the degree of similarity in relationships was measured by two indicators: level of education and occupation. Unsurprisingly, relationships tended to be homophilous (Tables 9.2 and 9.3).

Thus, the results are consistent with those of other surveys: the most highly qualified are associated with the most highly qualified and managers are more associated with managers; the tendency was particularly strong at the extremes, while the median categories (intermediate occupations, two years' post-secondary education) did not differentiate their associations to any great extent and could have been chosen by all the other categories. The degree of occupational homophily is greater in the cities and higher in Paris than in the provinces, which is consistent with Fischer's results and

---

[10] See, among others, E. O. Laumann, *Bonds of Pluralism: The Form and Substance of Urban Social Networks* (New York: John Wiley & Sons, 1973); R. S. Burt, "A Note on Strangers, Friends and Happiness," *Social Networks* 9 (1987), 311–331.

Table 9.2 *Educational homophily: Level of education of respondents and of the persons named (Toulouse survey)*

		Person chosen			
Respondent	< Upper secondary	Upper secondary	Two years' post-secondary	Four years' post-secondary	Total
< Upper secondary	56[a] / *49*	22 / *31*	14 / *17*	8 / *10*	100 / *29*
Upper secondary	30 / *16*	25 / *21*	26 / *19*	18 / *14*	100 / *17*
Two years' post-secondary	25 / *22*	23 / *33*	32 / *38*	20 / *26*	100 / *29*
Four years' post-secondary	16 / *13*	13 / *16*	25 / *26*	46 / *50*	100 / *25*
Total	33 / *100*	20 / *100*	24 / *100*	23 / *100*	100 / *100*

[a] In each cell, the top number is a percentage in rows; the bottom number in italics is percentage in columns. The more darkly a square is shaded, the more the frequency of this type of choice exceeds what would be expected if the choice was random.

Table 9.3 *Homophily of occupation: Occupations of respondents and the persons named (Toulouse survey)*

	Person chosen					
Respondent	Company dir., shop keeper, self-employed	Professionals and salaried managers	Intermediate occupations	White collar, manual	Inactive	Total
Company dir., shop keeper, self-employed	41[a] *25*	15 *5*	14 *6*	13 *4*	16 *4*	100 *7*
Professionals and salaried managers	11 *23*	42 *50*	18 *27*	13 *16*	16 *16*	100 *26*
Intermediate occupations	11 *18*	17 *16*	26 *30*	22 *20*	23 *17*	100 *20*
White collar, manual	13 *17*	10 *8*	14 *14*	42 *34*	22 *14*	100 *17*
Inactive	7 *17*	16 *21*	14 *23*	18 *25*	45 *49*	100 *29*
Total	12 *100*	22 *100*	17 *100*	21 *100*	27 *100*	100 *100*

[a] In each cell, top number is percentage in rows, bottom number in italics, is percentage in columns. The more darkly a square is shaded, the more the frequency of this type of choice exceeds what would be expected if the choice was random.

suggests there is a higher level of social fragmentation in the cities. Thus, all the surveys point to the existence of homophily of social status.

In the Caen survey, it was still too early to measure the young people's occupational differentiating behavior statistically. However, they were already very much aware of this trend toward dispersion in the social space following their departure from education. Gaël assessed the situation in wave 4:

Ten years ago, all my friends were in pretty much the same situation as me. We were all very similar. School, partying, not going to class, that was it, we really lived in a closed circle. We claimed to be tolerant, but in fact if you look a bit more closely it's obvious there was nobody from a completely different world in our group. And now I realize that the fact of working, of having been to university, of becoming a bit more open, well now I realize that really, among the people I've mentioned who are important to me, there really are some who come from completely different worlds.

Thus, the longer relationships have lasted, the more likely it is that occupational categories will be more diversified. After all, those relationships forged at a young age, the longest-standing ones, are the most heterogeneous from a socio-occupational perspective. The individuals concerned got to know each other during a period of relative "indetermination" and in some cases divergent trajectories thereafter have not been enough to separate them, particularly in the case of the most intense friendships. In other cases, however, the route taken after high school begins to create gulfs between friends, as Alban acknowledged:

It's strange, but we often associate with people with the same level of education. Michaël opted for a vocational training course. Maybe, in terms of relationships, we no longer had so much in common. So I stopped seeing him, he'd moved into a different world. It's not that I don't like him, but when you're talking with someone, if you're not hitting it off so well any more, you stop seeing each other.

The hierarchization of educational paths and qualifications creates divisions, as do those disciplines that often impart values, as in the case of Alice, who was studying law:

I chose my discipline, some people made the same choice as me, so that's something we have in common. There are certain affinities that are linked to an inclination towards law as well as to a certain idea of justice, of the things that are going on, of what is legal or illegal. So we meet to talk about these things because it's what interests us.

This choice of specialist discipline can lead to the emergence of new "worlds," as Emeline noted:

Anne was my best friend in high school, but things turned sour. Once we'd finished high school, she went to train as a social worker and I enrolled in the preparatory classes for entry to the HEC, she very quickly pigeonholed me: future capitalist, mercantilist, goodness knows what. After high school, neither she nor I said to ourselves that that was going to call things into question. It didn't even cross our minds. And when I saw the people in her year that was when I realized it was really a million miles away from what I might be myself or what the others might be. So she was really creating a gulf between the people she was associating with in Alençon and the people in Caen. And then, at one point or another, she had to take the plunge, come down on one side or the other. So it was logical for her to opt for the world of social workers that was her job. I felt that she was taking her future role as a social worker very seriously, she'd really taken a sharp turn to the left. And she'd pigeonholed me, as someone who understood nothing about social problems. That was something that was now central to her life, but that she absolutely could not talk to me about. So that was the end of that and the start of a new chapter.

And in a mirror image of this, Fleur felt it necessary for her friends to acknowledge her commitment to social work:

We're different now . . .. Talking with them now, I realize that Ludovic and Nicolas do not get why I want to be a youth worker, "There's no point," they're completely fixated on their interests, I can't talk to them about the things that are close to my heart . . .. And that bothers me, I like to talk about the things I stand up for, the things I see . . .

After university, workplace environments also play a part in the process of social differentiation, and young people are very sensitive to it. They learn to separate out their colleagues, who are more diverse than their school friends, using various criteria, as Violette did:

The people I've named are the one with whom there's the smallest age gap, Katy and Emma, for example. Julie, she's from the Calvados district as well, from Ouistreham, so that brought us together right from the start. That was one thing we had in common. And then now, there's work, there's the way we see lots of things, that brings us together, we're pretty much alike the two of us.

Above and beyond work, a "class" sentiment often emerges, which testifies much more broadly to the power of this process of social structuration, which produces a hierarchy of positions and plays a part in establishing social classifications. For this reason, the "soft segregation" based on the selection of peers and friends and the construction and continual reconfiguration of relational environments is certainly the manifestation of a deep-rooted process of social hierarchization that also manifests itself in people's private lives. This hierarchization manifested itself in various ways among the young people in the Caen panel, from cultural choices to forms of language, via leisure activities, choice of car, etc. Thus, Emeline interpreted the behavior of her former friend Eric, who was perhaps simply trying to please her, as a difference in social level:

I didn't want to meet up with Eric again because he'd become a detestable banker, I soon got tired of that. On one occasion, he'd come to Paris and he was showing off a bit, putting on airs and graces. One day we were going out together, he wanted to eat at the fancy Paris restaurants and drink in the coolest bars. That really pissed me off. So I broke off all contact with him.

Jérémie did not go any easier on his old friends:

There's some people I got to know, they're nouveau riche, upstarts, I can't stand them. Now they're living on a private estate, with a golf course and all that, they hang out with lawyers, people like that, I can't take any more of it, I don't like people who think they're God's gift.

Diane, who was from a more working-class background, saw her friend Emilie become "a lady," which was undoubtedly more painful for her than in the previous two cases:

Emilie was with her boyfriend, and now she's become a real lady. She doesn't acknowledge anybody any more, she has an apartment, she just does her shopping . . .. She also likes to act all la-di-da, she really thinks she's superior to everybody else.

However, many of the young people were also critical of people they regarded as "lower" than themselves, frequently accusing them of varying degrees of delinquent behavior, poor parenting, excessive alcohol consumption, etc. Thus, Jérémie mentioned two former friends who had "taken wrong turnings":

I saw Bruno when he got out of prison. There was a real coolness between us. I've never been back to his place to see him. He doesn't really want to get himself out of that situation, he just does what he wants. He wants to stay on the estate. Well, let him stay there. He knows the risks, they give him a buzz. I think that's the problem. Marco lived next door to my mother. He's really gone downhill, but badly, badly, badly. He separated from his wife. Now, quote – unquote, he's a "down and out." He's really down on his luck, completely changed. If you meet him, he looks down at the ground because he doesn't want to see us, he's ashamed.

Thus, the entry into adulthood very quickly crystallizes the social positions that maybe seemed less marked in high school. Such distancing acts also occur later in life, but undoubtedly at a slower pace.

Gender Similarity

The Toulouse survey shows the usual results for this type of homophily: men associate more with other men (62 percent, whereas the two sexes are more or less equally represented both in the survey population and among the people named) and women more with other women (61.2 percent, regardless of age and social level). A clear increase in homophily can also be observed in the United States when kin relationships are excluded.[11] And in the Caen survey as well, there was a clear though somewhat weaker tendency to associate with people of the same sex: 55 percent of the individuals named by the young people were of the same sex as themselves, 57 percent, if family and Ego's partner are excluded. Thus, young people would seem to be less homophilous in terms of gender than older people. The boys were more likely to associate with other boys: 62.2 percent of the individuals they named were boys, compared with 52.6 percent of those named by the girls who were girls (again excluding family and Ego's partner). Thus, girls were more likely to have mixed relational worlds.

Work is the decisive factor in this difference between men and women in terms of homophily: in the "Contacts" survey, the gap is no longer observed among those not in the labor market. Since men account for the larger share of the economically active population, work increases the likelihood of their finding themselves among other men, while it increases women's chances of coming into contact with men. This cannot be reduced to strictly work-based contacts, which were not taken into account in this survey. Thus, we are certainly dealing here with conversations of a personal nature, or even friendships that started in the workplace. However, this work effect has to be qualified to some extent by taking account of socio-occupational category and work environment, which vary in terms of the structural conditions they offer for mixing of the sexes. Working-class environments are, after all, hardly ever mixed, whereas offices are more likely to have men and women employed in the same jobs. In mixed or predominantly female environments, as in the teaching professions, for example, homophily persists, albeit to a lesser degree. This stability would appear to indicate that social structural explanations cannot account fully for the phenomenon, even though such factors are far from negligible. Thus, the persistence of homophily in relations with neighbors or in

---

[11] See P. Marsden, "Homogeneity in Confiding Relations," *Social Networks* 10 (1988), 57–76 and G. Moore, "Structural Determinants of Men's and Women's Personal Networks," *American Sociological Review* 55(5) (1990), 726–735.

contacts with vague acquaintances or tradespeople, which are spheres in which, on the face of it, there is no structural reason for a gender imbalance, confirms it is cultural and not simply structural in nature. Moreover, in the first wave of the Caen survey, when the young people were all still at high school or looking for their first jobs and thus in environments that tended to be mixed and egalitarian, the gender homophily was quite clear (57.9 percent of the individuals they named, excluding family and Ego's partner, were of the same sex as themselves).

It is also the case that the more intense a relationship becomes, the higher the level of gender homophily is. Thus, in the Caen panel, 64 percent of strong ties (excluding family and Ego's partner, a total of 6,789 relationships) were with people of the same gender, compared with 51.2 percent of weak ties. The share of relationships with people of the same sex also rises very steadily with the age of the relationship, rising from 53.4 percent in the case of ties established for less than a year to 67.8 percent for those that have lasted more than 10 years (thus, for these young people, relationships that began in childhood), again excluding family ties, of course. Similarly, in a survey of confiding relationships, it was found that 74 percent of such relationships are between people of the same sex.[12] In the same survey, friendships were also found to be characterized by high levels of homophily: 83 percent of women's best friends were women and 72% of men's best friends were men. In the case of these very intimate friendships, women are more homophilous than men, which is the opposite of what is observed for casual acquaintances or conversations. They tend to confide more in other women; men also confide more in other men but speak more to women than women speak to men. Overall, therefore, the strongest and longest-standing relations are more homophilous in terms of gender.

Thus, relationship choices tend to be of a piece with the major divisions of the social structure by age, gender, and social level. While individuals' integration in particular contexts and activities helps to explain this tendency, it cannot be reduced to mere structural determinism. There is also a "cultural" propensity to prefer people who resemble oneself in age, gender, and social status. It is not of course sufficient to be "birds of a feather" in order to "flock together," nor is it sufficient to resemble one another on those criteria alone. More personal qualities and characteristics play a role, of course. Thus, in the Caen survey, a wide range of arguments were put

---

[12] See A. Ferrand, L. Mounier, "Talking about Sexuality: An Analysis of Relations between Confidants," in M. Bozon and H. Leridon (eds.) *Sexuality and the Social Sciences* (Dartmouth: Aldershot, 1996), pp. 265–288.

forward as evidence of changes in relationships and the various forms of social segregation that often lay at the heart of such changes, either in speaking of relationships that had become less close or in explaining what kept them together. For example, Thibaut regretted that Maryline's current boyfriend was "a Parisian, a big show-off," which for him explained why she had changed and he no longer spent time with her. And Patrick spoke at length about the values associated with rap, which brought him close to his friends, while others spoke of their experiences, their values, their leisure activities, their emotional lives, their cultural tastes, and so on. Nevertheless, even though they cannot be reduced to them alone, relational preferences do reflect to some extent the major social divisions, which is an indication of their sensitivity to general tendencies within society.

VARIATIONS IN SIMILARITY AND NETWORK COMPOSITION

As we noted in the Introduction, relationships are not all homophilous in the same way. In the Toulouse survey, which focused on social support and exchanges, certain name generators were associated with socially very homogeneous relations (work discussions, personal problems), while others tended to be organized more by age group and gender (outings and leisure activities). Yet others were unaffected by differences in age, sex, or social position (care of the home, domestic tasks, advice on decisions, loans). The context in which relationships are first forged is also decisive. Table 9.4 summarizes the correlations obtained with different types of relationships. It will be noted that certain relations are scarcely homophilous at all (family relationships, casual acquaintances) while others are significantly more so (colleagues, friends).

As was noted in Chapter 1, family relations tend to be complementary, whereas those originating in the workplace or involvement in voluntary associations or friendships tend to be between people who resemble each other. On the other hand, neighborhood relationships and casual acquaintances are more or less non-specific in that regard. As we saw in Table 9.4, the intensity of the relationships also plays a part in determining the degree of homophily.

Thus, a person's network will be made up of individuals who resemble him or her in certain respects, some who are similar in other respects, others who are more complementary than similar, and yet others who have "points in common" not captured by our sociological indicators and which relate more to a shared history, musical tastes, life style, personality, etc. Two people cannot be alike in every regard, nor can personal networks be

Table 9.4 *Similarity and types of relations*[a]

Indicators of homophily Designation of relations	Same occupational category (aggregated data)	Same level of education	Same age (aggregated data)	Same sex
Family	–[b]	=	–	–
Colleagues	+	+	+	+
Neighbors	=	=	=	=
Associations	+	=	+	=
Friends	+	=	+	+
Acquaintances	=	–	=	=
Close ties	=	=	=	–
Others	=	=	=	=

[a] (+): significantly more; (–): significantly less; (=): not significant
[b] For example, family members are significantly less frequently in the same occupational category as Ego than the other individuals named.

totally homogeneous, which would indeed be difficult to bear. The system formed by these similarities and dissimilarities can be examined at the level of the network as a whole. It then becomes clear that, in addition to the dynamics of selection and influence, there are others that are likely to interfere with this tendency toward homophily. Other mechanisms come into play alongside homophily, causing network composition to vary; they include structural dynamics as well as effects of context and proximity, the constraints of which sometimes restrict the opportunities for making choices.[13] Some of these dynamics restrict homophily, in particular, by causing networks to become more diverse. However, the tendency to prefer people similar to oneself also has an intrinsic limit. Thus, Rachel Brooks points to the fact that young people tend "to manage the difference" when their friends diverge rather than excluding them as a matter of course from their networks.[14] In the Caen survey, in which the overall configurations of their networks were also discussed with the young respondents, it was clear that, far from bothering them or being seen as incoherence, the heterogeneous composition of their networks was in fact very much appreciated.

[13] See M. T. Rivera, S. Soderstrom, B. Uzzi, "Dynamics of Dyads in Social Networks: Assortative, Relational, and Proximity Mechanisms," *Annual Review of Sociology* 36 (2010), 91–115.

[14] See Rachel Brooks, "Transitional Friends? Young People's Strategies to Manage and Maintain Their Friendships during a Period of Repositioning," *Journal of Youth Studies* 5(4) (2002), 449–467.

Thus, Agnès testified to the diversity of the motivations behind her friendships:

With Pierre, perhaps we get on well precisely because we complement each other rather than because we've got lots of things in common. With Damien, I think we see things the same way, we have the same passions, we laugh at the same silly things. Valérie's dynamic, full of beans, we listen to the same kinds of music. What I have in common with Granville's group is the sea. And everything that goes with it, the beach, messing about in boats, volleyball, all that. Florence and I have done the same things, played basketball, learned to dance, we were in the same class and we've partied together. Samuel and I aren't going out together any more, but we still get on very well, we still tell each other what's going on. And yes, we had lots of things in common, for example he's got a swimming pool at his house, so we used to go swimming together, and motorcycling and walking, and music.

This is close to Bernard Lahire's notion of the plural actor,[15] which combines several cultural repertoires that are activated to varying degrees depending on the context and circumstances. In our view, this plurality is "embodied" in each personal network, whose diversity in various aspects is testimony to the different times and milieus individuals have experienced and from which they have retained relationships. The combination of these various strata helps to limit the tendency toward similarity, at least from the perspective of the person at the center, but without eliminating it altogether. But how is homophily of social position changing in today's social world?

WHAT CHANGES?

In order to have some idea of the current and future development of homophily, let us take homogamy as our starting point. Jeroen Smits, Wout Ultee, and Jan Lammers[16] studied the evolution of homogamy in sixty countries and tested three hypotheses: (1) the status attainment hypothesis, which postulates that educational homogamy is increasing in modern societies because education is very important economically and therefore constitutes an important criterion for choosing a marriage partner; (2) the general openness hypothesis, which predicts that educational homogamy will decline because increasing mobility, access to the welfare state, and the spread of mass communications will make the

---

[15] B. Lahire, *The Plural Actor* (Cambridge: Polity Press, 2011).
[16] J. Smits, W. Ultee, J. Lammers, "More or Less Educational Homogamy? A Test of Different Versions of Modernization Theory Using Cross-Temporal Evidence for 60 Countries," *American Sociological Review* 65(5) (2000) 781–788.

boundaries between social groups more permeable; and (3) the inverted U-curve hypothesis, which combines the two to predict that, as modernization spreads, so educational homogamy will first increase then decline. The results are complex. They seem to confirm the openness hypothesis, but the effects were quite variable depending on the national context. In fifteen countries, educational homogamy was declining; in thirty-eight others no change was observed and in seven it was increasing significantly. One important finding is that the tendency toward educational homogamy does not depend solely on the average level of modernization but also on its pace. Thus, the decline was more pronounced in rapidly modernizing societies than in those modernizing more slowly. In rapidly modernizing societies, the disintegration of the traditional social barriers based on inherited differences was not being offset by new barriers based on attained status. Moreover, education homogamy did not vary in those societies strongly influenced by Confucianism.

Recent studies have shifted the emphasis fairly radically by inverting the procedure and examining the social structure from a relational perspective with the aim of constructing a scale of occupations based on the spousal matches (of married or cohabiting couples) recorded in censuses, in this specific case, the Swiss household panel. These studies observe the frequency with which pairs of occupations occur and use this frequency as the basis for a horizontal chart of occupations (rather than the vertical one traditionally used in France). For example, if doctors frequently marry secretaries, these two occupations will be placed side by side. From this perspective, it is clear that occupation (and not just educational level and income) is a highly structuring factor but that its effects vary by gender and country.[17]

There are fewer results available for homophily. For confidential relationships, such that they can be captured by questions about people with whom important things are discussed, researchers compared the results of a 1985 survey and another in 2004 in the United States. They show that, when demographic changes are taken into account, homophilies of race, level of education, and age are stable (although young people are seeing fewer and fewer older people outside their families). Gender homophilia, on the other hand, seems to be decreasing.[18]

---

[17] M. M. Bergman, P. Prandy, D. Joye, "Theorization, Construction and Validation of a Social Stratification Scale: Cambridge Social Interaction and Stratification Scale (CAMSIS) for Switzerland," *Swiss Journal of Sociology* 28(1) (2002), 7–25.

[18] J. A. Smith, M. McPherson, L. Smith-Lovin, "Social Distance in the United States: Sex, Race, Religion, Age, and Education Homophily among Confidants, 1985 to 2004," *American Sociological Review* 79(3) (2014), 432–456.

It can reasonably be assumed that homophily has evolved in much the same way as homogamy, which persists with regard to educational level but has declined with regard to occupational category because of changes in the occupational structure, which has diversified and become less hierarchized than in the past. We return to this point in the Chapter 12.

*

*   *

In this chapter, which tackles a question that is central to "classic" sociology, namely social divisions and their reproduction, the sociology of relational dynamics offers new insights by assessing very precisely the way in which these divisions exert their influence to a greater or lesser degree on behaviors that appear, on the face of it, to be "free," such as the choice of partners and friends. The "soft segregation" that can be identified by measuring the degrees of similarity between the partners in a relationship, whether it be marriage, friendship, or mere acquaintance, is thus confirmed: the similarities tend to be greater than if the choice was purely random. Thus, relational matching is influenced by social divisions and tends to reinforce them. From this point of view, sociability and networks do not emerge as alternatives to social groups and do not totally breach their boundaries, as is sometimes stated. The most intense relationships, which are also the ones least fettered by context, as we have already seen, are sensitive to social divisions, sometimes even more so. Although it owes much to structuration by the contexts and milieus in which individuals first meet, homophily goes beyond them to assert itself as a cultural practice that contributes to the development of a preference for people "similar to oneself" in one way or another. While the existence within networks of a certain diversity of partners serves to modulate this homogeneity from the point of view of the individual at the center, it is nonetheless the case that relational spaces are, at least to some degree, sensitive to social segmentations. These particular forms of the reproduction of social divisions have consequences, the details of which we are now going to examine in terms of social resources.

10

Relationships and Networks As Resources

Relationships are not simply an expression of life in society and the pleasure of being together. They also have a "utility" dimension: in certain circumstances, they are a means of gaining access to resources. Individuals linked to each other in one way or another perform many services for each other and some do not conceal the fact that they expect or rely on such services. This then raises the question of whether a genuinely utilitarian attitude toward the management of relationships and networks can be identified. By analogy with the notions of economic capital and human capital (the latter term denoting primarily a person's individual competences), some authors have put forward the notion of "social capital" to denote the set of resources to which individuals might gain access through their personal network.[1] In the course of these studies, some authors have shown, for example, that "strong ties" have a protective effect in situations of social difficulty, whereas "weak ties" are more likely to generate new opportunities than anything else.[2] Nevertheless, the word "capital" encourages the belief that it is worthwhile investing in one's relationships in order to derive a benefit ("profit") from them or managing the structure of one's network reflexively in order to maximize its effectiveness.[3] However, this is verified empirically only in particular cases, such as that of certain sales representatives, for example. When individuals' ordinary relationships are examined, as we are doing in this book, it is not easy to find any indications

---

[1] J. S. Coleman, "Social Capital in the Creation of Human Capital," *American Journal of Sociology* 94 (1988), 95–120. Pierre Bourdieu also used this notion in "Le Capital social, Notes provisoires," *Actes de la recherche en sciences sociales*, 31 (1980), 2–3.

[2] This idea has been developed notably by Nan Lin. Cf. his book *Social Capital: A Theory of Social Structure and Action* (Cambridge: Cambridge University Press, 2001).

[3] This is the point of view of Nan Lin (see note 2) and other network analysts such as Ronald Burt.

of utilitarian behavior. Generally speaking, people do not forge interpersonal ties out of self-interest. Although relationships can indeed be powerful vectors for resources, one of the reasons is that they are not experienced solely as such. This "effacement" of utility is actually essential for social relations, which are based on this ambivalence. Moreover, it is not necessary to adopt utilitarian hypotheses in order to analyze what relationships can provide in the way of resources. After all, even when they are played out disinterestedly, relationships frequently prove to be crucial supports in certain situations. However, these resources, in the sense in which we understand them, can also, in certain cases, be constraints as well. Although we intend to take relational resources seriously, we will be very careful not to adopt the fairly common reductive approach that emphasizes purely utilitarian interpretations.

A brief review of the theory is needed if we are fully to understand the link between relationships and resources. The resources that can be accessed through relationships are not the same as "personal" resources such as property, earnings, qualifications, or even knowledge and expertise. These resources are connected to an individual by formal title deeds or forms of incorporation, whereas relationships are first and foremost commitments to other individuals that may, under certain circumstances, give access to various resources, temporarily transforming the relationship itself into a resource. As many authors have already noted,[4] the following conditions have to be met if a relationship is to give access to a resource: (1) the relationship has to exist, (2) Alter has to have the resource, and (3) Alter has to be willing to make it available to Ego.

Drawing on the "social capital" metaphor, therefore, we might speak of "social" resources, even though this expression is not wholly satisfactory since "personal" resources obviously only have a meaning in the social world and are consequently, in that sense, equally "social." We will adopt it, however, to facilitate our argument. It will be clear, given what we have written since the beginning of this book about networks and circles, that the notion of "social" resource may just as well denote the resources accessed through involvement in circles as those accessed via networks. The difference between the resources that might sometimes be accessed via chains of relationships and those accessible within a circle is that, in this latter case, all members of a circle potentially have the same access to these resources, whereas in the case of relationships, it is often necessary to link

---

[4] Lin, *Social Capital.*

together relationships whose only point in common is the intermediaries who make the linking possible. For example: I need a drill to put up some shelves. Whether I own one or buy one, it will be a "personal" resource as defined above. If I'm a member of a DIY club, I can borrow one of the club's drills provided I obey the rules and procedures of that particular circle. In that case, I'm clearly using the circle as a "social" resource: I can only borrow the drill because I'm a member of the circle. After all, I can also ask a friend or a neighbor to lend me his or, if he hasn't got one, to point me in the direction of one of his acquaintances who might lend me one. Even if I don't know the owner of the drill I end up with, the fact of having been recommended by my friend or neighbor may be sufficient for him to lend me his equipment. I will have mobilized a relational chain with just one link in it if the friend or neighbor has the drill I'm looking for, two links if it's one of their acquaintances who lends me it, three links if it's a friend of a friend, and so on. Thus, the drill as personal resource in the first case can be replaced in the second and third cases by the drill and the circles or relationships that enabled me to gain access to it as "social" resources. This demonstrates the ambiguity of social resources, which is inherent in the very notion of social capital, namely, the fact that they invariably involve two resources that are virtually inseparable, an initial one that provides access and a second one obtained through the first. The second might be said to be "embedded" in the first. The argument could of course be developed further by imagining the market as a vast circle with its own particular rules governing the transfer of property rights, but that would take us too far away from the subject under discussion here. Let us stick with the distinction between "personal" and "social" resources. It follows that there are two types of "social" resources, namely, those associated with a circle, which might be described as "collective" resources, and those linked to dyadic relationships, which might be described as "relational." It is these latter, with their particular significance and complexity that we are going to analyze in this chapter.

Located on the margins of the economic sphere (insofar as its boundaries can be mapped), "ordinary" exchanges of goods and services constitute the most visible part of the flows of resources arising out of interpersonal ties. Running errands, lending money, chauffeuring children, providing assistance with computers: many studies have born witness to the importance of these exchanges, particularly within the family.[5] The provision of

---

[5] S. Arber, C. Attias-Donfut, *The Myth of Generational Conflict: The Family and State in Aging Societies* (London: Routledge, 2000).

information is also an absolutely crucial type of resource, particularly in economic activity. In many cases, relationships play an essential role in obtaining jobs or finding customers, suppliers, and partners of all sorts for those running businesses. Without adopting a totally calculating attitude toward relationships, people know they play an important role in their activities and are mindful of that. Another type of resource, finally, is more fluid and difficult to describe. The reference here is to those resources produced by the interactions between individuals and their relational environment and the influences they exert on their attitudes, behaviors, and life choices. Personal networks can, after all, be regarded not as a source of assistance but rather as a set of individuals likely to influence Ego's trajectory and to play a part in his/her decision-making by putting forward ideas and giving advice. For example, a friend can indeed provide a service or some information leading to a job. However, he may also simply give advice, suggest an option, open up an unexpected new path for the future, or, conversely, deter or put a damper on things. Sometimes, the influence is less explicit, as when one takes someone as a model or hero or, conversely, a deterrent. And sometimes the pressure also turns out to be more diffuse, emerging from a group or social circle that is taken as a reference point, which follows a particular fashion trend or affirms a norm. Relationships and personal networks can be the mediums through which these forms of influence are transmitted.

Furthermore, social ties are one of the foundations of social solidarity. The fact that parents bring up their children and give them the means to become independent, just as, having become adults, those same children help their elderly parents, that we do not leave sick people untreated, elderly people without assistance, and the weakest unaided, are all examples of social solidarity. It varies considerably in form and scale depending on the societal context, but it is never totally absent, even in the most tragic situations. In the modern world, life in society involves a host of institutions and community amenities – schools, roads, hospitals, etc. – that fulfill some of these needs in one way or another. However, while part of this solidarity is mediated through collective or instituted channels, another part is conveyed through interpersonal ties and the exchanges of resources that occur between individuals. It is important to be mindful of the fact that there are two sides to solidarity, just as there are to the notion of resource. For Diane – one of the young people in the Caen panel, who did not dare move far from her depressive, alcoholic mother for whom she was a carer – it was a burden that prevented her not only from seeking work outside her small village but also from going out with her friends, moving in with her boyfriend, etc. In such situations, networks can be as much a trap as a positive resource.

It is important to underline the fact that the relationships within which economic activities are deeply embedded, or those that underpin the various forms of social support or influence, are no different from those previously described. Whereas studies in economic sociology or surveys of mutual aid or influence have captured the efficiency of such relationships in a specific context, and in many cases, by means of analyses of specialized networks, we have sought to reconstruct their origins and incorporation into more multifaceted networks. In this way, we can gain a better understanding of the origin and construction of those relationships. This will facilitate understanding of the origins and construction of relationships, which, in certain contexts, will prove decisive. Family relationships, friendships, and acquaintances made during leisure activities, whose dynamics have been investigated here, are those that may one day become suppliers of resources.

Our two main surveys were not designed with a view to measuring the use of resources, even though they do provide some new information in that regard. In the remainder of this chapter, therefore, we will also be drawing on other studies. However, two other surveys we carried out in Toulouse and the South of France can be used as sources of information on particular aspects.

RELATIONSHIPS IN THE LABOR MARKET

Interpersonal relationships play an important role in the labor market. In the United States, Granovetter's classic survey[6] of 282 white-collar workers in the Boston suburbs who had changed jobs and moved home showed that a majority of them (56 percent) had found their new jobs through personal contacts, while the others were divided more or less equally between those who had used formal methods, such as job advertisements, and those who had approached employers directly. Furthermore, about one-third of the personal contacts were family members or friends (categorized as strong ties) while two-thirds were linked to work (weak ties). In France, Michel Forsé, who analyzed the responses to a question asked in INSEE's employment survey, concluded: "Besides human capital, which remains a fundamental factor, social capital plays a part in everything

---

[6] M. S. Granovetter, *Getting a Job: A Study of Contacts and Careers* (Cambridge, MA: Harvard University Press, 1974).

concerning employment and its role should never be neglected."[7] However, he notes that the effective ties in disadvantaged milieus are often
strong ties and that work-based relationships are brought into play more
often in more advantaged milieus. In INSEE's 2004 employment survey in
France, jobs found "Through family, personal or work-based relationships"
accounted for 21 percent of responses and "By activating a previous
work-based relationship" for a further 16.2 percent, making a total of
37.2 percent of new jobs found through personal relationships, past or
present. It should be noted that surveys of this type generally overestimate
"unsolicited applications," which is the least precise response, particularly
in a survey in which respondents are able to tick only one box. In a similar
survey in the United States,[8] where respondents could tick several boxes,
relationships were mentioned by more than 50 percent of them. In the
survey on business start-ups that will be presented later, 64 percent of the
new recruits were found mainly through social relations. Thus, interpersonal relations play an essential role in the labor market.[9] The only cases
where relations are practically neutralized are those professions to which
access is obtained through anonymous competitive examinations, as in the
French public service.

The use of relationships in this way varies considerably by economic
sector and size of firm. The largest firms use formal means (recruitment
consultants, tests, etc.) in order to guard against the risks associated with
hiring the wrong person, which does not, incidentally, completely exclude
putting relationships to use. Small firms do not use the same methods
because of the costs involved, but the use of relationships provides another
form of confidence. Let us take the example of a small pancake restaurant:

Every time I've hired someone, it's been through people I know. And I've never
placed an ad. I've never been to the job center when I was looking for someone, I've
always done it through customers who knew someone who was looking for work.
They're people who come and eat here from time to time, the ones I talk
to ... [talking about a recent hire] I got out my notebook and called a guy who'd

---

[7] M. Forsé, "Capital social et emploi," *L'Année Sociologique* 47 (1997), 143. See also
A. Degenne et al., "Les relations sociales au cœur du marché du travail," *Sociétés Contemporaines* 5 (1991), 75–98.

[8] P. V. Marsden, "Core Discussion Networks of Americans," *American Sociological Review*
52(1) (1987), 122–131.

[9] See the studies by C. Marry, "Origine sociale et réseaux d'insertion des jeunes ouvriers,"
Formation-Emploi 4 (1983), 3–15 and "Les jeunes et l'emploi, force et faiblesse des liens
forts," in L. Coutrot and C. Dubar (eds.) *Cheminements professionnels et mobilités sociales*
(Paris: La Documentation Française, 1984), pp. 300–324.

done a placement here. When he was sixteen or seventeen, he'd done a two-week work experience placement with us. So I knew he could make pancakes and all that. Then I said to myself: "I'm going to see, I'll ask him to come by." As he didn't have a job, I asked him if he was interested . . .. I told him about the drawbacks. Obviously, in that respect, it was the hours. Since I couldn't offer him many hours, obviously the pay wasn't that great.

Small firms tend to favor personalized relationships because the employer deals with everything and knows his employees. The same applies to firms that provide very specific services. Even though there may be a formalized organizational structure, it is generally underpinned by the personalized working relationships that are essential if all the work required is to be carried out. This can be illustrated by the example of a manager in a construction company:

I can't hire guys who haven't been trained in my company. We work on monuments. So my workers have to be up to speed with the latest techniques, if you like. I hire them when they're young because adults are no good to me. They're not at all suited to our company, to our work. I hired a guy last summer. Well, he couldn't work with us. He didn't have the skills to do this kind of work. The guys I train, they know our methods, how we work.

In the Caen panel, several questions on the search for a job or work experience placement show the extent of the informational resources that young people may have at their disposal. Of the 371 jobs these young people held over the four waves of the survey, 37.7 percent were found through personal relationships (10.5 percent through family members, and 27.2 percent through other relationships). Of the rest, 43.9 percent were found through various organizations (the National Employment Agency, local youth employment services, temp agencies, companies, and job advertisements) and 18.3 percent through direct approaches (unsolicited applications, knocking on doors, ringing numbers in the telephone book, etc.). The share of family connections declined over the four waves of the survey from 17.2 percent to 5.5 percent in favor of other relationships, organizations, and unsolicited applications. If work experience placements are included, the share of organizations rises slightly to the detriment of relationships. Individual situations vary considerably. Some young people basically rely on their families, when they have sufficient resources at their disposal. This was the case for Elodie, whose biogeneticist father was able to find her various jobs at very different levels as her knowledge and skills developed. This was also the case for other youngsters who went down the same path as their parents. This group included Suzie, who worked in the same automotive components factory as her parents; Paul, who was working in a bank like his father; and Alice, whose mother was a nursing auxiliary and was able to find casual jobs in the hospital while she was studying. Others relied mainly on friends and acquaintances, as did François, who had gone to Norway and got into the habit of using all the means at his disposal, including a wide range of friends and acquaintances, some of whom he had met only very recently. Yet others relied largely on public bodies (the National Employment Agency, local youth employment services, young people's information and guidance centers, etc.), as did Marine, whose network did not provide much in the way of resources. And for some, the assistance came from a very wide range of sources, including public bodies, family, and friends. This was the case for Joël, a seasonal waiter, who was perpetually looking for new jobs and deployed all possible resources to that end. In terms of level of job, it should be noted that manual jobs were found mainly through public organizations, while white-collar jobs tended to be obtained through family contacts. Jobs in intermediate occupations were obtained mainly by means of unsolicited applications, while craft workers, shop workers, and managers made more use of non-family contacts.

This panel enables us to observe how the use of relationships evolved over time as the young people embarked on their working lives. As the school-to-work transition progressed, the most immediate strong ties were gradually replaced by more distant, work-based relations as resources on which to draw.[10] This was the case, for example, for Victor, whose father was a farmer and (remarried) mother a shopkeeper, and who in the first wave limited his horizons to the resources provided by strong ties:

I think my mother could help me run her shop. Or my father, in farming. But that's not really my thing . . . .. My sister works at McDonalds, but it's difficult to get in there.

In the second wave, his horizons had broadened slightly, but the relevant relationships for him were still family ones. However, it was beginning to dawn on him that the work experience placements he would have to do at the business school to which he had just been admitted might open up prospects for him in future:

Of my current relations, I don't think there's really anybody who could help me find a job. Perhaps Cyril, my brother-in-law, who knows lot of people in pretty much all the companies. There's always my stepfather, who has a shop, and my

[10] Cf. L. Mounier, "A quoi peuvent servir les relations sociales des jeunes?," *Agora* 17 (1999), 47–62.

father, who's a farmer. Otherwise, as far as pulling strings is concerned, I very much believe in it, so later on I'll use the contacts I'll make during my placements in the next few years . . .

As he became upwardly mobile, Victor did indeed call on some more appropriate relations, moving from the strong ties in occupations that did not really appeal to him to weak ties with more suitable connections. In the third wave, he had found a temporary position as head of sales through his friend Nicolas, who had held the post before him, and then a job as project manager that he obtained through his business school. He was also able to call on an even more distant connection if necessary:

I could get in touch with Michel, Sabrina's uncle, who's HR director at the Family Allowance Office, they've got a big IT department. I think he could help me get a job in that department.

In the fourth wave, Victor was indeed working at the Family Allowance Office, in a managerial position. While many young people follow similar trajectories as the resources they are able to access become more closely linked to their work, others, and particularly the less well qualified, find it more difficult to move upward and their close family and friends remain crucial.

We can also examine the relative centrality[11] of relationships in the Caen survey by comparing the relationships that proved helpful in finding jobs with that of the others. This analysis shows that, for the totality of strong ties, the average of the relative centralities is higher for those relationships that were a source of assistance (0.299 for assumed assistance,[12] 0.297 for actual assistance[13]) than for the others (0.259). However, if family and Ego's partner are excluded, centrality is, conversely, lower for actual assistance (0.180) than for relationships that did not provide assistance (0.182), and only very slightly higher for assumed assistance (0.185). Thus, the assistance was provided both by a relatively central core of family helpers and less central, more dispersed non-family relations. Furthermore, as far as job search is concerned, Alter's connections with a professional world close to Ego or one that may further his objectives have to be taken into account as well. It is here, in particular, that weak ties, or even

---

[11] Relative centrality = (number of connections to Alter) divided by (size of network –1).
[12] When the young people were questioned about the people who might help them find a job.
[13] When the young people were questioned about the people who had actually helped them find a job.

friends of friends whom one has not yet even met, can gradually be brought into play through one or more intermediaries, thereby generating that "strength of weak ties" that can be a source of new information. This is what Nicolas experienced when the family of his partner Véronica found him a job as soon as he arrived in Spain:

> The family network was activated and they all looked all over the place for some work for me, and that's how Gino came along, he's the father of a friend of Véronica's sister. He said: "No problem! I need more workers right now!"

A friend's parents, a cousin's colleagues – ties that are sometimes very indirect and not always mentioned as ties in a young person's network – can be activated simply because they work in the right place or know the right person strategically placed to act as intermediary. Thus, Solange contacted a friend of her mother's who worked at the employers' union ("She knows a whole load of employers") and Christophe called on his friend Arnaud, who is manager of a tennis club and "sees all the people who are well informed about job offers pass by." However, these individuals still have to be motivated to help, which may, conversely, bring a person's strong ties back into play. This is the argument put forward by Clara, who said she would call

> mainly on family, and then on people who are keener to help you than others. There are people who say they'll help you but when it comes to the crunch they all disappear . . .

Thus, the core of strong ties and the periphery of weak ties play complementary roles in the search for work. Depending on the resources available to Ego and Alter and also on the phase of the career trajectory, some will be more easily activated and efficient than others.

Access to jobs is one case in which social networks play an important "economic" role. It is not the only one. Social relations are also very important in daily life at work. In some cases, a firm's entire organization depends on the structure of its cooperative and consultative relations.[14] However, personal networks are not confined within the boundaries of organizations but are constantly crossing them. This is why personal networks like those we are investigating here cannot be regarded as separate from economic networks.

---

[14] E. Lazega, *The Collegial Phenomenon: The Social Mechanisms of Cooperation among Peers in a Corporate Law Partnership* (Oxford: Oxford University Press, 2001).

CROSSING ORGANIZATIONAL BOUNDARIES

When it comes to accessing jobs, chains of personal ties cross organizational boundaries, enabling employers to establish contacts with potential recruits. This capacity for crossing organizational boundaries can be observed in other cases, for example, in innovation activities, which are comparable in many respects to craft activities, both being characterized by low levels of standardization, the importance of personal relations, and spatial proximity effects. Clearly, relationships are mobilized in economic activities other than innovation. Through the notion of embeddedness,[15] economic sociologists have sought to demonstrate the important role relationships play in all areas of economic life. Innovation activities are taken here simply as an example, one that has the added advantage of having been investigated extensively from the perspective of social networks.

In a study of collaboration between CNRS research institutes and industrial firms,[16] Marie-Pierre Bès and Michel Grossetti reconstructed 130 case histories of collaborative ventures between CNRS research institutes and industrial firms on the basis of interviews with the various protagonists. In 44 percent of these cases, the relationship between the two organizations (research institute and firm) was established via a relational chain involving at least one link that crossed the boundaries of the organizations, that is, one that cannot be inferred from relationships within the organizations. Some of these relationships were family ties, while others were friendships originating in contexts completely outside the professional sphere; yet others were ties established at university, between individuals in the same year group or between a professor and student, or had their origins in a previous job and involved former colleagues who had remained in contact with each other when one or both had moved on. These various situations can be divided into three categories: non-work-related relationships (family, friends, etc.), those established at university, and, finally, those linked to work. The first category was the smallest (19 percent of cases), while the other two accounted for more or less equal shares of the remaining situations (40 percent and 41 percent respectively).

---

[15] M. S. Granovetter, "Economic Action and Social Structure: The Problem of Embeddedness," *The American Journal of Sociology* 91(3) (1985), 481–510.

[16] M. Grossetti, M.-P. Bès, "Encastrements et découplages dans les relations science – industrie," *Revue Française de Sociologie* 42(2) (2001), 327–355. For an English summary, see Michel Grossetti, "Proximities and Embedding Effects," *European Planning Studies* 16(5) (2008), 613–616.

In all the cases investigated, the researchers or the industrialists had drawn on relationships with people outside their organization. In doing so, they had had to cross organizational boundaries and hence place themselves to some extent in contradiction to or at least a position of some tension with those boundaries. When the relationships brought into play were work-based, or involved ties formed at university, this hardly constituted a problem. The interviewees found it normal to draw on outside relationships at work, particularly if the objective was to find partners for collaborative projects. However, in some cases, we had to dig a little deeper with our questions and cross-check statements in order to ascertain that the collaboration in question had indeed originated in a relational chain. In several cases, the researchers we were interviewing preferred to highlight their own reputations, insisting that they had been contacted solely on the basis of their skills. In a few cases, the industrialists were also reluctant to mention, without prompting, that they had made use of their social relationships. It is likely, moreover, that despite our attempts to clarify matters, this way of establishing contacts remained slightly underestimated. Nevertheless, the relationships alluded to up to this point were broadly work-based. On the other hand, when the relationships brought into play originated in contexts far removed from the world of work, a second boundary was crossed, namely, that separating the work context from the other contexts in an individual's life, such as family, voluntary or community activities, and friendship circles. In this case, there was considerably greater reluctance to discuss these contacts, although some interviewees found it quite natural to report on their use of ties located outside of the workplace. The reluctance of some interviewees to mention the relationships, and particularly those unconnected with their work, was due to this crossing of boundaries, which can be experienced as a form of transgression. Even though those involved in innovation activities are being increasingly encouraged to seek collaboration outside their organizations, such collaboration is not supposed to be reliant on personal contacts.

In another study,[17] we examined situations in which individuals attempting to set up companies accessed resources that they did not

[17] M. Grossetti and J.-F. Barthe, "Dynamiques des réseaux interpersonnels et des organisations dans les créations d'entreprises," *Revue Française de Sociologie* 49(3) (2008), 585–612; M. Grossetti, J.-F. Barthe, N. Chauvac, "Studying Relational Chains from Narrative Material," *Bulletin de Méthodologie Sociologique* 110 (2011), 11–25.

themselves possess. Of the 53 companies studied,[18] the number of situations in which resources were accessed turned out to be 16.4 per start-up
history on average, making a total of 870. The first result was that social
relations play a dominant role in company start-up processes: 57 percent of
the situations in which resources were accessed involved bringing into play
the founders' personal relationships. These relationships were more
evident in the initial phase, before the articles of incorporation were filed
(64 percent of the situations involved personal relationships). In the
following phases, there was more space for mediation resources, that is,
resources enabling the actors to coordinate with each other (54 percent of
situations in which resources were accessed involved such mediation in the
second year of the company's existence). This reflects the new organizations' gradual decoupling from their founders' social relations. It was as if
the organizations were gradually succeeding in becoming independent
from the founders' relationships, as if the initial embeddedness in their
personal network, which had been crucial during the start-up process, was
gradually giving way to a new set of non-relational organizing principles.
The relationships brought into play were mainly work-related (73 percent
of cases), although they were fairly frequently given affective connotations
(34 percent of them were described as "work-related friendships"). The
company founders relied massively on their personal relationships to
resolve the problems involved in setting up their businesses. Consequently,
they were constantly being obliged to juggle the boundaries of the organizations of which they themselves or those with whom they had a connection were members and to operate on the borders between what could be
described as ordinary mutual aid, on the one hand, and the normal
functioning of businesses and markets, on the other.

MUTUAL AID

For all that, relationships are not merely channels through which resources
can be accessed. Part of their content, as we have already said, resists the
utilitarian logic. Nevertheless, the exchange of resources remains an element not only of relationships but also, more generally, of what might be
called the social bond. Let us leave the world of work for the moment and
return to "ordinary" mutual aid. While relationships can be drawn on in

---

[18] These companies were selected for their innovative character, as evidenced by the fact
that they had received innovation grants or were located in an enterprise zone or business
incubator.

"entrepreneurial" situations, as we saw above, they are also important when illness, unemployment, or family breakdown strikes, when they often prove to be crucial in enabling those affected to overcome the ensuing difficulties. Everyone can remember occasions where they have lent a hand during a house move, acted as intermediary in a transaction, or lent money to a friend. Surveys show, incidentally, that we remember the aid we have given more easily than the aid we have received.[19] But what is mutual aid? If someone asks their neighbor to help them move a piece of furniture, it is clear to both that this is a request for aid. If neighbors have a conversation during which they mention their children's education or health, it is possible that in the course of that conversation useful information might be passed on, or perhaps the mere fact of talking about it will bring relief or help them clarify their ideas. In this case, however, they will not speak of mutual aid, even though exchanges of this kind are essential to their equilibrium.

It should be noted that it is difficult to speak about exchanges of resources outside of the context within which they take place; any attempt to measure such exchanges with a universal instrument would seem to be doomed to failure. The aid a reasonably affluent middle-class family that wants to send their daughter to the United States to improve her English might expect to obtain from their network is likely to be expressed primarily in terms of information and contacts. Thus, their personal network is likely to include educated people who travel, etc. This has nothing to do with the assistance an elderly lady might expect from those around her. She is more likely to expect help with getting about, doing her shopping, or dealing with administrative formalities. This assistance may then come from her close circle (relatives, neighbors, etc.). When pupils are choosing which courses to take at school, parents and teachers are expected to influence the process, but sometimes it is the advice of a classmate or the example of a friend they spend their free time with that proves to be decisive. This is why, when conducting surveys, one has to scan a wide variety of everyday interactive situations. It is also clear that the support is closely linked to the problems people encounter and that, consequently, the characteristics of the networks (homophily, stability, etc.) generated by questions about support are also very closely linked to these living situations and needs. Moreover, various studies have shown that the time frame of the assistance is important. The assistance provided and the long-

[19] A. Degenne, M.-O. Lebeaux, "L'entraide entre les ménages, un facteur d'inégalité sociale?," *Sociétés Contemporaines* 8 (1991), 21–42.

and short-term implications for networks differ depending on whether the life event in question is a natural disaster,[20] the loss of a job,[21] or a time-limited or chronic illness.[22] Furthermore, since it is usually pre-existing relationships that are called on to provide assistance, it is dependent on those relationships, that is, on the personal networks of the beneficiaries of the assistance.

All developed countries have put in place welfare policies that aim to redistribute a proportion of national wealth and to compensate to some extent for resource inequalities. There are considerable differences between these countries in what the state provides and what is left to private initiative. Various comparative studies have shown, in particular, that the family plays a greater role in Southern European countries. In the case of France, specialists in kinship[23] conclude that there is a certain complementarity between public and private solidarity. For them, family solidarity has been maintained because of the state system of social protection. Private assistance complements the benefits and services provided by the welfare state but could not replace it because the burden would be too heavy and the objectives are different. The financial support provided by families can be likened to a parental strategy for combating the risk of a son or daughter experiencing social downgrading.[24]

Mutual aid is a complex phenomenon that depends on the situations of both helper and helped and the nature of the relationship between them. Prouteau and Wolff write that "to receive aid from a third person predisposes recipients to offer assistance to others themselves. Thus, informal voluntary work helps to preserve reciprocity in networks; since it is also a way of establishing and maintaining interpersonal contacts, it responds to motivations of a relational nature."[25] Even when it is the vector for a very considerable amount of assistance, the relationship in question remains

---

[20] V. A. Haines, J. S. Hurlbert, J. J. Beggs, "Exploring the Determinants of Support Provision: Provider Characteristics, Personal Networks, Community Contexts, and Support Following Life Events," *Journal of Health and Social Behavior* 37(3) (1996), 252–264.

[21] T. Atkinson, R. Liem, J. J. Liem, "The Social Costs of Unemployment: Implications for Social Support," *Journal of Health and Social Behavior* 27 (1986), 317–331.

[22] P. Willmott, *Social Networks, Informal Care and Public Policy* (London: Policy Studies Institute, 1986).

[23] C. Attias-Donfu, "Rapports de générations. Transferts intrafamiliaux et dynamique macrosociale," *Revue Française de Sociologie* 41(4) (2000), 643–684.

[24] N. Herpin, J. H. Déchaux, "Entraide familiale, indépendance économique et sociabilité," *Économie et Statistique* 373 (2004), 3–31.

[25] L. Prouteau, F.-C. Wolff, "Les services informels entre ménages: une dimension méconnue du bénévolat," *Économie et Statistique* 368 (2003), 3–31 p.3.

dominant. From this point of view, there is no reason to regard market and non-market exchanges as diametrically opposed to each other. As we have seen, they can both be mobilized in different ways. Any social interaction can be interpreted as having a dimension of mutual aid, while any instance of mutual aid can be seen as an aspect of life in society. As we noted earlier, above and beyond tangible exchanges of material goods, services, or even information, relationships also provide the framework for exchanges of ideas, feelings, and mutual influence. It is to this less tangible aspect of exchanges that we now turn.

INFLUENCE

To what extent do relationships influence behaviors and decision-making? This is a question that has always interested sociologists, but it is difficult to measure. The psychological theory of social evaluation, which states that people learn to evaluate themselves by comparing themselves with others, has been little used in social network analysis.[26] Some studies have recognized the importance of "significant others" in socialization processes,[27] but usually without going any further, either in identifying those "others" (usually it is only parents who are mentioned) or investigating the ways their influence is exerted. Combining this approach with detailed analysis of personal networks may help us to understand how decisions are made and plans constructed, particularly at key moments, such as the transition into adulthood.[28] This concept of influence can have several meanings. One person may directly suggest to another that they should adopt a particular behavior, either by exerting pressure or encouraging them to learn it. An item of information diffused by the media may influence the behavior of those receiving the message. This is what is at stake in the diffusion of information process.[29] The fact of being a member of a group or a social circle may lead someone to adopt a particular type of behavior

---

[26] C. D. Gartrell, "Network Approaches to Social Evaluation," *Annual Review of Sociology* 13 (1987), 49–66.

[27] G. H. Mead, *Mind, Self, and Society*, ed. Charles W. Morris (Chicago: The University of Chicago Press, 1934).

[28] L. Bernardi, "Channels of Social Influence on Reproduction," *Population Research and Policy Review* 22 (2004), 527–555.

[29] E. Katz, P. Lazarsfeld, *Personal Influence* (Glencoe: Free Press, 1955), showed that the message was all the better perceived and had a greater chance of exerting influence if it were subsequently passed on by someone close to that person or by someone they trusted; this is what is known as the "two-step flow" theory.

in order to strengthen their integration into the group through imitation and conformity. In an even more roundabout way, a person might imitate certain individuals she knows who "embody" particular life styles, some-times without even being aware of doing so.

We referred in Chapter 9 to studies that have sought to evaluate the part played by influence, on the one hand, and selection, on the other, in the homogenization of networks. When individuals connected to each other in some way adopt similar behaviors, is it the result of a choice based on their initial resemblance or of influence gradually exerted by one over the other? Undoubtedly, both play a part. One has only to think of long-standing couples, for example, who, although they initially got together because of a certain degree of homogamy, end up after several years by resembling each other much more. It may be more "economical" to reduce the divergences. However, above and beyond this imitation effect, Alexis Ferrand and Sophie Tazé[30] have shown that behaviors and opinions are intrinsically associated with relationships: our thinking is shaped by others and evolves with others, and our opinions change depending on who we are talking to. This is not to say that individuals are constantly changing their minds; rather, these authors take the view that opinions are formed through interaction and do not exist prior to it. They demonstrate, using an original survey procedure, that the more heterogeneous an individual's relation-ships are, the more ambivalent and pluralist their opinions and attitudes are likely to be.

In the Caen survey, influence can be evaluated on the basis of two questions. Firstly, each young person was asked, with reference to the list of all the individuals they had mentioned: "Which of these people would you ask for advice on personal problems (for example, emotional prob-lems, decisions that have to be made)?" Another question was asked a little later about those turning points when the respondent had had to make a choice: "Are there any individuals who influenced your choice? Who?" Thus, an initial speculative response to an imagined scenario could be compared with answers related to actual events, choices that had really been made.[31] Friends, who accounted for 62.8 percent of the relationships mentioned in the personal networks, featured less (51.4 percent) among

---

[30] Cf., among others, A. Ferrand, "Réseaux de discussion hétérogènes et pluralisme cogni-tive," *REDES* 10(2) (2005); S. Tazé, A. Ferrand, "Les savoirs profanes sur le sida: des incertitudes rationnelles aux certitudes relationnelles," *Sociologie Santé* 26 (2007), 31–48.

[31] We are of course leaving to one side those unconscious influences that act on us in the form of models, norms, fashions, etc.

the influential relationships (speculative or real). Mothers and fathers, on the other hand, who accounted for 4.9 percent of the total ties mentioned, accounted for no fewer than 18.3 percent of the influential relationships. Friends featured more in the scenario, accounting for 55.4 percent of the imagined advisers, whereas parents accounted for only 13.6 percent. However, when it came to advice actually received, parents' share rose to 24.8 percent and to 40 percent if the speculative and actual advice are added together. Thus, in the imagined scenario, it was their friends, closer to them emotionally and a greater presence in their everyday lives, to whom their thoughts turned, whereas, in reality, it was their parents who proved to be more influential. Brother and sisters and boy/girlfriends also emerged as significant influences. Thus, in decision-making situations, it was close friends and family who influenced Ego. More than half of the influential relationships involved older individuals: approximately 57 percent were older than Ego, whereas older people's share in all relationships mentioned was 49.4 percent.

The young people were then asked openly: "Why them?" and "Why not the others?" The answers to these two questions enabled us to identify what gave the "influencers" this (possibly excessive) power to intervene in the decision-making. The main reasons given referred to the quality of the tie ("he's my best friend," "we adore each other," etc.): 72 percent of the responses fell into this category, whereas 31 percent focused more on Alter's qualities (including his/her competence) and 6 percent referred to the similarities between Ego and Alter. The fact that competence appeared to have less effect on the capacity to exert influence than the quality of the relationship, and, in particular, its emotional intensity, is an important finding and is an encouragement to those investigating social capital to look beyond Alter's resources and to take the characteristics of relationships into consideration.

If we now shift the focus from this relational or dyadic dimension to the level of the networks themselves, it soon becomes evident that these influences and the reasons given by the same person for turning to particular members of his/her network vary considerably. Serge, for example, would seek advice from friends who differ in their views:

I think that with all my friends in fact, if I really had a major decision to make, I would talk about it in order to obtain a range of views, to get completely different opinions, because they're different people so they must necessarily have different opinions. But to be absolutely certain, to make sure they're not mistaken .... Perhaps my mother and father are maybe the two people I would listen to most.

This plurality and distribution of influences seem not only tolerable for these young people but to be actively sought after. This reflects, once again, the notion that individuals are a combination of several social identities produced by the various contexts in which their socialization took place. The various members of an individual's personal network are the personifications of the various layers and contexts of their lives. The opacity of roles within people's set of social circles enables them to manage a large part of the divergences between different parts of their networks. After all, work colleagues do not have the same experience or the same image of an individual as his or her neighbors or family. Thus, individuals are able to juggle their various identities, displaying in each context just one part of their full identity, as long as the various spheres of their lives remain disconnected from each other, as their various partners do not meet each other and the contradictions are not exposed. Consequently, the degree of opacity in a network is an important factor to be taken into consideration. Network density, that is, the degree of interconnection between the Alters, or the centrality of individual relationships can be used as approximate measures of this opacity. After all, if the friends know each other, they will communicate among themselves and the network will be less opaque and more unified. Biographical events may even be more synchronized, as Laura Bernardi and her colleagues[32] show in their study of peer influence on the decision to have a child. In the Caen panel, the average degree centrality of the "influential" relationships was higher (0.330) than that of the "non-influential" relationships (0.243). The gap narrows if family and Ego's partner, for whom degree centrality is generally higher, are excluded: centrality is 0.219 for non-family influencers and 0.173 for non-family non-influencers. The average of these centralities is higher for actual than for speculative influence, whether or not family are included. Those relationships that are sources of advice are more central, for example, than those that are sources of assistance with job searches. If each of the networks now becomes the reference point for estimating degree centrality by constructing specific medians, it can be shown that, excluding family and Ego's partner, most (56 percent) of the influential relationships have a low relative centrality.[33] Thus, within each network, and if only non-family

---

[32] L. Bernardi, S. Keim, H. von der Lippe, "Social Influences on Fertility. A Comparative Mixed Method Study in Eastern and Western Germany," *Journal of Mixed Methods Research* 1(1) (2007), 1–27.

[33] Relative centrality = (number of connections to Alter) divided by (size of network −1). Degree centrality is deemed to be low if it lies below the median for the network in question.

ties are counted, it tends to be the "peripheral" relationships that are more influential. Here too, therefore, the influence on Ego has two components, one consisting of very central relationships, the other of "outsiders."

This relative dispersion is important. After all, the existence of a number of possible options is due to the "structural holes"[34] that divide the various parts of the network and prevent them from communicating with each other, thereby avoiding any confrontation between heterogeneous sectors as well as, we might add, between the different "self-images" associated with them. For many of these young people, therefore, it seemed preferable to seek advice from a range of people from unconnected milieus. This was the case for Clotilde:

Seeing as how he's a bit outside it all, there's no problem with Mathieu. It shouldn't be something that concerns people who know each other too well either.

Thus, in order to avoid interference, there is a preference for seeking advice from people who are not involved and who have nothing to do with the problem or with the immediate protagonists. Thus it was that Nadège preferred to seek advice from disinterested work colleagues when she was faced with making a very personal decision:

It was the decision on whether or not to have a child. I could've talked to my mother about it, but I didn't really want to because I knew she would get carried away immediately, she would say "yes darling, that's fantastic, I'm going to be a grandmother" ... I talked about it a bit at work precisely because they were outsiders who were going to give me advice on something .... Sometimes you ask someone who knows the situation well for advice, but this time I wanted to take advice from people completely unconnected with the whole thing.

Alexis Ferrand[35] has demonstrated the value of these distant confidants, "outsiders" who can be seen as neutral but also as minority vectors of alternative options. He notes that recipients of sexual confidences are either the partner or close friend or someone completely unconnected with the couple. Mario Small also insisted on the relevance of weak ties and opportunity contexts on confidence.[36] Thus, network structure not only

---

[34] R. S. Burt, "Structural Holes and Good Ideas," *American Journal of Sociology* 110 (2004), 349–399.

[35] See A. Ferrand, *Confidents. Une analyse structurale de réseaux sociaux* (Paris: L'Harmattan, 2007).

[36] M. Small, *Someone to Talk to* (Oxford: Oxford University Press, 2017); M. L. Small, C. Sukhu, "Because They Were There: Access, Deliberation, and the Mobilization of Networks for Support," *Social Networks* 47 (2016), 73–84; M. L. Small, "Weak Ties and

shapes the normative pressures on an individual but may also encourage the emergence of innovative sources of ideas.

Now, as we saw earlier, as the young people in the Caen panel entered adult life, their network density diminished, the networks became increasingly dissociated and the Alters became less and less connected with the other members of the network. Thus, the tendency was for the networks gradually to become increasingly dispersed. The young people increasingly saw their friends one-to-one or in twos rather than in larger groups and their friends became less and less likely to know each other. At the same time, influence began to become more dispersed as well. Among the 1,358 influential relationships, the average relative centrality fell from 0.344 in the first wave to 0.262 in the fourth wave; if family ties are excluded, it fell from 0.240 to 0.152 for the influential relationships. These developments tend to produce increasing opacity between the Alters within a network, to make the advice given more diverse, and to create greater opportunities for Ego to juggle his or her various identities.

The evolution of the influential relationships in Antoine's network bears witness to this dispersion (see Figures 10.1 and 10.2). In the first wave, his influential relationships (circled with dashed line in the graph) all spent time with each other. It is likely, therefore, that they had convergent views or that the ensuing disharmony was difficult to manage.

In the fourth wave, on the other hand, the influential relationships were more dissociated from each other. Thus, Antoine was able to obtain advice from Emmanuel or Aïcha that differed markedly from that given by Sébastien or Denis, who knew nothing of the other's advice.

Thus, four major forces have been identified, each of which played a part in linking relational and identity-related processes for the young people. The dynamics in question are: (1) selection, which led them to choose partners relatively similar to themselves; (2) influence, which encouraged them to heed the advice given by individuals with whom they had a significant emotional tie, as well as on occasions that given by people relatively unconnected with the issues at stake; (3) network composition, which made available a range of contrasting options provided by the various unconnected parts of their networks; and (4) dissociation, which caused relationships to become increasingly disconnected and fostered the opacity required for the composition dynamic to unfold.

the Core Discussion Network: Why People Discuss Important Matters with Unimportant Alters," *Social Networks* 35 (2013), 470–483.

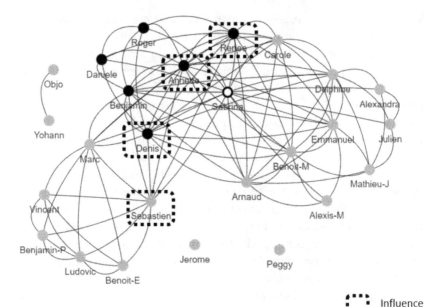

Fig. 10.1 The network of Antoine in the Caen panel (wave 1)

These four forces – influence, selection, composition, and dissociation – interact with each other within the dynamic of personal networks and socialization processes. As they gradually learned to monitor their networks for a certain degree of social homogeneity, which was no longer provided by the high school context, the young people also become increasingly selective in their social interactions and more and more sensitive to the social differentiations associated with their adult roles; they listened to and followed some of the advice given by those emotionally closest to them or by a few more imaginative outsiders, while at the same time ensuring that their networks remained sufficiently diverse to give them the possibility of changing or of simply remaining ambivalent, without being obliged by an overly cohesive and transparent network to confront blatant contradictions. This could be a summary – admittedly a broad-brush one – of the combined effect of these four complementary dynamics at work in relational processes.[37] They interact with each other

---

[37] C. Bidart, "Dynamiques des réseaux personnels et processus de socialisation: évolutions et influences des entourages lors des transitions vers la vie adulte," *Revue Française de Sociologie* 49(3) (2008), 559–583.

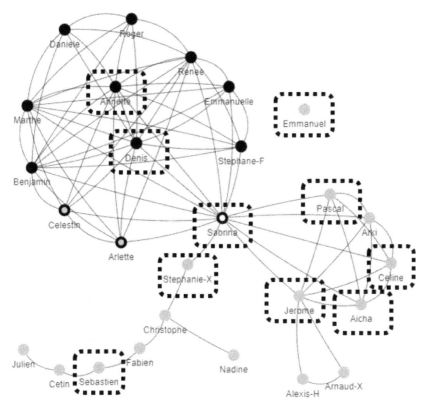

Fig. 10.2 The network of Antoine in the Caen panel (wave 4)

to establish the connections between relationships and networks that underpin the various modes of resource circulation.

*

*   *

Networks and resources are closely linked but are not one and the same thing. Relationships are an essential source of support, in both economic activity (finding a job, setting up a business, establishing contacts between organizations, etc.) and daily life. Nevertheless, it has to be emphasized that an individual's network constitutes a resource, which, even if called on frequently, is not generally managed or regarded as such. Mutual aid is one of the forms this resource takes, but moral support and influence, whether through advice or example, are also important forms. Thus, personal networks help to inform decision-making, particularly in situations of uncertainty. More negative forms of resources also exist, akin to constraints, curbs, or dissuasive influences.

The circulation of these resources is linked to the quality of the ties and to network structure at least as much to the Alters' qualities. Our analysis has enabled us to single out, in particular, the complementary effects of a core of strong central ties, often family relationships, and a more peripheral segment of weak ties unconnected with the others. For all that, social networks are not so many sets of inert channels through which resources flow, automatically advantaging those who are "well placed" within the structure. The affective and, on the face of it, "free" nature of these ties fosters trust and the circulation of influence or assistance. This is why the expression "social capital," which has become common currency, may prove to be misleading. Networks are complex social forms that may be "helpful" in certain circumstances and not in others. Above all, they are extremely diversified. Moreover, the process of dissociation that is at work during the transition into adult life tends to increase the range of options still further. It is, paradoxically, this very complexity that gives personal networks their strength.

The question of the resources provided by an individual's ties and network is the most familiar part of network analysis. The sociology of relational dynamics broadens its perspective considerably by showing that these resources depend on pre-existing relationships, as well as on contexts, social milieus, other forms of resources, mode of integration into groups, stages of the life course, etc. Far from regarding networks as a totalizing level of analysis, it focuses rather on the dynamics of embeddedness and decoupling, particularly with regard to the organizations whose boundaries they cross; in conjunction with innovation processes, these dynamics play a part in the creation of resources. The notion of resource can also be extended to include its "dark" side – namely, the constraints created by networks and relationships, those that bind more than they aid. However, relationships also provide less tangible resources through the options they make available as examples, the opinions they provide, and the diverse influences for which they are the vectors. In terms of dynamics, one can see, in particular, how the processes of selection, influence, network composition, and the evolution of network structures combine. Here too, it is the combination of these different points of view that imparts such richness and depth to a sociology that connects the various dimensions of the social.

11

Unequal Networks

If relationships can be resources, how are those resources distributed? Are there "relational inequalities" as there are income inequalities? After all, as we have noted on various occasions in the course of the preceding chapters, when it comes to relationships, as in the other areas of social life, not everyone is equal. The environment in which one is brought up, the education one receives, the occupation one enters, the events that punctuate one's life, and, of course, the choices one makes all help to shape networks that bear the marks of these experiences. Those networks may be large or small, family-centered or more open, dense or not so dense. Some are made up of well-off individuals, others of less advantaged people. Some extend over a large "social area" that encompasses a wide range of milieus, while others are concentrated around a very small universe. This was clearly evident in Chapter 2, for example, when we compared Agnès's network with that of Sonia. Since an individual's network plays a part in shaping how resources circulate, all these differences may also be sources of inequality. How are these inequalities linked with the inequalities associated with the "personal resources" on which the standard indicators of social hierarchies are based? Do relational inequalities compensate for those related to education level, income, or even gender and other characteristics? Or, conversely, do they merely reinforce them? These are the questions we shall be addressing in this chapter, first from a static and then from a dynamic perspective.

UNEQUAL NETWORKS

This question of relational inequalities is investigated here from five points of view: network size, network composition in terms of the roles and social status of the Alters, structure, and the role of mutual assistance.

Variations in the Number of Relationships

One simple way of assessing relational inequalities is to examine the variations in the number of relationships mentioned by respondents from the various social categories. The variations presented here are drawn from the Toulouse survey, but the same tendencies can be observed in all surveys, and, in particular, in the large-scale lifestyle surveys carried out by INSEE. The Tables 11.1 and 11.2 use the standard indicators of socio-occupational category and level of education.In both cases, the differences are very significant: the higher one rises in the hierarchy of occupational statuses or educational levels, the more the number of names cited increases.

Table 11.1 *Average number of relationships by Ego's socio-occupational category (Toulouse survey)*

Socio-occupational categories	Average number of relationships
Agricultural workers, craft workers, shop workers, and company directors	25.9[a]
Managers and higher intellectual professions	35.9
Intermediate professions	29.2
Clerical and manual workers	21.5
Inactive	22.8
Total	27.5

[a] For example, agricultural workers, craft workers, shop workers, and company directors cite 25.9 people on average.

Table 11.2 *Average number of relationships by Ego's level of education (Toulouse survey)*

Level of education	Average number of relationships
Lower than baccalaureate	21.4[a]
Baccalaureate	24.2
Two years' post-secondary education	28
Four years' post-secondary education	36.6
Total	27.5

[a] For example, individuals whose level of education is lower than the baccalaureate cite 21.4 people on average.

Let us examine the most extreme situations in terms of network size. We will begin by investigating the most circumscribed networks. In the Toulouse survey, there is not really anybody who could be regarded as isolated. The individuals who cited the fewest relationships mentioned at least three (only two actually reported fewer than five) and declared they could get assistance in various areas of their lives. This type of survey, which is sampled on the basis of the residents in certain streets who are telephone subscribers,[1] disregards certain situations that might give rise to more pronounced isolation (dependent elderly people, people of no fixed abode, recently arrived immigrants, undocumented workers, highly mobile individuals, etc.). Among the respondents who cited fewer than ten names (22 of a total of 399 individuals surveyed), half were elderly people (11 were over 65) with low levels of education (10 of the 11 did not have the baccalaureate). This combination of characteristics is important. After all, advancing age was clearly associated with a decline in relationships only for those with little formal education (qualifications lower than the baccalaureate). It is true that this applies to the overwhelming majority of the relevant generations (the share of holders of the baccalaureate in each generation did not exceed 20 percent until the 1980s). However, it is important to point out that the over-65s with university degrees did not experience any particular shrinking of their networks. The other half consisted of individuals under sixty-five, a good many of whom (six out of eleven) had at least the baccalaureate (four had a two-year HE qualification and one even had a four-year degree) but whose shared characteristic is that at the time of the survey they were all in relatively unskilled jobs (five clerical or manual workers) or were not working at all (three inactive, one housewife). Of the remaining two, one was a craft worker, the other a technician. Here, therefore, it is less the level of qualification that counts than the type of employment (or lack of employment). Finally, almost all the respondents (sixteen out of twenty-two) with these circumscribed networks lived in the most working-class district that featured in the Toulouse survey.

This analysis can be clearly illustrated by reference to the three most circumscribed networks. The first is that of a man of thirty-one, a skilled worker born in Toulouse but who had only returned there in 2001 (a few weeks before the survey) after having lived in the United States. There were just five people employed at his workplace and he was living alone. He

---

[1] This procedure, which was still working very well in 2001, would be less satisfactory in the age of the mobile phone.

cited only three names: his father (retired) and a couple in which the man was a childhood friend in the same type of occupation. In his case, the effect of his occupation was reinforced by his recent mobility, which explains the absence of weak ties and hence a network reduced to very strong ties. It may well be that if we were to have questioned the same person again a few years afterward he would have cited more relationships. The second very restricted network is that of a woman aged seventy, retired, of foreign origin (Europe), who had arrived in Toulouse in 1971 and was living with her husband (aged sixty-five) and one of her sons (aged twenty-seven and a civil service clerical worker). She cited four people, including her other son, who was thirty-eight and a skilled manual worker who had passed the baccalaureate and was living with his partner but had no children, and a man aged thirty-five, who was not in employment and living with a partner, also without children; she had met him five years previously in the course of associative activities and he also knew her son. The third network is that of a thirty-one year-old woman, a housewife who had left school before the baccalaureate and was living with her husband (a thirty-year-old engineer) and her two daughters aged five and one. She cited five people, including a thirty-three-year-old female neighbor, a housewife and mother like herself, a thirty-three-year-old craft worker and a twenty-five-year-old farm worker who were relatives of her husband and, finally, a forty-four-year-old woman, a service worker to whom she could entrust the care of her house and with whom she could also discuss personal problems. This third example, which is fairly typical of certain housewives' situations, neatly rounds off this brief illustration of what the statistical analyses describe.

By way of comparison, we turn now to the large networks. Of the fifty-one respondents who listed more than forty-five relationships, 70 percent were managers or in possession of a four-year degree. Their age distribution is fairly similar to that of the population as a whole, with a slight concentration in the 46–64 age group. The same applies to gender. Thus, it is among the indicators of social hierarchy that the characteristics that best explain these large-scale networks are to be found.

Let us look more closely at the three largest networks. The first is that of a forty-nine-year-old man, who was living in the city center. He was a technical manager in a private-sector company and holder of a two-year degree; he was born in Toulouse and studied there. He had come back to the city in 1997 after having lived in five other places. He was working in a firm with seven employees; he traveled frequently on business throughout France (once a week on average). He was living with a man aged thirty-nine who was working in a liberal profession.[2] He cited 141 individuals, 134 of them in response to the question on social activities (going out, entertaining, etc.). Of these, the subsample procedure led to the identification of a work colleague living with a partner and their children whom he had known for fifteen years, an old friend (aged forty) working in a liberal profession, living with a partner but no children and to whom he spoke about his personal problems, and a thirty-year-old women, also in a liberal profession, whom he had known for six years and with whom he also discussed personal problems. He mentioned only six people in his family, to whom he did not feel particularly close. We did not investigate gays or lesbians specifically, but it can reasonably be supposed that this characteristic comes into play in certain cases when it goes hand in hand with affiliation to a community of similarly oriented individuals. The second largest network is that of a retired woman aged seventy-two who was living in a rural area where she had arrived in 1955. She was born in Paris, where she was at university for four years. She had lived and worked in eight towns and cities, some of them abroad. She was living with her husband, aged eighty-one and also retired. She listed ninety-one relationships, many of them relating to outings (55) as well as to domestic tasks (10) and leisure activities (10). Thirty-five of the people she cited were part of her family. Among these relatives, she mentioned her husband, her son (aged fifty-four, liberal profession), who was living five-minutes' travel time away, and a neighbor aged ninety-four. She also listed a person no longer alive: a man aged seventy-eight and retired, whom she had known for fifty-three years since her time at university and who had died. This example of a woman who maintained a vast network of family, friends, and neighbors shows that networks do not necessarily shrink with age, particularly for those with university degrees. The third example of a large network is that of a thirty-four-year-old academic who was living in the city center with his thirty-year-old wife, a business executive. Born in Paris, he had attended university there before moving to Toulouse in 1994. He was working in a team of six people. He listed eighty-eight people (71 for outings/nights out, 22 for leisure activities, 5 for work-related discussions – i.e., his colleagues – and just 3 family members, all regarded as close). Among the individuals cited were his wife, a neighbor working in one of the liberal professions and living with a partner, their children, and a female primary school teacher whom he had known for five years because they were members of

---

[2] There were 7 people living with a same-sex partner out of the 221 living with a partner.

the same community association. He also mentioned a lost relationship, a fifty-five-year-old man in the same profession whom he had known for thirteen years and with whom he had fallen out.

Thus, examination of the extreme cases confirms the statistical trends (higher level of education and/or managerial or executive status) but with additional characteristics emerging that were not perceptible at the aggregate level but which seem to play a role nevertheless – homosexuality, in the first case and high mobility, in the second. The third case is more general: the academic profession is one of those whose members have the most extensive networks. This brief examination of the variations in network size in the Toulouse survey confirms the general analysis: it is the social hierarchy (degree and occupation) that best explains the variations, even though it is often accompanied or modulated by other relevant factors.

The respondents in the Caen survey were too young for their professional positions or level of education to be taken into account, since some were still in education. However, the same trend for network size to increase with social position is confirmed if social origin as measured by parental occupation and level of education and the education/training pathway taken (economic and social baccalaureate, vocational baccalaureate or training scheme for the young employed) are included in the analysis. After all, the average network size fell from 46 for respondents from the higher social categories to 41.5 for those from the intermediate categories and 33.4 for those from the working classes. Average network size for respondents who had obtained the economic and social baccalaureate was 43, for those who had taken the vocational baccalaureate it was 36 and for those who had completed a training scheme (without the baccalaureate) it was 28. The smallest networks, those with fewer than 30 members, represented 34.5 percent of the panel's total of 287 networks, but 72.7 percent of these small networks were those of working-class respondents. We have also seen that the differences were very large: the smallest network had just 6 people in it, the largest 131.

Similarly, the "Contacts"[3] survey had earlier revealed the strength of social hierarchization:

When it comes to sociability, the various socio-occupational categories are hierarchized with a quite unusual degree of precision, regardless of gender . . . . It is true that sociability is positively correlated with income, but it is even more highly

---

[3] Carried out by INSEE between May 1982 and May 1983, among a sample of 4,701 people.

correlated with level of education, since it is in the intellectual segments of the higher social classes that sociability reaches its peak. Professors, artists and senior civil servants rub shoulders with members of the liberal professions despite being less well-off than they are, while corporate managers, whether on the adminis-trative or sales side, tend to stay in the background and engineers, as usual, occupy an intermediate position. The cultural hierarchy of sociability is no less visible, one rung below, among the lower middle classes. Here too, it is reflected in a pro-nounced contrast between the world of business, which is relatively less sociable, and the public service, which is richer in relationships.[4]

Moreover, these differences would also appear to be cumulative:

Despite the privileged ties that link certain types of relationships at certain stages of the life course and despite the gender division of labor, there is a considerable degree of consistency between the various components of sociability. For example, individuals who maintain a large number of friendships are also the ones who are most likely to go out with colleagues, to invite neighbors into their homes and to be involved in associative activities and thereby to engage in extensive personal discussions over the course of a week . . .. When it comes to social relationships, therefore, to those who have, more is given – and this law is stronger than the time constraints that might force individuals to scale back their investment in relationships.[5]

Thus, there are "accumulators" who succeed in overcoming time con-straints in order to maintain relationships with more people than the others.

Variations in Network Composition

Networks differ not only in size but also in composition. Furthermore, differences in the number of names mentioned and in the distribution of relational roles within networks are very closely linked to the questions asked in the name generators. After all, as we saw in Chapter 2, differences in numbers are determined primarily by certain types of relationships, namely those linked to work, leisure activities, and friendships.

In the Toulouse survey, the number of family members cited does not vary in a linear fashion with education level. It declines slightly among holders of the baccalaureate compared with those who do not have it, but

---

[4] F. Héran, "La sociabilité, une pratique culturelle," *Économie et Statistique* 216 (1988), 18. See also A. Ferrand, A. de Federico de la Rúa, "Methods of Social Network Analysis," in G. Caselli, J. Vallin, and G. Wunsch (eds.) *Demography: Analysis and Synthesis*, vol 4 (Cambridge, MA: Elsevier Academic Press, 2006), pp. 745–764.

[5] Héran, "La sociabilité, une pratique culturelle," 15.

rises again among those with higher levels of education. On the other hand, the share of friends increases with Ego's level of education. It declines slightly among holders of the baccalaureate compared with those who do not have it, but rises again among those with higher levels of education. The family accounts for half of the average number of 21.4 relationships cited by those who left education before the baccalaureate and 40 percent of the average of 28 names cited by those with the highest levels of education, which is proportionately lower. In purely numerical terms, however, those with the highest levels of education cite more family ties (13.9 compared with 10.8), just as they cite more names in general. The intermediate categories cite fewer family ties (nine to ten, or approximately 36 percent). This question of the distribution of relationships in terms of roles in networks is important in that it enables us to distinguish "assigned" relationships (family and neighbors) from those that are more freely chosen (friends, hobbies, and leisure activities), the colleague category being located between the two. Table 11.3 shows the average number of relationships cited in each of the categories by level of education.

Social origin is more significant in the Caen survey, in which social status as measured by parents' occupation and level of education is strongly correlated with the share of family members in individuals' networks. This share rises from 24.6 percent for the young people from the higher social categories to 27 percent for those from the intermediate categories and to 29 percent for those from the working classes.

Here too, a cumulative effect can be observed. In the Toulouse survey, the share of family relationships in all relationships gradually decreases as the total number of relationships increases. In the Caen survey, similarly, the share of family members in the smallest networks (fewer than thirty relationships) is 31.6 percent compared with 26.6 percent in the others. Thus, the smallest networks are also more concentrated around family, which can only foster the reproduction of social inequalities. The tendencies revealed in these two surveys are consistent with the results of the "Contacts" and EPCV surveys. Thus, network size is not the only factor that is sensitive to social inequalities. The "reach" of an individual's resources (whether they are concentrated on assigned relationships, i.e., family or neighborhood, or dispersed across various milieus and based on more "constructed" relationships), the distribution of relational roles within networks and the intensity of these contacts are also variously distributed depending on social hierarchies.

Furthermore, having relationships is one thing, but having relationships with people of different social statuses is quite another thing. In a revue of

Table 11.3 *Types of relationships by Ego's level of education (Toulouse survey)*

Level of education	Family	Colleagues	Neighbors	Members of associations	Friends	Acquaintances	Others
Lower than baccalaureate	10.8[a]	1	1	1.9	8.1	2.2	1.7
%	50	5	5	9	38	10	8
Baccalaureate	8.8	2.5	1.2	1.5	9.8	2.2	1.3
%	36	10	5	6	40	9	5
Two years' post-secondary education (Bac + 2)	9.9	2.1	1.1	1.3	10.8	3	1.4
%	35	8	4	5	39	11	5
Four years' post-secondary education (Bac + 4)	13.9	3.2	1.4	1.9	15.2	3	1.2
%	40	9	4	5	42	8	3
Total	11	2.1	1.2	1.6	11.1	2.7	1.4
%	40	8	4	6	41	10	5

[a] For example, or individuals whose level of education is lower than the baccalaureate, the average number of Alters who are family members is 10.8, or 50 percent of all relationships cited.

several surveys carried out in the United States, China, and Germany, Nan Lin[6] shows that there is always a correlation between a respondent's social status and that of the individuals he or she cites. He concludes from this that social capital depends on an individual's initial position within the social hierarchy. And indeed, it is seldom that one sees individuals in a disadvantaged situation who have relationships likely to give them access to valuable resources, which prevents social capital from reversing the tendency toward reproduction. This is what Rose, one of the young people in the Caen panel, experienced when she was looking for a job: her relationships were either disconnected from the world of work or even a hindrance to finding employment – her brothers were in prison. Thus, when asked whether she could ask the people she spent time with for help in finding a job, Rose replied:

No, not really, because they all work in the maintenance agency and the problem is that my brothers did some bad stuff there, so that's finished, it's definitely a non-starter. My mother doesn't work, so no help there . . .. And the others, my friends, most of them are unemployed or don't really have a job or they've just changed job, so there's no one who can help me, not really, no . . . Jérémie, for his part, was able to find help, but only for a casual job: To tide me over, yes, but not for a proper job. For a proper job, I don't know anybody high enough up for that . . .

Thus, social segmentation, reinforced by the effects of the homophily described previously, sometimes prevents a personal network from becoming sufficiently extended to compensate for initial inequalities. Moreover, it is tempting to think that there is an automatic relationship between having advantaged individuals in one's network and thereby having access to valuable resources and using those resources to obtain information or recommendations. However, those resources have to be exploitable, friends have to want to get involved, which is not always the case. People who have extensive networks that include among their membership individuals who are socially well placed are usually part of the same world. Thus, over the four waves of the survey Agnès, the daughter of a company executive, and possessor of the most extensive network in the Caen panel, was able to count on twenty-five people for help if she was looking for a job, including two company directors, nine people in managerial or intermediate occupations, three white-collar workers, seven students, and four retired individuals. In contrast, Sonia, the daughter of temporary agency workers in sales who had the smallest network in the panel, was able to count only on

[6] N. Lin, *Social Capital – A Theory of Social Structure and Action* (Cambridge: Cambridge University Press, 2001).

her mother and two retired neighbors, who advised her when she was looking for a placement. Thus, the support relationships provide usually favors those who are already advantaged and only rarely helps to reduce inequalities.

Network Structure

A network structure in which all the Alters belong to the same social universe confines the person at its center to that same milieu, whether they be poor or more comfortably off. According to Granovetter's theory,[7] the individuals in this "homogeneous" universe all have at their disposal the same information and the same potential resources. They are employed in similar kinds of professions, live in the same kinds of areas, and meet only people of their own kind. They constitute a community that is more or less comfortably well-off and more or less cultivated, but redundant – as a result of its members' participation in the same circles, that community will eventually give birth to a carbon copy of itself. If we are looking for a process that will enable inequalities to be overcome, it has to be based on a network that not only provides access to a range of different milieus and enables its members to cross boundaries but is also constructed in such a way that the members of Ego's network do not all know each other and do not all spend time with each other, since this simply gives rise to a redundant network.

Network density is a general indicator of this confinement or openness. In the Caen panel, the young people's average network density follows a very clear trend, ranging as it does from 0.22 for the networks of those from the higher social classes, to 0.26 for those from the intermediate classes, and to 0.31 for those from the working classes. The higher social classes have a greater presence among the dissociated networks, while the intermediate classes are more likely to have centered networks and the working classes to have dense networks; the composite networks are more evenly distributed among each of the categories. Thus, the working-class networks are denser and redundant, while those in the higher social classes are more dissociated. Once again, capital is given to those who already have it. In other words, a network that is going to stimulate exchanges and to be constantly providing access to new milieus must be not only diverse and relatively dissociated but also "open."

---

[7] M. S. Granovetter, "The Strength of Weak Ties," *The American Journal of Sociology* 78 (1973), 1360–1380.

We are dealing here with a form of inequality that differs in kind from inequality of income or education, since it has its roots in the relational dynamic. If we examine the transitions from one wave to the next of the Caen survey between the various types of networks that were identified there, it is evident that the higher social classes clearly dominate the process of dissociation, while the working classes equally clearly dominate the process of network centralization. Over time, therefore, the dynamics of network structuration further reinforce the specific characteristics that reflect the social categories in which the networks originated. A "good" network is undoubtedly one that opens up new horizons and enables individuals to cross clan and milieu boundaries in order to experience other cultures and gain recognition within them. A very dense, redundant network will offer nothing more than a sort of static relational coziness, a "haven" of highly interconnected fellow creatures that may give a feeling of security but will in fact be more fragile because it is unlikely to accommodate change. If the individual relocates or changes their lifestyle, they will find themselves isolated. In a more diversified network, one that is open but also pluralist, the people and circles in which a person is recognized will in turn give access to other people who themselves have networks of the same kind. Once again, the process is cumulative. Thus, Patrick, after having "sweated blood" for some years establishing himself as a musician, suddenly saw his relational resources begin to take off dramatically after a concert at the festival "Printemps de Bourges":

It's people I've worked with or people who are in the music business or the people in charge of the venues, people who've heard about us or friends of friends of friends who have friends who know people . . .. Sometimes we get phone calls, we don't know who's given them our number, but still . . . it's happening and we've not tried too hard to understand why.

Thus, it was the peripheral ties whose connections he did not control that opened up these new resources for Patrick. This is one of the specific characteristics of relational resources: the intersecting relationships of which networks are made up and their structural dynamics enable individuals to transcend traditional inequalities. At the same time, however, since these characteristics of networks are themselves dependent on social positions, they are rooted in them. Networks can alleviate inequalities but they can also reinforce them.

Mutual Aid and Inequalities

From everything that was said in Chapter 10, it will readily be sensed that mutual aid is not going to be sufficient to reduce social inequalities.

Table 11.4 *Family financial assistance relative to total consumption by household social category*

	Average consumption in €	Assistance offered in €	% share of consumption
Self-employed	19,167[a]	548	2.8
Business manager, liberal profession	34,280	1,282	3.7
Intermediate occupations	25,951	284	3.2
White-collar/clerical workers	18,383	446	2.4
Manual workers	19,457	424	2.2
Total	22,934	660	2.9

[a] For example, in 2000, a self-employed worker spent on average 19,167 euros per year. He received 548 euros in family financial assistance, representing 2.8 percent of his consumption.
SOURCE: Insee – Family Budget survey (2000)

Drawing on the INSEE Lifestyles survey, Alain Degenne and Marie-Odile Lebeaux[8] wrote that mutual aid between households, far from alleviating inequalities, was – on the contrary – a factor in social inequality. Data from the 2000 Family Budget survey led to the same conclusion, by showing that the assistance offered to corporate executives and managers is on average three times greater than that offered to white-collar and manual workers (See Table 11.4):It was noted in Chapter 10 that resources, including those linked to personal networks, were unequally distributed. Thus, it would be illusory to regard mutual aid as a remedy for inequalities.

DYNAMICS THAT FOSTER INEQUALITIES

The old adage that "Whoever has will be given more" can also be interpreted in dynamic terms. Relational inequalities cannot escape the influence of social inequalities, but network dynamics tend to widen these inequalities still further. We examine this question first with regard to the contexts in which relationships are established, then with regard to the

---

[8] A. Degenne, M.-O. Lebeaux, "Does Social Capital Offset Social and Economic Inequalities? Social Capital in Everyday Life," in Henk Flap and Beate Völker (eds.) *Creation and Returns of Social Capital: A New Research Program* (New York: Routledge, 2004), pp. 51–73.

changes in networks over time, and finally, from the point of view of the effects of life events.

Social Differentiations in the Establishment of Relationships

The contexts in which relationships are established vary in their social composition. Some are relatively homogeneous, others much more diversified. The individuals met in these contexts resemble or differ from each other to varying degrees in terms of position and social origin, level of education, gender, and age. These contexts and the opportunity structures that arise out of them are the mechanisms through which social characteristics are mediated and transformed into the characteristics of personal networks and sociability in general. A university, for example, brings together people of very similar ages and levels of education, whereas in a family or neighborhood both these factors are more diverse. Some people get to know many of their friends at work, while others are more focused on their neighborhood. We will now consider these contexts in terms of the social characteristics of the individuals interviewed. By investigating the variations in the contexts in which ties are established, we can begin to understand the origin of relational inequalities. In the final analysis, these inequalities exacerbate the more familiar forms of inequality, such as educational level and income.

As far as the Caen panel is concerned, the differences in the contexts in which relationships are established can be analyzed with reference to social origin as identified by parental occupation and level of education. The lower social categories tend to establish their friendships in their neighborhood, while the higher ones tend to make theirs in the course of their education, whether at school or university. In the case of work, leisure activities, outings and evenings out, and associative activities, there are no clear differences in social milieu. Meeting someone through a third person is more specific to the higher and intermediate social categories. The same tendencies can be observed in the Toulouse survey. Here, respondents' occupations are known, which makes it possible to verify that the relative shares of the various contexts differ depending on the type of job held. Unsurprisingly, what varies the most is the share of relationships that originated in education and in work, which is much greater for managers and those in intermediate occupations. The same tendency can be observed when education levels are analyzed (see Table 3.2). While the less well qualified tend to establish most of their relationships among family members and neighbors or through intermediaries, the more highly qualified tend to establish their relationships through their involvement in associative activities, at university, or at work. Once age and social level are taken into account, these tendencies do not vary by gender (Table 11.5).

The contexts that produced most relationships for the most highly qualified were university and work (and, to a lesser extent, associative activities). Thus, it is not sociability per se (introductions through friends) that creates the most differences but rather the contexts associated with certain circles. This statement requires some qualification, since the various occupational contexts give rise to very different levels of constraint. Generally speaking, however, the impact of contexts is an unavoidable fact for everyone. For the most highly educated, nevertheless, most of the

Table 11.5 *Variation in the contexts in which relationships are established by level of education (Toulouse survey) (%)*

Context of first meeting	Respondent's level of education				Total
	Lower than baccalaureate	Baccalaureate	Two years' post-secondary education	Four years' post-secondary education	
Same family	34.8[a]	30.5	27.4	26.9	30.0
Association	4.7	7.1	3.9	7.4[b]	5.5
School	3.0	5.6	5.9	5.6	4.9
Neighbor	9.5	5.6	7.4	6.4	7.5
Grew up together	1.4	0.4	0.9	1.3	1.1
Through children	8.5	4.9	7.4	5.1	6.8
Higher education	0	6.8	5.4	9.7	5.0
Through husband/ wife	7.1	6.4	6.1	6.9	6.6
Through a friend	14.4	15.4	12.4	7.9	12.4
At work	10.1	11.7	15.7	18.4	14.0
Other	6.5	5.6	7.6	4.3	6.1
Total	100	100	100	100	100

[a] For example, respondents with a level of education lower than the baccalaureate met 34.8 percent of the people they cited within their own families.
[b] The shaded cells indicate salient values in each row.

people they cited whom they first met at university or at work were regarded as friends at the time of the survey (and not as schoolmates or colleagues). In other words, these relationships arose both out of the constraints and opportunities associated with a particular context and of a process whereby friendly relationships leading to the development of affinities became "decoupled" from the original context. If networks are generally larger in the "higher" occupational and educational categories and if members of those categories have more relationships, it is undoubtedly because, firstly, they are involved in more varied circles and, secondly, they tend, to a greater extent than the less well educated, to "extract" numerous dyadic relationships from these contexts. Thus, the contexts in which relationships originate determine a large share of the differences in network composition. They provide the opportunities and settings for meeting people but also determine the degree of homogeneity of those who may be encountered there.[9] In other words, relational inequalities are constructed through participation in the various contexts, which vary socially to a greater or lesser extent from the outset, and in the ways in which relationships are "extracted" from those contexts. Let us further clarify the dynamics at work in these differentiated processes of network evolution.

The Smallest Ones Shrink

Relational inequalities are constructed as relationships are forged through the processes described in earlier chapters. Even though families are obviously very unequally endowed when it comes to relationships, these differences in relational resources widen further at the beginning of adult life. And unfortunately, network dynamics also prove to be vectors for the reinforcement of social inequalities. In the Caen panel, the networks of the young people from working-class backgrounds were smaller but were also the ones that regenerated themselves the least: 56.5 percent of the 200 transitions between two waves of the survey led to a reduction in network size for them (compared with 40.6 percent for the higher social categories). In each transition between two waves of the survey, a greater share of the stock of new ties originated in the higher social categories than in the lower ones. Moreover, 68 percent of the smallest networks (fewer than thirty ties)

---

[9] See G. Mollenhorst, B. Völker, H. Flap, "Social Contexts and Personal Relationships: The Effect of Meeting Opportunities on Similarity for Relationships of Different Strengths," *Social Networks* 30 (2008), 60–68.

shrank during these transitions, which confirms that this process does indeed have a cumulative aspect to it.

These differences develop and are reinforced through two interacting processes. The first sees the emergence of group-based relationships. Higher education and work experience, which are important "breeding grounds" for relationships, are strong differentiating factors in individual trajectories. Most of the variations in average network size by social status are constructed in the course of this process. The causality is bidirectional: involvement in a variety of groups creates more relationships and those relationships in turn generate links with more groups. More specifically, relationships explain how individuals gain access to certain types of higher education, internships, and, above all, jobs within which new relationships are created in turn. The second process is the densification of networks through introductions and sociability. This process explains in part why social relations tend to be cumulative: outside the phases of rapid network reconstitution, the more people one knows, the more opportunities there are to create new relationships. Conversely, as is demonstrated by Sylvie, who cited only three non-family ties, these opportunities to create new relationships are reduced when one's friends themselves have few friends:

Séverine is basically someone who was very withdrawn, she was living with her parents, she never went out, so she didn't have any friends except for me so I didn't get to know anyone through her.

Homophily, in this respect, reinforces inequalities. After all, relationships are a resource only to the extent that those individuals brought into play through them have resources themselves. The more similar relationships are, the less easy it becomes for the more impecunious to access a wide and substantial range of resources through their social relationships. Thus, it is clear, from listening to the narratives of the young people in the Caen panel, that various factors come together to trigger the processes leading to a reduction in network size and confinement in the disadvantaged segments of the social space. Family problems (excessive drinking, domestic violence, etc.) are more common and more intractable in these social categories, as is well known, and they constitute a "heritage" that makes the transition to adulthood more difficult. Disputes with the extended family, which are also more frequent than in the other social categories, have the effect of cutting off one source of solidarity. The interviews are also peppered with stories of quarrels with neighbors and disputes of various kinds; young people from the lower social categories reported more relationships cut off because of disputes than their counterparts in the other categories. These young people were also less involved in activities, such as group leisure activities, sport, music, or associative activities, that might have expanded their networks. At most, Kévin had been involved for a long time in a boxing club, while Alexis talked on CB radio with people he had never seen "in the flesh." They never went on holiday or traveled, which meant they had no opportunities to meet different people from those they encountered in their daily lives. In some cases, they were becoming increasingly isolated in their impoverished situations; Diane, for example, had seen virtually all the young people leave her village:

I'm the only one left in C., everybody's leaving C., everybody's trying to make a life for themselves and they're succeeding in doing so, and now there's only me left in C. . . .. If I could find somewhere to live in C., I'd be happy, but . . .. All the same, I'd like to find somewhere, make a life for myself as well, get a good job, have a car and a nice home . . .

Diane had little education and was unable to leave her depressive and alcoholic mother; between the first two waves of the survey, her network shrank from twenty-one to just six ties. In order to gauge the differences between these "working-class" networks and those of more socially advantaged young people, it is enough simply to recall all the social circles with which Agnès, the daughter of a bank executive and a hospital manager, was associated; as we have already seen, she had the largest network in the panel, with a total of 131 relationships. Her relational environment included several circles linked to the Caen high school from which she was to retain a core of friends as well as several others linked to Granville, where she spent most of her weekends, which were divided up on the basis of the dominant sporting activity (football, wind-surfing, volleyball, etc.). In addition, Agnès went to race meetings with her grandfather, where she met another group made up of adults and young people. She quickly added her university and Parisian friends and then her friends from work, while at the same time maintaining her old high school friendships and those from Granville and the racecourses, circles into which she subsequently introduced her partner Olivier.

Unfavorable Events for the Unfavored

Over and above their social and cultural disadvantages, young people from the lower social categories experience biographical events in the early years of their adult lives that typically restrict their social interactions even further. They are, after all, more likely than their counterparts from the higher social categories to find themselves unemployed, to experience early parenthood, to have family feuds, or even to suffer health problems. Sylvie had experienced several of these situations:

For three years I went through, not exactly hell but it's true that a lot of things happened, like the birth of my son, splitting up with his father, going to court about visiting rights for the child, rows with my parents, they were terrible, between my son's father and then my parents, so that was a very, very difficult period of my life that upset me deeply, and then not finding a job, being unemployed and still today there are other things to deal with that are very, very hard . . . . I had a lot of problems with my friends when my son was born: Séverine and Fabrice know my child's father, they don't get on at all, that affects things. And because I have a child, I have a lot less time for myself and so a lot less time for my friends.

For her, these adverse situations were all connected with each other and constituted a real process of social disqualification.[10] Other young women found themselves in the same situation, unemployed and with children, including Marine, who already had two children in the second wave and five by the third wave. Examination of the networks that diminished in size shows that these trajectories were characterized by recurrent periods of crisis and "bad patches."[11] Furthermore, the effects of these difficult periods on relational practices emerged clearly in the interviews. This was the case for René, for example, who went through a difficult period between the second and third waves following the death of his father, his breakup with his partner Pascale, who was suffering from depression, and his expulsion from his nursing auxiliary training program. His network shrank from twenty-six to fifteen ties, in particular, because he reacted to this sequence of difficult biographical events by distancing himself from a certain number of his ties:

All the same, I've been shaken up by everything that's happened to me. It was a real blow what happened with Pascale, it did my head in, things like that. So now I don't make plans any more. And anyway it's going to be like that everywhere, even at work. I won't be a nursing auxiliary and I won't be part of the social world. I won't be doing good works any more. I won't be leaving my mark on anything,

---

[10] S. Paugam, "The Paradox of Exclusion: Crossed Considerations on the Contemporary Forms of Broken Social Links," in Marc Humbert and Yoshimichi Sato (eds.) *Social Exclusion: Perspectives from France and Japan* (Melbourne: Trans Pacific Press, 2012), pp. 20–31.

[11] C. Bidart, D. Lavenu, "Evolutions of Personal Networks and Life Events," *Social Networks* 27(4) (2005), 359–376.

I won't leave a telephone number or whatever. Or maybe just for a casual relationship, but not written down in my notebook. Now I have an unfortunate tendency to burn everything once I've moved on. Still, it's not all bad. It means less cards to send at Christmas . . .

Sonia, who, as we have seen, had the smallest network in the panel, or Diane, who saw her friends leave without being able to move herself, also experienced processes of disaffiliation leading to a loss of social and relational resources.

Even the way of considering other people, of entering into contact with them, and of constructing relationships is affected by these events and bad patches. Thus, Joël had become both restrictive and mistrustful in his relations with others, a development he linked to his "darker" view of things:

Everybody's grown up, matured, so I'm perhaps less trusting, I contact people less, I'm more mistrustful . . . I prefer to have a more closed circle of friends but, in terms of feelings, friendships that are more intense, more real, rather than having lots of people you vaguely know, like when you go to a club and say hi to half the people there but without really knowing them at all well . . . and without knowing what kind of mischief I might get mixed up in with them the day after, or what fate might have in store for me.

Thus, mistrust and withdrawal, which are more characteristic of disadvantaged populations, here further compound the process of individuation described above. Disputes, which are more frequent in the lower social categories, as we have already noted, have the effect of not only paring down networks but also restricting relational processes and openness to others.

Escaping One's Social Destiny

Nevertheless, a person's social "destiny" can sometimes be thwarted and a positive outcome achieved. Even though they are not statistically significant, some individuals whose lives start off badly are able to turn them around, and these exceptions deserve to be mentioned, if only to conclude this chapter on a slightly more optimistic note.

When we met Katia in the first wave of the Caen survey, she was involved in legal proceedings against her mother and stepfather because of the physical abuse she had suffered. She was thirteen before she got to know her biological father and half-brothers, one of whom had since been to prison and was undergoing treatment for heroin addiction. What she and her brothers had in common, she said, was "hatred." She had lived in a social welfare hostel for young people, and then on the streets. She had been hospitalized for depression following a suicide attempt. She had then worked as a gardener and during the first wave of the survey was just completing a work experience placement. And then Katia met Marion. Their love story gave Katia her zest for life back but also encouraged her to return to education and even to work to "help others," since it was now important for her to look after unhappy or handicapped people. So, she trained as a special needs teacher and then worked in a facility for people with intellectual disabilities. Katia had kept in touch with two female friends from her time in the social welfare hostel; they had helped her get off the streets but it had been difficult to maintain the relationships:

As I was suffering from depression in the hostel, I burned quite a few bridges. And when I was depressed, I didn't want to see Magali. There was only Valerie who was persistent, she came to see me regularly in hospital. She was the one who didn't want to burn any bridges. Seeing how I was, I cut off a lot of people. Even now, I don't really feel a need to see certain people again, simply because of the impression I left behind when I was in the hostel.

However, her partner Marion's family represented for her "more than just friends, they're a second family." Her network initially comprised various groups of Marion's friends, and then gradually filled up with the ties she herself made at work and those they built up together in other contexts (leisure activities, travel, associative activities). Katia became reconciled with her mother, introduced Marion to her own family and "picked up the pieces" while at the same time developing new relationships of her own. From the second wave onward, Katia was indeed more peaceable and according to her it was love that gave her the strength to extricate herself:

There are many things that contribute to a person's happiness, but love is the most important one. Personally speaking, that's what got me out of my situation, what picked me up when I was at a very low ebb . ... Marion and I talked an enormous amount, she opened my eyes to my family, she taught me to judge them less, not to be so hard on them, she helped me to see the positive aspects. She's given me so much, so much personal well-being, she's enabled me to feel better and to settle down as well.

Katia and Marion entered into a civil partnership, bought a house and continued to spin out love's sweet dream – with lots of friends around them. Thus, the vicious circle disadvantaged groups often suffer, in which their already restricted networks become even sparser through mechanisms that are themselves differentiated by social origin, can sometimes be broken following a happy encounter, say, that gives a person fresh heart and offers them access to new resources and different worlds. Other cases proved to be equally "atypical" in terms of social destiny. Alice, the daughter of a manual worker and auxiliary nurse from the West Indies, became a commercial lawyer in Paris. The French national education system certainly played a major part in shaping her upwardly mobile trajectory, but so too did her extensive family network that was highly diversified in terms of occupations and also very multicultural; it included a number of musicians as well as some individuals who were highly influential in her development (her "lineage" as she described it) and who, according to her, have been the cornerstones of her upward mobility. Alice also frequently mentioned people she had met at her piano lessons. Thus, her very open personal network was not a restricting factor, nor was it an obstacle to her social mobility. Mention should also be made of Patrice, son of a gardener father and housewife mother, who, after having worked in carpentry jobs that he struggled to carry through, retrained in industrial design, strongly encouraged by a teacher who understood and supported him. His personal network also expanded from forty-six to sixty-four ties and comprised various people who were able to find him placements. On the other hand, these young people who "hung on in there" and defied the mechanisms leading to the social reproduction of inequalities were not, at least at the fourth wave of the survey, involved in romantic relationships.

Conversely, some of the more advantaged young people experienced downward mobility. Colette, the daughter of doctors who spent a long time flitting from one degree course to another, never getting beyond the first year, before finding a job at FNAC; or Florence, whose parents were also doctors and who was still finding her way in life, were going through a sort of latency period as far as their career plans and the transition into adulthood in general were concerned. Their networks were relatively limited in size and diversity and, in both cases, their parents constituted their main resources (and effective ones they were too). For these two young women, the dynamic that generally favors the well-off classes had not come into play and their relative inertia had prevented them from replenishing their networks after the significant losses of relationships that accompanied their departure from education.

Network composition and the degree of homogeneity and dispersion play a large part in determining modes of socialization and access to diverse social worlds. As we have seen, the processes whereby network homogeneity is reinforced often work to the disadvantage of the working classes. Nevertheless, here too, certain events can disrupt these statistical regularities. Thus, Simon experienced a sudden opening up of his social world during his military service:

When I joined the army, I said to myself: "Shit, I'm an old man, I'm spending my time, all my time, with the same people repeating the same old stuff the whole time," so I said to myself: "This has to stop, it can't go on, I have to meet other people." Because at the end of the day, there were only four of us who hung out together the whole time, we were so bound up with each other that we weren't even trying to make new friends. Every time a new person turned up, it only took a couple of days and we were fed up of them, so we made sure it was just us four, every time the new person was kicked out in thirty seconds. But ultimately, I find it better to meet different people, that's what I discovered in the army, I turned up with forty totally different guys, ranging from someone who couldn't read or write to a guy who was going to be a police superintendent when he left the army, so I listened to everything, all the people I met, I met some engineers, I realized it was much more interesting than staying with my little gang of four, a closed group where we didn't see anything.

Thus, in the course of this rite of passage (now abrogated in France), well known for revealing the extent of the social world, Simon's universe suddenly broadened and he was certainly expecting to reap the benefits of this openness to new relationships.

*

*   *

If a few stories that end happily lighten the impact of the social reproduction of inequalities to some extent, it is nevertheless true that in the majority of cases, social differentiations are strongly linked to relational configurations and their dynamics. What the analyses in this chapter show is that the more personal resources an individual has (for which socio-occupational category and educational level are the proxy indicators here), the more relational resources he or she has. To those who have, more is given. Obviously this is only a statistical link: there are individuals with abundant personal resources whose networks are relatively restricted (e.g., 30 percent of the business managers or executives with a qualification that required four years' post-secondary education in the Toulouse survey cited fewer than twenty-six relationships) and, conversely, relatively disadvantaged individuals whose networks are fairly extensive (37 percent of the manual or clerical workers without the baccalaureate cited more than twenty-five relationships). If the extremes are disregarded, it is clear that three-quarters of respondents cited between twenty-five and forty-five relationships, which is not such a wide range. However, size is not everything: as we saw in Chapter 9, individuals connected to each other tend to have similar levels of resources at their disposal, which obviously means that those with the most personal resources are connected to individuals who also have significant resources. The tendency toward social similarity increases the inequalities caused by differences in network size and composition. Thus, relational inequalities are very real and tend to be distributed in the same way as those linked to personal resources. It might even be said, albeit with a slight degree of exaggeration, that to some extent accumulating dyadic relationships is "the preserve of the rich," since highly educated individuals in "favored" professions have more extensive and diversified networks. What is more, they are the ones who cite the highest proportion of people regarded as "close," which reinforces the notion that they have a heightened perception of dyadic relationships and networks, while in the less advantaged social categories ties are more often perceived as integrated into circles. It can be hypothesized, moreover, that extensive and diversified networks go hand in hand with specific cultural representations and "relational skills," which make it easier to establish and maintain interpersonal relations.

What are the dynamics at work in the linkage between the two sorts of resources – personal and relational? It is evident from our analysis that they interact permanently with each other and mutually reinforce each other. Personal resources influence the circles with which people affiliate themselves and the interpersonal relationships they establish. These relationships give access to new resources, which in turn open up new horizons, and so on. The resources to be found in circles and relationships are permanently caught up in processes of embedment and decoupling, selection of ties, affiliation to and disaffiliation from certain circles, and network composition. As we have seen, these dynamics are socially oriented. While some young people from working-class backgrounds have large groups of friends in high school, like their classmates from the higher social categories, they tend to break away from them more quickly as they enter the labor market and get married earlier; they lose the ties associated with a circle when they leave it, they are more restrictive in limiting their close ties to family members, and they meet fewer people in adult life. However, the opposite can also happen: some of these relationships give them access to opportunities to pursue their education or to apply for interesting jobs that will increase their personal resources. In this case, the adjustment between network and resources will be "upward." However, these processes of adjustment between their social interactions and their social status generally serve to reinforce the divisions between the different social milieus. In most cases, moreover, the fact of living in the midst of one's social environment into which established friends introduce others produces a form of social segregation; this segregation may be "soft" but it is nevertheless insidious, since it tends to keep people in their own milieus. We have also seen this process at work in the breakdown of relationships when social distancing occurs, particularly at the start of the working life. This is reminiscent of a standard hypothesis in social network analysis, whereby the "strong" ties that offer protection in difficult situations at the same time lock individuals into relatively homogeneous "social worlds." The complementary hypothesis is that "weak" ties, conversely, make it easier to break with these homogeneous relational worlds. However, since these weak ties do not fall from the sky but originate in circles and contexts, they can play a part in fostering social mobility only for those who have been able to gain access to those circles and contexts, which usually occurs through changes in an individual's personal resources (through the acquisition of new skills, for example).

These results and analyses are rather overwhelming, depressing even. After all, when one thinks of social relations and networks, social inequalities are not the first things that spring to mind. One tends to imagine rather a world of solidarity, reciprocity, and affinities freely established on the basis of pleasure and fine sentiments. This is still true, of course. And yet, if the sociologist's tools are brought into play, one pretty quickly comes face to face with the regularities and dynamics of social differentiation. In this respect, sociologists do not always show themselves in a good light, particularly when they "take the magic out of" social relations based on friendship and sociability that one would like to believe are free of such determinations. And yet it is possible, using reasonably rigorous methods, to understand these relationships a little better, including their paradoxes. Clearly, it is important to measure inequalities, particularly by investigating income and education hierarchies, and essential to analyze the way in which the education system reproduces, reduces, or amplifies differences in social origins. However, it is equally important to apprehend, as we have attempted to do in this chapter and the previous ones, the detailed processes through which these inequalities manifest themselves, are reinforced, or in some cases modified under the influence of the day-to-day workings of ordinary social ties and life trajectories.

We have devoted this chapter to inequalities because it seemed to us important to remember that social relations are not immune to that particular reality and also because the analysis of the dynamics of relationships and networks in which we have been engaged enables us to understand it better. In particular, a sociology of relational dynamics enables us to identify and understand the actual mechanisms at work in relationships between individuals and their sensitivity to the differences in status that loom over them. However, it also enables us to see how these individuals can, in some cases, reshape those inequalities, nullify or even transcend them as they construct their network and make use of the resources they uncover there. Maybe these social constructions will gradually help to make the boundaries more flexible or narrow certain divides? Nothing is less certain. Nevertheless, there is more to the social world than inequalities, and this is even more true of networks.

Furthermore, the very notion of inequality, which is a typically French intellectual construct, is far from exhausting the broader question of differences in resources, which cannot be reduced to a hierarchy or even a set of hierarchies, and even less to a simple division into social classes. For example, the attempt Bourdieu and the many sociologists who followed in his wake made to reduce cultural practices to effects of social position has been challenged by certain sociologists. In fact, it is often by taking account of trajectories and networks that it is possible to make advances in the identification of inequalities. The sociology of relational dynamics most certainly has an important role to play in this regard. And finally, the question of resources is itself just one aspect of social logics and networks.

Thus, relational inequalities are connected in a multiplicity of ways to inequalities in personal resources. They sometimes reinforce them by forming barriers and "niches" that make social mobility even more difficult. At other times, despite everything, whether it be through a shared leisure activity, a period of time spent in a socially mixed world, or just a chance encounter, they diminish them by opening a "window" through which new resources capable of redirecting the expected path of a person's life course can flow.

12

Networks Online and Offline

At the beginning of the 1990s, the Internet was starting to become fairly widely used in academic circles. This development raised questions within the community of social science researchers who were studying social networks. For the first time in its history, this community was faced with a significant change in forms of communication. After all, even though the strand of research represented by network analysts can be traced back to the nineteenth century at least,[1] no systematic study of interpersonal relations and the networks they constituted existed from the time the telephone came into use.[2] Among the questions that were raised as the Internet started to become widely used was of course that of the changes in relational structures (connectivity, size, density and composition of personal networks, etc.) that might occur as a result of the increasing diversification and sophistication of communication technologies.

This problematic question to which, as we shall see, there has been no generally satisfactory answer despite the existence of many interesting studies, resurfaced in a more pressing way in the 2000s following the emergence of social networking services such as Facebook, services that are now commonly known as "social media." In 2015, according to a survey conducted by the Pew Research Center, 65 percent of Americans

---

[1] L. Freeman, *The Development of Social Network Analysis: A Study in the Sociology of Science* (Empirical Press, 2004).

[2] Nevertheless, mention should be made of the efforts of Claude Fischer, author of one of the most important studies of personal networks, C. S. Fischer, *To Dwell among Friends* (Chicago: The University of Chicago Press, 1982), to analyse the early stages of the diffusion of the telephone and its effects on practices, particularly those linked to sociability: C. S. Fischer, *America Calling: A Social History of the Telephone to 1940*, (Berkeley: University of California Press, 1993). One of his conclusions was that the telephone did not significantly change the development of relationships in geographical space.

were using online social networking sites; the figure for 18–29 year-olds was 90 percent and 35 percent for the over-65s.[3] In France, a 2014 survey put the share of users in the population at large at 48 percent, 88 percent for 18–24 year-olds, 26 percent for 60–69 year-olds and 7 percent for the over-70s.[4] These figures suggest that registering on a social networking site (overwhelmingly Facebook) is becoming as commonplace as owning a telephone. These services enable users to adopt a more reflexive approach to managing a range of social relationships, normally grouped together under the heading of "friends."[5] Thus, it is certainly possible that they promote changes in relational structures or at least in the forms of involvement in interpersonal relationships.

As ever in the social sciences, it is difficult, impossible even, to isolate the effects of a single factor on historical developments. Nevertheless, those developments can be analyzed and a few hypotheses advanced as to the weight to be attributed to the factor under consideration. This is what we will be attempting to do in this chapter. To kick-start our deliberations on recent changes in personal networks and their possible links to communication, we will briefly review a number of studies that offer some clues as to how networks have developed over the long term and the type of changes that have accompanied the adoption of new tools in the past. We will then use our data to analyze some recent developments. For this chapter, we draw on two recent original surveys in addition to the two on which our analyses have so far been based. The first is a questionnaire-based survey conducted in January and February 2014 among 2,700 young people aged between 15 and 25 living in the Toulouse area. This survey comprised name generators based on exchanges of tips about music, the list of people respondents regarded as important to them, and people encountered online. For each person cited (four on average), respondents were asked to say if they were someone with whom they could discuss important matters. The second survey is a detailed questionnaire filled in during face-to-face interviews by some 470 individuals aged 60 and over (the oldest was 100 at the time of the survey) in the Toulouse area. This questionnaire comprised six name generators, including the standard question on the individuals with whom respondents are able to talk about important

---

[3] A. Perrin, "Social Networking Usage: 2005–2015," Pew Research Center, October (2015), www.pewinternet.org/2015/10/08/2015/Social-Networking-Usage-2005-2015/.

[4] www.arcep.fr/uploads/tx_gspublication/etude-CREDOC-diffusion-TIC-2014.pdf.

[5] For convenience sake, we have put Facebook "friends" between quotation marks.

matters. This question can be used to make comparisons with a 2008 survey of the US population by the Pew Research Center.[6]

RELATIONSHIPS AND PERSONAL NETWORKS: A HISTORICAL PERSPECTIVE

Let us begin by going back over the past: have dyadic relationships and personal networks always been what they are today? Harrison White, one of the fathers of "modern" social network analysis believes that the notion of a dyadic relationship was constructed historically at the same time as that of the individual from which it is inseparable (an interpersonal relationship presupposes that individual persons exist).[7] It can reasonably be hypothesized that these notions did not emerge at the same time in all social strata.[8] It is probable that they developed earlier in the wealthiest milieus and later in the others, even though certain notions, such as friendship, for example, are extremely long-standing.[9] In certain periods and in certain milieus, the notion of interpersonal relationship undoubtedly had little meaning, nor did that of personal network either, even though the existence of inter-family[10] or inter-group ties can be established. However, the extent to which individuals were confined within groups should not be exaggerated, even in the most ancient times. Nor should their freedom of movement and ability to forge networks stretching over wide geographical areas be underestimated. It is sufficient simply to reread the portrait of the shepherd Pierre Maury that Emmanuel Leroy-Ladurie paints in his study of an Occitan village to realize that an illiterate shepherd in the fourteenth century could cover considerable distances during transhumance and, in the process, build up an enormous and

---

[6] K. N. Hampton, L. F. Sessions, E. J. Her, L. Rainie, "Social Isolation and New Technology. How the Internet and Mobile Phones Impact Americans' Social Networks," Pew Internet and American Life Project (2009), www.pewinternet.org/files/old-media//Files/Reports/2009/PIP_Tech_and_Social_Isolation.pdf.

[7] White, *Identity and Control: How Social Formations Emerge* (Princeton: Princeton University Press, 2008).

[8] See, for example, Norbert Elias, *The Society of Individuals* (Oxford: Blackwell, 1991, [1987]).

[9] A. A. Silver, "Friendship and Trust As Moral Ideals: An Historical Approach," *European Journal of Sociology* 30 (1989), 274–297.

[10] As in John Padgett and Christopher Ansell's classic study, "Robust Action and the Rise of the Medici, 1400–1434," *American Journal of Sociology* 98 (1993), 1259–1319.

[11] E. Leroy-Ladurie, *Montaillou: Cathars and Catholics in a French Village 1294–1324* (London: The Scolar Press, 1978).

diversified network of colleagues, supportive relationships, and friends well beyond his family circle and the microcosm of his home village. Similarly, the young noblemen of the French Renaissance used to visit Europe to make themselves known to the different royal courts and there were frequent international exchanges of letters between scholars. The increasing use by historians of the notions and methods developed by social network analysts should shed further light on this question of dyadic ties in different historical contexts.

For the last century, some authors have attempted to formulate a comprehensive answer to the question of how social relationships evolved in a period that saw increasing use of the telephone and then of electronic communications. Thus, Claude Fischer has taken stock of the evolution of family and friendly relations in the United States over the last decades, based on numerous published surveys. He shows that while the number of close family relationships and formal gatherings have declined over the decades, neither the overall quantity of personal relationship, or their quality, has diminished.[12] Lee Rainie and Barry Wellman have also tried to compare the changes linked to electronic communications with longer-term historical trends.[13] They consider three successive "revolutions," namely, the recent ones based, firstly, on the Internet and, secondly, on the mobile telephone and then the older one involving (non-digital) "social networks." Rainie and Wellman include some very interesting summaries of various surveys of social practices and of the use of communications technologies. However, what they have to say about the evolution of personal networks remains largely in the realm of hypothesis and still has to be verified with diachronic data. The work of the historians mentioned above shows that dyadic relationships are not a recent innovation, even though the way people perceive them may have changed.

Let us turn now to the present: are personal networks changing in a world in which means of communications are very rapidly becoming increasingly sophisticated? The problem is that we have very little perspective and very few reliable studies on the subject. Consequently, all we can do (in some cases) is outline a few trends and (more usually) put forward some hypotheses by drawing on findings on the evolution of social networks in general and the effects of earlier electronic means of communication (email, instant messaging, and so on).

---

[12] C. S. Fischer, *Still Connected: Family and Friends in America since 1970* (New York: Russell Sage Foundation, 2011).

[13] L. Rainie, B. Wellman, *Networked: The New Social Operating System* (Cambridge, MA: MIT Press, 2012).

IS THE WORLD SMALLER?

One way of approaching the recent evolution of social networks is to examine quantifiable indicators such as connectivity (the relative ease of contacting an unknown person within the global network) and the size of personal networks.

This is the standard "small world" question.[14] It has been known since the 1960s and the famous study by the psychologist Stanley Milgram[15] that social networks have a particular structure, one that is characterized by a high degree of connectivity: relatively few intermediaries are needed (around five in Milgram's study) to reach any point in a network. This question applies only indirectly to personal networks. Rather, it concerns what are known as "large networks" or relational chains. It is addressed here because a number of interesting studies are becoming available that draw on data on users of social networking services such as Facebook and Twitter as well as MSN instant messaging.[16] These studies suggest that the average number of intermediaries is slightly lower than in Milgram's study (between three and five). This finding has sparked a number of hasty comments about the shrinking of the social world. In light of the differences in the construction of the data and the populations investigated, all that can be said is that the order of magnitude is similar and that the structure is indeed a "small world" one.[17]

DOES THE EXISTENCE OF ELECTRONIC MEANS OF COMMUNICATION INFLUENCE THE SIZE OF PERSONAL SOCIAL NETWORKS?

The orders of magnitude established by the surveys have been noted. They are as follows: a few close relationships with people with whom one is willing to share important things, even secrets; 15 people, if those to whom one speaks regularly in the course of a month are added; between 40 and 50 relationships if the people whom one sees in the course of various

---

[14] For a review of research on this subject, see Sebastian Schnettler, "A Structured Overview of 50 years of Small-World Research," *Social Networks* 31 (2009), 165–178.

[15] Milgram, "The Small World Problem," *Pscyhology Today* 1 (1967), 61–67.

[16] L. Backstrom, P. Boldi, M. Rosa, J. Ugander, S. Vigna, "Four Degrees of Separation," (2012), http://arxiv.org/abs/1111.4570.

[17] In general, it is considered that below sixteen intermediaries, which would equate to a network structure in which the ties were random, networks are indeed "small-world" structures.

activities are included; between 100 and 200 ties if we add the people whom one seldom sees but who could be asked to make introductions; and, finally, more than 1,000 if we count the people encountered in the course of life whose names one knows and who could be contacted on the basis of past interactions. We should add that some psychologists believe there is a cognitive limit of about 150 on the number of stable ties that can be maintained at the same time.[18]

What about changes in the size of personal networks? A recent controversy divided opinion among network analysts on the evolution of the first of these circles, that of the confidants. In their analysis of data from the General Social Survey (GSS), the large-scale social survey conducted regularly in the United States, three authors observed a decline (rounding down, from three on average to two) between 1985 and 2004 in the number of people with whom respondents discussed "important matters." They concluded from this that social isolation was on the increase.[19] Their analysis was critiqued by Claude Fischer, who took them to task for not having taken account of methodology effects that explained the apparent variations.[20] Lee Rainie and Barry Wellman also critiqued this article using findings from the Pew Research Center surveys in the book cited above (see note 13). One of the surveys carried out by that organization in 2002 does, after all, include the same question as that in the GSS.[21] Rainie and Wellman draw on this study to argue that, while the results are similar to those of the GSS (an average close to two), significantly fewer people mentioned no names at all and, in particular, that Internet and mobile telephone users cited more names and were less likely to be "isolated" (no names mentioned). Referring similarly to the GSS, Zhao concludes that internet users and, to an even greater extent, heavy email users, have more

---

[18] R. I. M. Dunbar, "Coevolution of Neocortical Size, Group Size and Language in Humans," *Behavioral and Brain Sciences* 16(4) (1993), 681–735; R. A. Hill, R. I. M. Dunbar, "Social Network Size in Humans," *Human Nature* 14(1) (2002), 53–72.

[19] M. McPherson, L. Smith-Lovin, M. E. Brashears, "Social Isolation in America: Changes in Core Discussion Networks over Two Decades," *American Sociological Review* 71 (2006), 353–375.

[20] C. S. Fischer, "The 2004 GSS Finding of Shrunken Social Networks: An Artifact?," *American Sociological Review* 74(4) (2009), 657–669. See also the authors' response: M. McPherson, L. Smith-Lovin, M. E. Brashears, "Reply to Fischer: Models and Marginals: Using Survey Evidence to Study Social Networks," *American Sociological Review* 74(4) (2009), 670–681.

[21] K. N. Hampton, L. F. Sessions, E. J. Her, L. Rainie, "Social Isolation and New Technology," *Pew Internet & American Life Project* (2009), www.pewinternet.org/Reports/2009/18-Social-Isolation-and-New-Technology.aspx.

social contacts than non-users, both online and offline. Only users of instant messaging services keep their ties exclusively online, which prompts him to argue that analyses should be differentiated depending on the systems and technologies being used.[22] Confidential questions were also used in the GSS in 2010 with information on investigators. Researchers analyzing the results show that the number of names cited is very sensitive to investigator effects and recommend that this indicator no longer be used.[23]

In the 2001 Toulouse survey, one of the name generators, in particular, was very similar to that in the GSS. It concerned people with whom respondents were able to discuss "personal problems." The average number of names cited in response to this question was 2.6 (from 0 to 12). For the 18–25 age group (49 respondents), the average was 3.8. In the 2014 survey of young people aged between 15 and 25, if only the same age group is considered (18–25, 1,116 respondents), the name generators on sharing music, important relationships, and online encounters generated on average slightly more than four relationships, with three of whom respondents believed they could discuss "important matters." The difference in methods and the small size of the 2001 sample make precise comparison difficult, but the order of magnitude is similar. If the 2001 question (discussion of "personal problems") can be regarded as close to the notion of "confidant" that was being alluded to in mentioning discussion of "important matters," then the balance tips slightly in favor of a reduction rather similar to that observed in the GSS. However, that is a mere hypothesis.[24]

---

[22] Z. Shanyang, "Do Internet Users Have More Social Ties? A Call for Differentiated Analysis of Internet Use," *Journal of Computer-Mediated Communication* 11 (2006), 844–862.

[23] A. Paik, K. Sanchagrin, "Social Isolation in America: An Artifact," *American Sociological Review* 78(3) (2013), 339–360.

[24] On the basis of these data, these two surveys can be compared with that carried out by the Pew Research Center. In order to do this, the cases where we have more than five names cited have to be recoded in the same way as in the American survey, in which the number of names was limited to a maximum of five. By doing that, we obtain a total of 3.2 names for discussions of "personal problems" for the 2001 survey and 2.7 names for discussion of "important matters" for the 2014 survey. For the same age group (18–25), the average obtained in the American survey was 1.8 (for 275 respondents in this age group, without weighting). The survey of over-60s in the Toulouse area tends in the same direction: slightly fewer than 27 percent of the respondents cited no names in response to the question about persons with whom they could speak about important matters, whereas the share for the same age group in the American survey was 30 percent. All this suggests

In the 2001 survey, finally, those respondents who used email with at least one of the individuals they cited had more relationships than the others. In the 2014 survey, furthermore, those respondents who also had at least one of the individuals they named as a "friend" on a digital social networking site (generally Facebook) had more relationships in general than the others and also more relationships that enabled them to discuss important matters (3 on average, compared with 1.1).[25] These results are consistent with those obtained by Rainie and Wellman. Facebook users are even said to be more involved in community activities, to maintain or even strengthen face-to-face relationships, and to have more social support.[26] However, this hypothesis has given rise to some debate. After all, internet use spread from the higher social categories to the lower ones and from young to old, which may help to explain why social inequalities in terms of offline sociability have been reproduced in online interaction.[27] Thus, it is not the Internet, it is argued, that fosters sociability and solidarity, as the "cyber-optimists" say, but rather its diffusion that has followed the same tendencies as those governing social inequalities in relations in general: internet users are better educated, wealthier, and younger. After all, the 2014 Toulouse survey also shows that, while 15–25 year-olds make extensive use of social networking sites in order to maintain their relationships with people of their own age group (in 84 percent of cases, the age gap between Alters and respondents was less than five years) and younger, this is less the case with older people (39 percent were at least five years older). In any event, the effects of age and time period must be closely investigated and isolated.

As far the other levels of relationship are concerned, particularly weaker ties, few studies are available. Mention should be made, nevertheless, of a meta-analysis carried out by a team of German psychologists of 277 surveys of personal networks conducted between 1978 and 2012.[28] According to these authors, the networks observed diminished in size over the period

---

differences tending in the same direction as the comparison between our 2001 survey and Fischer's, namely, toward fewer isolated individuals in France.

[25] The difference is still significant when parents' educational level is neutralized.

[26] B. Wellman, A. Quan-Haase, J. Witte, K. Hampton, "Does the Internet Increase, Decrease, or Supplement Social Capital? Social Networks, Participation, and Community Commitment," *American Behavioral Scientist* 45(3) (2001), 436–455

[27] N. H. Nie, "Sociability, Interpersonal Relations, and the Internet: Reconciling Conflicting Findings," *American Behavioral Scientist* 45(3) (2001), 420–435.

[28] C. Wrzus, M. Hänel, J. Wagner, F. J. Neyer, "Social Network Changes and Life Events across the Lifespan: A Meta-Analysis," *Psychological Bulletin* 139 (2013), 53–80.

during which these surveys were conducted, except in the case of family ties. Thus, their arguments tend in the same direction as that of the authors who believe that the number of confidants is declining.

The upshot of these various studies is that we still do not know whether or not there has been a significant change in the number of confidants and, more generally, of strong ties. If there has been a decline, however, then those who are kitted out with the most advanced means of communication are better protected against it than the others. Thus, the following hypothesis begins to take shape: there has been a reduction in the number of strong ties and an increase in isolation in the least advantaged social categories (who are on average less well "kitted out," or at least they were at the beginning of the 2000s) and hence an increase in relational inequalities in a context in which there has been a slight reduction generally in strong ties.

For the other types of ties, there are few very persuasive studies. It is possible (probable even) that the reduction in strong ties has been counterbalanced by an increase in weak ties: it would appear that, with the help of the new communication tools, people tend, through sporadic interactions, to keep alive more of the weak ties that in the past could easily have become dormant. However, many recent studies show that there is not necessarily any compensatory relationship between online and offline ties or between strong and weak ties. On the basis of a literature review on the subject, Scott Campbell concludes that: "mobile communication indeed favors close personal ties, but not necessarily at the expense of network breadth."[29] Two representative surveys conducted in Great Britain show that network size is not really changed by the use of digital technologies and also that online networks are ultimately shaped by constraints and tendencies similar to those that shape offline networks. They remain firmly rooted in contexts and, as far as strong ties are concerned, replicate the communication behaviors of offline networks. Only relatively few networks have greater numbers of weak ties, particularly among young people. Adults, for their part, pay greater attention to the quality of ties.[30]

---

[29] C. W. Scott, "Mobile Communication and Network Privatism: A Literature Review of the Implications for Diverse, Weak, and New Ties," *Review of Communication Research* 3(1) (2015), 18.

[30] R .I. M. Dunbar, "Do Online Social Media Cut through the Constraints That Limit the Size of Offline Social Networks?" *Royal Society Publishing Open Science* (2016), https://doi.org/10.1098/rsos.150292.

ONLINE ENCOUNTERS?

Online activities involve interactions with strangers, and these interactions can lead to relationships. What is more, there are sites designed specifically to enable people to meet each other, whether for romantic or sexual purposes or simply to share common interests and activities.

An American survey published in 2015 found that 57 percent of 13–17 year-olds had established friendships on the Internet (the share for boys was slightly higher, particularly through video games).[31] A rather older study found that from the 2000s onward, 22 percent of American couples had got together after meeting online. The proportion was significantly higher for gay couples (over 60%).[32]

In a French survey carried out in 2014, 27 percent of respondents said they had formed new relationships thanks to the Internet, the proportion among 18–24 year-olds being 54percent.[33] In the same survey, 10 percent of respondents declared they had had a romantic encounter initiated through the Internet. Another survey[34] found that 9 percent of French couples who had got together between 2005 and 2013 had first met online, with the share reaching more than 30 percent for gay couples.

In our 2014 survey of 15–25 year-olds, there were 566 couples in all. The proportion who had met online was 6.5 percent but rose to 22 percent for gay couples. In our survey of over-60s, only one of the more than 6,000 relationships had started online (it led to the formation of a couple).

An additional wave of the Caen survey carried out in 2015 provides some information on the use of Facebook by respondents now in their forties[35] and how it compares with their offline relationships. The majority of them denied that they had "friends" on Facebook whom they had never previously met. Thus, the share of "friends" met on Facebook was marginal and in the majority of cases they were introduced through third parties,

---

[31] A. Lenhart, A. Smith, M. Anderson, M. Duggan, A. Perrin, "Teens, Technology and Friendships," Pew Research Center, August (2015), www.pewinternet.org/2015/08/06/teens-technology-and-friendships/.

[32] M. Rosenfeld, R. Thomas, "Searching for a Mate: The Rise of the Internet As a Social Intermediary," *American Sociological Review* 77(4) (2012), 523–547.

[33] www.arcep.fr/uploads/tx_gspublication/etude-CREDOC-diffusion-TIC-2014.pdf.

[34] M. Bergström, "Sites de rencontres : qui les utilise en France? Qui y trouve son conjoint?," *Population & Sociétés* 530 (2016), www.ined.fr/fichier/s_rubrique/25008/population.societes.530.site.rencontres.conjoint.fr.pdf.

[35] Seventeen individuals who were users or former Facebook users were questioned, their relational networks reconstituted again using the same procedure and their practices explained at length in an additional module of the interviews.

making them friends of friends or of acquaintances. Thus, it took the combined effect of a pre-existing network and Facebook for a relationship to be forged. This is undoubtedly a major difference between this group and the teenagers, although even for the latter group contexts are also important.

On the other hand, new relationships forged via Facebook are more numerous among certain forty-somethings, typically artists or freelancers and self-employed workers in general, who use it strategically as a resource for their work. These users are aware of the stock of readily identifiable and accessible resources that Facebook offers, the selection it makes possible depending on the interests posted, and the community-building it facilitates. They often end up meeting in person, particularly since most Facebook "friends" tend to live nearby. Thus, context, occupational status, cultural identity, and spatial proximity, but above all, their combined effect, are still relevant. Facebook amplifies and accelerates their selection effects as a number of "useful" relationships develop. It helps to highlight the fact that social ties can function as resources. Many Facebook "friends" are clearly taken on for utilitarian purposes, which is much rarer (and morally frowned upon) in the case of face-to-face relationships. Even for others, respondents are often looking for "something of value" in their Facebook friends' publications and the practical or cultural discoveries they make possible, and links regarded as "of no interest or value" are removed from time to time.

Facebook also brings out "latent" or potential ties situated within social circles. By providing immediate access to a large quantity of information on the profile, it enables users to identify a colleague in a business, a cousin in a large family or a friend's husband. This tie can then be registered and easily contacted. This functionality is undoubtedly more important and discriminating for forty-somethings, who tend to individualize relationships, than for young people, who approach them in a more collective and undifferentiated way.

Very many people also look for and find childhood friends on Facebook. In this case, the interpersonal relationship in question already has a history but has dropped "out of sight." However, a process of selection comes into play very quickly following the initial resumption of contact, in which the profile information and posts will be decisive. After all, some of these reactivated dormant ties will not get past the hurdle of shared tastes and interests as revealed in a user's posts and very quickly become dormant again. Thus, these reactivated relationships are also subordinated to the contexts of everyday life: either they become part of them if they are compatible with current interests or they become dormant again. Thus, the emergence of new relationships on Facebook is far from being something apart from the contexts of everyday life. We are not dealing with a separate, virtual universe. On the contrary: the effects of pre-existing networks and of visual contact, the specific nature of certain occupational milieus or leisure activities, the resource function, which proves to be central here, and the selection processes that have taken place all root Facebook in the real social world.

THE EMERGENCE OF "VERY WEAK TIES"?

Rather than being part of an ill-defined crowd or social circle, ties on Facebook are named, individualized, and immediately contactable without commitment. Above all, however, and this is another specific feature of Facebook, a considerable volume and variety of information can be accessed immediately. It would take several months or even years to exchange such a volume of information in a face-to-face relationship. It would even be unthinkable to broach certain subjects in relationships that are frequently routinized. True, this information is biased: users display only what they want to display. But even if it is biased, it still plays a crucial role in determining whether a relationship is to be pursued or abandoned. What takes place on Facebook is a dense, many-sided process of disclosure; it costs little and is further augmented by the fact that this information is not controlled. Thus, many people discover that their "friend" also loves boxing, Japanese literature, or permaculture. The most inquisitive Facebook users draw on the wide range of information posted by their "friends" to fashion a sort of customized magazine for themselves. This volume of information is sometimes the only motivation, the only driving force for these online relationships.

In many cases, after all, these "friends" who have been discovered or rediscovered on Facebook often come with less emotional "baggage" than friends one meets face-to-face. The expressions used in talking about them can be unappealing and often disparaging. Some are described as "enforced," particularly the spouses of friends or relatives. Interactions are limited for the most part to birthday greetings, posting a "like" from time to time or making use of the resource that has been identified. These "friends" have little history or commitment, but also little perspective. The exchanges are not always sufficient to become a genuinely committed and durable relationship, as Solange described:

You have the impression of knowing each other without knowing each other, of following their lives without seeing them . . .. It's nice at the time, but that's not necessarily going to bring us closer together. At the moment, it hasn't necessarily brought me close to anyone.

Whereas a relationship implies a commitment to recognize each other and to pick up the thread of that accumulated acquaintanceship when next the occasion presents itself, it is perfectly possible on Facebook to consider not sharing anything more, to freeze a relationship, or even to leave it to one side out of sheer inertia. Thus, Facebook also serves as a sort of relational "antechamber": contact is made, and then one waits to see if the feeling is mutual, if the information gleaned is useful or relevant, if the person has the same tastes, if there are reasons to revive a dormant link, if the contact can go any further. If this is the case, then the exchange can be sustained and the relationship supplemented with this information, which can lead in turn to the emergence of new topics of conversation. If not, then the link may simply lie moldering "in a corner" or be gently removed. The strength of Facebook may be that, among other things, it occupies that space between the crowd or social circle, on the one hand, and, on the other, relationships that have become solidified by a history played out in social contexts. Ties established or revived online, which tend to be centered more on exchanges of information and resources, often remain online. Nevertheless, they are certainly real relationships if the exchanges are sustained over a minimum length of time, but they are more strategic, more fragile, and less emotionally charged than face-to-face relationships. Ultimately, Facebook widens the gap between strong and weak ties: it supports the selection processes that constitute the formers' specificity (especially for the forty-somethings) while at the same time boosting the flows of information from diverse sources that constitute the specificity of the latter.

THE HOMOPHILY OF ONLINE TIES

Another question that the use of online tools might raise is whether or not it changes the relational selection process: are these ties more or less similar, and by what criteria? This brings us back to the issue of homophily or, to put it another way, the preference for people who are "the same as oneself."

A study of 980 Israeli adolescents shows that relationships forged on the Internet are on average slightly weaker and a little less homophilic in terms of gender and that they bring together individuals located further apart from each other spatially; on the other hand, when they are homophilic in terms of gender, then they are stronger.[36] Another study comparing personal networks obtained by means of standard name generators and the Facebook networks of the same respondents (212 American college students, aged 21 on average) seems to show that the latter are more homophilic in terms of race.[37] It is known that online dating sites provide information on the social characteristics of the individuals who register with them, which should encourage homophily (homogamy when dating leads to the establishment of a couple, except for gender and age, where the difference is normed). However, it is also known that some people use these sites for more transient encounters, for which social characteristics are less discriminating than physical appearance or availability.

Over and above variations in methods and survey environment, therefore, these surveys coincide on a number of points. The first point is that online interactions have become an important context for the establishment of interpersonal relationships, particularly romantic relationships. The second point is that the diffusion of social networking sites is ongoing and that in 2015 frequency of use varied very significantly with age. The third point is that the establishment of interpersonal relationships through online contact is particularly significant in the case of encounters involving forms of homophily for which partners are scarce, which can be seen in the high rate of online contacts for homosexual relationships. All of this suggests that the increased opportunities electronic media provide have served to strengthen the adjustments between individuals' interests and tastes, leading to the establishment of more homophilic relationships. Above and beyond couples' gender homophily, it is very probable that the same phenomenon also fosters homophily in terms of educational level and social status, and hence also greater segregation based on the same criteria. Kobayashi and Boase even suggest there is an association between the frequency of texting and a decline in the tolerance of diversity of

---

[36] G. de Mesch, I. Talmud, *Similarity and Quality of Social Relationships among Adolescents* (Haifa: The University of Haifa, 2000).

[37] N. Park, S. Lee, J. H. Kim, "Individuals' Personal Network Characteristics and Patterns of Facebook Use: A Social Network Approach," *Computers in Human Behavior* 28 (2012), 1700–1707. See also E. Hargittai, "Whose Space? Differences among Users and Non-users of Social Network Sites," *Journal of Computer-Mediated Communication*, 13(1) (2007), 276–297.

opinions among young Japanese.[38] Other authors have studied personal networks of 3,000 Dutch teenagers from Facebook. For them, Facebook's extensive networks have much the same characteristics as the core networks usually studied, but are slightly less segregated in terms of gender and ethnicity.[39]

As we have seen, what takes place on Facebook is a dense, many-sided process of disclosure; it costs little and is further augmented by the fact that the information made available is not controlled. Thus, the selection factors are both more numerous and more varied than those usually measured in surveys. The attraction to certain profiles rather than others is often based on subtle cultural distinctions. However, eclectic mixes are precisely what constitutes many contemporary cultures. The sharing of common interests in leisure activities, technologies, the arts, etc. will play a very important filtering role in shaping sociability, alongside social milieu and level of education.

As we saw in Chapter 9, another way of approaching the changes in homophily is to observe homogamy, which has been investigated for longer and more systematically. In France between the 1970s and the 1990s, homogamy related to social origin declined but that related to educational level did not.[40] There is no research that enables us to determine whether couples who get together after meeting online are more homogamous. As far as homophily more generally is concerned, there are few findings available. In a comparison of various surveys, a French researcher suggests that homophily based on socio-occupational category has declined but that "homophily based on age has increased."[41]

It might reasonably be hypothesized that homophily is following the same trend as homogamy, which has remained the same for educational level but declined for socio-occupational categories as a result of changes to

---

[38] T. Kobayashi, J. Boase, "Tele-cocooning: Mobile Texting and Social Scope," *Journal of Computer-Mediated Communication* 19(3) (2014), 681–694.

[39] B. Hofstra, R. Corten, F. van Tubergen, N. B. Ellison, "Sources of Segregation in Social Networks: A Novel Approach Using Facebook," *American Sociological Review* 82(3) (2017), 625–656.

[40] M. Forsé, L. Chauvel, "L'évolution de l'homogamie en France: Une méthode pour comparer les diagonalités de plusieurs tables," *Revue Française de Sociologie* 36(1) (1995), 123–142. See also M. Bouchet-Valat, "Patterns and Trends of Educational and Occupational Homogamy: Evidence for France Based on Yearly Surveys (1969–2011)," Spring conference of the Research Committee on Social Stratification and Mobility (RC28), Trento (Italy), May 18, 2013.

[41] O. Godechot, "Plus d'amis, plus proches? Essai de comparaison de deux enquêtes peu comparables," *Document INSEE*, no. 0004 (2000), 40.

their structure, which has become more diverse and less easily reducible to a hierarchy than in the past. Fischer's survey, which focused on the effects of mass urbanization on the forms of social solidarity, showed that urban dwellers' networks were a little different from those of people in rural areas (who were supposed to represent the past). The former were less dense and composed of more homophilic relationships in terms of age (young urban dwellers spent less time with older people), educational level (the more highly qualified were less likely to spend time with those with few qualifications), and occupation. Urban dwellers saw less of their neighbors and families but said they had more friends.

One of the ways of interpreting these differences is to say that urban dwelling lowers the constraints on interactions, thereby making people freer to construct their relationships. When the material and social restrictions that enforce a certain degree of diversity are lifted and when geographical distance and linguistic and other barriers exert less influence on interactions, there are more opportunities to establish homophilic relationships, that is, to be free to choose friends with similar tastes and behaviors. When relationships are more freely chosen, there is greater scope for genuine affinities to come into play. As a result, relationships tend to be more homophilic. This is particularly the case with tools such as Facebook, which give immediate access to a much greater diversity of options and milieus than even towns and cities could offer.

As far as network structure is concerned, it is probable that the evolution of communication technologies has had an effect similar to that of urbanization described by Fischer. It emerged from research carried out more than fifteen years ago on the use of the Internet for the purpose of establishing relationships[42] that intensive internet users tended to have less dense networks than non-users. As with improvements in transportation, therefore, the use of electronic communications tends to increase homophily and to disperse relationships more widely, particularly among the most highly educated segment of the population, by making it possible to maintain distant homophilic relationships.

COMMUNICATING FROM AFAR . . . OR FROM NEARBY

The telephone is one of the most commonly used means of long-distance communication, but it has undergone significant changes in the last twenty

---

[42] M. Grossetti, "Communication électronique et réseaux sociaux," *Flux* 29 (1998), 5–13.

years. Zbigniew Smoreda has summarized the results of several studies of the link between network geography and use of the telephone in its various forms (landline or mobile).[43] He sums up one key finding in a very simple expression: "The more time you spend together, the more you talk on the phone." The telephone is not a substitute for face-to-face interaction; rather, it supplements such contact and sometimes makes it easier. Smoreda shows that, in all the surveys, telephone use becomes significantly less frequent beyond a distance of about thirty miles and extremely infrequent when the two parties are not in the same country, whereas "snail mail" and email remain heavily used, albeit at somewhat reduced levels. However, these surveys were conducted before applications, such as Skype, which allow users to communicate by voice and video over the Internet, came into widespread use. By making long-distance exchanges easier, the Internet has also reshaped the technical environment within which ties are maintained.[44] In an experiment in Ethiopia, researchers gave telephones to members of a rural community. They show that this speeds up exchanges but that calls remain local for day-to-day coordination.[45]

Moreover, as Zbigniew Smoreda shows, the various means of communication tend to coexist rather than replace each other: those to whom we write tend also to be those with whom we speak on the telephone (65 percent of those with whom the Toulouse respondents telephoned several times a week also exchanged emails with them several times a week; the percentage in the opposite direction was 86 percent. For face-to-face exchanges, the corresponding percentages were 53 percent and 79 percent). The people with whom one communicates a great deal are those to whom one feels close – their strong ties. Modern telecommunications technologies seem mainly to be used as a means of maintaining such ties better when the parties live far apart, which is not necessarily reflected in any significant spatial expansion of networks.[46] Even with online relationships, space is important. In a recent article presenting the findings of an analysis

---

[43] Z. Smoreda, "*Sociabilités ordinaires, réseaux sociaux et médiations des technologies de communication,*" PhD thesis, Université Paris-Est (2008).

[44] See, in particular, C. Licoppe, Z. Smoreda, "Are Social Networks Technologically Embedded? How Networks Are Changing Today with Changes in Communication Technology," *Social Networks* 27(4) (2005), 317–335.

[45] P. Matou, Y. Todo, T. Ishikawa, "Emergence of Multiplex Mobile Phone Communication Networks across Rural Areas: An Ethiopian Experiment," *Network Science* 2(2) (2014), 162–188.

[46] See the synthesis article by D. Mok, B. Wellman, J. Carrasco, "Does Distance Matter in the Age of the Internet?," *Urban Studies* 47(13) (2010), 2747–2783.

of a German social networking site similar to Facebook, the authors observed that the variable that best explains the existence of ties is geographical distance: measuring distance in car travel time, the number of people named drops by 91 percent for each additional 100 minutes traveled.[47]

COMMUNICATING MORE QUICKLY, STAYING PERMANENTLY CONNECTED

The main change wrought by electronic communications technologies seems to concern the timing of interchanges. Simplifying things somewhat, it could be said that digital technologies do not so much expand space as accelerate time. Communication is made so easy that all ties are potentially accessible all the time, leading to virtually continuous interchanges where previously interactions were separated by intervals during which people were more or less uncontactable.[48] It would certainly seem that social relations are evolving toward the notion of permanent contactability; ties that used to be activated from time to time between periods of variable length when no interactions took place are becoming "permanently accessible," using weak signals to draw attention to themselves.

The proliferation of means of communication enables individuals to manage their relationships and ways of engaging with others in a more sophisticated way than in the past, when many relationships could all too easily be reduced to relational roles (family, neighbors, colleagues, friends, etc.). This sophistication has probably gone hand in hand with increased reflexivity regarding ties and social networks. People develop a certain conception of their networks and their popularity based on their contacts list, the frequency of their calls, and the links offered by Facebook.[49] This may foster more strategic relational behaviors, which, in turn, may

[47] C. Lee, T. Scherngell, M. J. Barber, "Investigating an Online Social Network Using Spatial Interaction Models," *Social Networks* 33 (2011), 129–133.

[48] C. Licoppe, "Two Modes of Maintaining Interpersonal Relations through Telephone: From the Domestic to the Mobile Phone" in J. Katz (ed) *Machines That Become Us: The Social context of Communication Technology* (New Brunswick: Transaction Publishers, 2002), pp. 171–186.

[49] This is particularly true of adolescents: see D. Boyd, "Why Youth (Heart) Social Network Sites: The Role of Networked Publics in Teenage Social Life," in David Buckingham (ed.) *Youth, Identity, and Digital Media Volume* (Cambridge, MA: MIT Press, 2007); and I. Mizuko, S. Baumer, M. Bittanti, D. Boyd, R. Cody, B. Herr, H. A. Horst, P. G. Lange, D. Mahendran, K. Martinez, C. J. Pascoe, D. Perkel, L. Robinson, C. Sims, and L. Tripp (with J. Antin, M. Finn, A. Law, A. Manion, S. Mitnick, D. Schlossberg, S. Yardi), *Hanging*

exacerbate a fundamental paradox of social relations, namely, the fact that sociability appears to be intrinsically disinterested while at the same time constituting an essential social resource. Ambivalence, a fundamental component of social ties, prevents this contradiction from making social life impossible. Thus, "demystifying" ties may prove to be problematic. Nevertheless, it can be imagined that users of these platforms would be able to invent new ways of recreating this ambivalence, if only by dividing "friends" into groups, selecting options, etc.

It remains the case that a new category of very weak ties may be emerging and becoming established, ones that are emotionally unengaged but directly geared to the circulation of informational resources at least. They are usually kept in reserve and remain relatively inactive; in some cases, they are transient but they undoubtedly constitute a form of social capital in the true sense, particularly potential. However, the effectiveness of these resources, particularly in the event of real need or an emergency, remains to be proven, since the tie is not substantiated by a shared history, experience, the social norm, indebtedness, or trust – all factors that could help to trigger a desire to help.

*

* *

If we extrapolate from these trends and hypotheses, it might be thought that social networking platforms are not going to change personal networks radically. They make them more tangible and more manipulable. It is likely that they encourage the rapid renewal of the weakest ties and the diversification of relational experiences. They probably also reinforce the more general trends in the evolution of interpersonal relations and networks that developed with urbanization, although the surveys do not permit much in the way of historical generalizations. These trends have multiple causes, which can in no way be reduced to the changes in means of communication but also include changes in the education and earnings hierarchies, family structures, flows of goods and ideas, and collective commitments. While we may reasonably not agree completely with Wellman's theory that "a social network revolution" took place after the Second

Out, Messing Around, Geeking Out: Living and Learning with New Media (Cambridge, MA: MIT Press, 2009).

World War, we can agree that the Internet and mobile phones have strengthened the dynamics at work in social relations in general.

Thus, the effect of digital networks on social networks is simply to extend the scope of the changes already taking place, which are linked to many other factors. These changes seem to be tending in the direction of a slight reduction in strong ties, an increase in weak or even very weak ties and, in particular, a strengthening of relational inequalities and homophily. Whether digital or not, networks help to reinforce social inequalities and tend to encourage the formation of like-minded groups and increased social segregation. The hypothesis that digital platforms are a sort of extension of urbanism still seems interesting. If this were so, the development of digital platforms would amplify the tendencies already observed in the transition from rural to urban dwelling. We would then be heading toward a better equipped and more connected world, with more frequent, more continuous, and quicker communications, but one that is perhaps more segregated. This suggests that it would be useful to combine, to a greater extent than hitherto, analyses of networks, both online and offline, with investigation of the ways in which ties are embedded in geographical and social space.

However, just as the social world in general is not made up solely of interpersonal relationships, so the Internet and mobile phones do not exclusively support dyadic ties. They may also foster the establishment of groups and of new forms of democracy.[50] In order better to assess whether the prevailing tendency will be toward the formation of like-minded groups or toward greater embeddedness in collective forms, further empirical studies will be required.

---

[50] D. Cardon, *La démocratie internet. Promesses et limites* (Paris: Seuil, 2010); M.-L. Geoffray, *Contester à Cuba* (Paris: Dalloz, 2012).

Conclusion

Relationships are an intrinsic part of people's life histories and are themselves histories. They are born and then undergo change, becoming specialized or generalized, stronger or dormant before eventually dying. To consider a relationship at a given point in time is like pausing a film and freezing a frame. However, the story of an encounter and the subsequent relationship generally constitutes the most important aspect of its current existence. A relationship's current content is an expression of the experiences, memories, emotions, trust, and changes that have accumulated over time. This content determines in turn its future, its durability, and its development. The relationship extends a longer or shorter distance into the future, evidence of a commitment, which, being tantamount to a promise, also gives it its current color and substance.

The overall configuration of individuals' networks also evolves. They shrink or expand, become dissociated, polarized or recentered. Their form depends on the fate of each relationship and on the renewal of their various elements as well as on structural dynamics that form gradually changing combinations. Gaps widen, bridges form, connections multiply, groups split up, and the overall system changes profile. It becomes more cohesive or more diversified, surrounding the individual with a homogeneous cocoon or a multi-faceted mirror offering him or her a range of options.

Personal histories leave their imprint on relationships and networks, and the interconnections between them tell of unions, separations, withdrawal, reconciliation, fracture lines, and adjustments that go beyond these individuals. For, as we have seen, relationships are not created just anywhere, at just any time or with just anybody. Society, with its divisions, marks out relational landscapes, cities and neighborhoods, occupations and leisure activities, styles and families, cultures, social circles, and divides that "sift out" the possible contacts and the unlikely encounters. However, this relational landscape does not do everything: some relationships cross the metaphorical mountains formed by social groups or the passage of time; they defy boundaries and bear witness to the room for maneuver individuals enjoy in matters of sociability. Although they tend to follow certain patterns, which it is the sociologist's job to reveal, relational choices can be neither wholly reduced to nor rendered fully stable by those patterns. A network is always a complex combinatorial structure, characterized by diversity as well as by selection and influence.

It is true, as we have seen, that educational level and occupation continue to exert their influence, even when "cushioned" by these relational choices and their particular dispositions. In general terms, the networks of the wealthy and those of the poor differ from each other, and sometimes even reinforce social inequalities. However, we have also seen that life histories, events, and chance encounters can modify network profiles and temper the influence of individual endowments and their reproduction. Travel to distant places, a love affair, or joining a band can reverse a social destiny and enrich or reconstruct a relational environment that will help to put a life trajectory on a different course. Personal networks are both the fruit of and the breeding ground for social trajectories. In this respect, they constitute an "intermediate level" between the individual and society; our objective in this book has been to shed light on the evolution of such networks by putting into practice the principles of a sociology of relational dynamics.

To that end, we decided not to separate relationships and networks from the worlds and constructs they pass through but rather to analyze their dynamics as they become decoupled, embedded, individuated, or connected with each other. The complexity of the social world cannot, after all, be reduced to relationships and networks alone. They are in constant interaction with contexts, social circles, and organizations, which, with the various forms of segmentation and social hierarchies that accompany them, leave their mark on the very birth of social ties, on individual preferences, on affinities, and on relational cultures. Formalized institutions and organizations are connected to relationships and networks while at the same time maintaining a certain autonomy, even though their boundaries are porous. Nor are social circles, which are more fluid, to be confused with systems of bonds or ties; rather, they testify to a "common motivation" that transcends the individuals that constitute them. Any investigation of network dynamics must consider these connections, otherwise it reveals only a skeleton whose actions and development remain poorly understood. Thus, our aim here has been to give some examples of this constantly moving substance and to outline some significant sequences. From this point of view, our contribution lies perhaps above all in the empirically based construction of concepts and tools that can be used to analyze relational dynamics. This exercise may lead to deliberations that are sometimes complex; nevertheless, it remains essential to an understanding of reality that is neither overly simplistic nor reductive and that is not limited to conceptual promises either. It is certainly challenging, if only from the point of view of conceptual clarity and the reader's peace of mind, to investigate relationships and networks concurrently, without isolating them from the contexts, without ignoring the impact of individual attributes, without emptying ties of all their substance and leaving only the pipes visible, without forgetting the relevance of the overall structure but without ignoring its sensitivity to life events, and all the while adopting a dynamic perspective. However, this is where our experiences and dissatisfaction as researchers have taken us.

In the tradition of network analysis, and particularly studies of personal networks, on which we have drawn extensively in analyzing our own data, we have not sought to nurture a sociology of sociability in which social relations are merely practices like any others that can be analyzed on the basis of variables such as age, gender, or level of education. Rather, we have adopted a "relational" approach to the social world, which considers the dynamics of relationships between social entities rather than their distribution within a static space. This undertaking was inspired by the hypothesis that interactions (between individuals, between groups and institutions as well as between social facts themselves) produce social forms capable of sustaining themselves on a long-term basis.

Of course, no survey, not even a longitudinal one, is able to reveal the emergence of or transformations taking place in large social structures, such as nations or institutions. However, in observing encounters, interactions, and relationships between individuals, we have been able to see changes emerging that have a profound effect on their lives, their choices, their trajectories, and their social rootedness. Their relational environments and identifications change together depending on their position in the life cycle or the impact of unforeseen events. Forms of solidarity and modes of social contact change, relationship configurations become more or less centered or dissociated, and network profiles evolve with the passage of time and as a result of events and setbacks.

This approach gives full recognition to individuals, who are not merely mediums for the transmission of information drawn from a random survey but real individuals observed in their relational environments, which change and that they change. Chance plays a part in these analyses, with individual action remaining central. However, in order to go beyond the case study stage and build up, with others, a deep understanding of relational dynamics, more has to be known about relations between individuals and, more generally, between what Harrison White calls identities.[1] It is to this knowledge that we wanted to make our modest contribution by identifying dynamics, analyzing sequences, and locating relational tendencies likely to acquire a degree of generality by virtue of their possible recurrence and reproducibility. Other individuals in a similar life sequence might experience comparable dynamics as their relationships become decoupled, multiplex, or individuated and their networks become centralized or dissociated. This is what we invite our colleagues to test after us.

Relational surveys are more difficult to carry out than opinion polls or behavioral surveys. This is why they are rare; however, they are the only way to improve understanding of relations between individuals and between social entities. Consequently, it is important to emphasize the methodological rigor that these relational surveys require: substantiated construction of name generators, informed choice of individual and relational characteristics and indicators, relevance of mixed methods making it possible to combine the qualitative, quantitative, and structural dimensions, etc.

Of course, what we have observed is still subsumed within the macro-level social structures and more general forms of determinism, which bring their full force to bear on microsocial phenomena. It remains the case, nevertheless, as we bring our analysis to a close, that an original approach centered primarily around the dynamic of this "intermediate level" of relationships and personal networks, an approach we claim as our own and believe we have implemented here, appears to be a meaningful one. Much is revealed, after all, by observing interpersonal relationships and social networks. A relationship is indeed a story, full of experiences, emotions, and motivations that are ultimately converted into actions. However, a relationship is also a link between elements of the social world that would otherwise be isolated. In that respect, it helps to weave the social fabric, to ensure that we can bear to live alongside each other, to work with and for others in constructing hospitals, stage plays, scientific knowledge,

---

[1] H. C. White, *Identity and Control: How Social Formations Emerge* (Princeton: Princeton University Press, 2008).

etc. The most formal bodies, the most well-established institutions and the most abstract dynamics can also be analyzed from the point of view of the social networks they bring into play, the relational tendencies that underlie them, and the "mainspring" or motivating force of the ties they produce. The same is true of a nation-state's constitution, the founding of companies, the search for a job, family disputes, and committed, loving relationships. This perspective enables us to reconcile formal structures, individual plans, and the power of emotions, which are all dimensions that social scientists have investigated in depth (particularly the first two) but often separately from each other. It has also been our aim to conceptualize and analyze how social structures are considered, understood, and adapted at the level of actual individuals and how they are conceptualized and enacted in life histories, which, taken in conjunction with their relational environments, are part of history in the making.

Of course, the present volume is far from exhausting all the avenues it has opened up. Although our surveys and analyses have provided the foundation for some significant advances, particularly in respect of relational dynamics, these sources have their limitations, which will have to be pushed back.

Firstly, our longitudinal data are concentrated on just one particular stage of the life course, namely the transition into adult life. This prevents us from analyzing the other stages in as much detail, although fortunately we do have more standard static data for them. More generally, longitudinal surveys are constructed and used far too seldom and should be significantly developed. A trend in this direction can currently be discerned. It is true that they are unwieldy affairs that require long-term commitment, but their advantages far outweigh their costs. They make it possible to observe actual rather than reconstructed changes taking place in networks and to measure structural changes that cannot possibly be captured retrospectively. They are the only way to compile a register and examination of defunct relationships, which are undoubtedly at least as significant as those that are maintained. Thus, increasing use should be made of these methods, and they should be applied to all stages of the life course. We have sought in this book to exploit to the full two original French surveys and an extensive literature on personal networks. However, we have used mainly French data, even though the Toulouse survey enables us to make a comparison with the United States, where more studies have been carried out. Personal networks in the United States and in France are fairly similar, but the average characteristics of networks differ somewhat in other countries. What is described here holds true for a wealthy democratic country but not necessarily for a poor country or one with a totalitarian regime.[2]

We have also left out of our analysis "marginal" situations, such as life on the streets, the recent immigration of people with few if any qualifications, some of whom are illegal, highly dependent individuals, etc. Further studies are certainly required in order fully to understand the dynamic of relationships and social networks in these particular situations. It might then be necessary to focus more closely on certain populations (exiled and excluded individuals, leaders, etc.). A narrower focus could also perhaps be used to explore in greater depth certain life events, such as divorce, migration, or unemployment, for example. It remains the case, nevertheless, that above and beyond the figures that delineate the overall characteristics of networks and above and beyond specific situations and arrangements, the dynamics of relationships and networks and the processes whereby they are constructed and evolve seem to be fairly widely generalizable. Thus, despite their limitations, our sources have enabled us to construct a comprehensive overview of the principles currently animating the establishment and development of social ties and networks, one that is to the best of our knowledge without any real precedent.

There is every reason to believe that the dynamics described throughout this book will, for a long time to come, remain the basis for the establishment of personal networks, regardless of how sophisticated communications technologies become. It is even likely that it will be increasingly difficult to investigate the social world without taking into account the murmuring of ties being made and unmade.

---

[2] B Völker, H Flap, "Weak Ties As a Liability: The Case of East Germany, *Rationality and Society* 13 (4) 397–428.

References

Adams R., Allan G. (eds.). (1998). *Placing Friendship in Context*. Cambridge: Cambridge University Press.

Allan G. (1979). *A Sociology of Friendship and Kinship*. London: G. Allen & Unwin.

Arber S., Attias-Donfut C. (2000). *The Myth of Generational Conflict: The Family and State in Aging Societies*. London: Routledge.

Atkinson T., Liem R., Liem J. J. (1986). The Social Costs of Unemployment: Implications for Social Support. *Journal of Health and Social Behavior* 27: 317–331.

Attias-Donfu C. (2000). Rapports de générations. Transferts intrafamiliaux et dynamique macrosociale. *Revue Française de Sociologie* 41(4): 643–684.

Backstrom L., Boldi P., Rosa M., Ugander J., Vigna S. (2012). Four Degrees of Separation. http://arxiv.org/abs/1111.4570.

Berger P., Kellner H. (1964). Marriage and the Construction of Reality: An Exercise in the Microsociology of Knowledge. *Diogenes* 12(46): 1–24.

Bergman M., Lambert P., Prandy K., Joye D. (2002). Theorization, Construction and Validation of a Social Stratification Scale: Cambridge Social Interaction and Stratification Scale (CAMSIS) for Switzerland. *Swiss Journal of Sociology* 28(1): 7–25.

Bergström M. (2016). Sites de rencontres: qui les utilise en France? Qui y trouve son conjoint? *Population & Sociétés* 530. www.ined.fr/fichier/s_rubrique/25008/population.societes.530.site.rencontres.conjoint.fr.pdf.

Bernardi L. (2004). Channels of Social Influence on Reproduction. *Population Research and Policy Review* 22: 527–555.

Bernardi L., Keim S., von der Lippe H. (2007). Social Influences on Fertility: A Comparative Mixed Method Study in Eastern and Western Germany. *Journal of Mixed Methods Research* 1(1): 1–27.

Bessin M., Bidart C., Grossetti M. (eds.). (2010). *Bifurcations. Les sciences sociales face aux ruptures et à l'événement*. Paris: La Découverte.

Bidart C. (1997). *L'amitié, un lien social*. Paris: La Découverte.

— (2008). Dynamiques des réseaux personnels et processus de socialisation: évolutions et influences des entourages lors des transitions vers la vie adulte. *Revue Française de Sociologie* 49(3): 559–583.

(2009). En búsqueda del contenido de las redes sociales: los "móviles" de las relaciones', "A la recherche de la substance des relations: le ressort du lien." *REDES, Revista Hispana para el Análisis de Redes Sociales* 16. http://revista-redes.rediris.es/pdf-vol16/vol16_7.pdf.

(2013). What Does Time Imply? Contributions of Longitudinal Methods to the Analysis of the Life Course. *Time and Society* 22(2): 254–273.

Bidart C., Charbonneau J. (2011). How to Generate Personal Networks: Issues and Tools for a Sociological Perspective. *Field Methods* 23(3): 266–286.

Bidart C., Degenne A., Grossetti M. (2017). Personal Networks Typologies: A Structural Approach. *Social Networks* 54: 1–11.

Bidart C., Lavenu D. (2005). Evolutions of Personal Networks and Life Events. *Social Networks* 27(4): 359–376.

Bidart C., Longo M. E., Mendez A. (2013). Time and Process: An Operational Framework for Processual Analysis. *European Sociological Review* 29(4): 743–751.

Bidart C., Pellissier A. (2002). Copains d'école, copains de travail. Evolution des modes de sociabilité d'une cohorte de jeunes. *Réseaux* 20(115): 17–49.

(2007). Entre parents et enfants: liens et relations à l'épreuve du cheminement vers la vie adulte. *Recherches et Prévisions* 90: 29–39.

Bigot R., Croutte P. (2014). La diffusion des technologies de l'information et de la communication dans la société française. www.arcep.fr/uploads/tx_gspublication/etude-CREDOC-diffusion-TIC-2014.pdf.

Blau P., Schwartz J. E. (1984). *Crosscutting Social Circles: Testing a Macrostructural Theory of Intergroup Relations*. Orlando: Academic Press.

Bott E. (1971 [1957]). *Family and Social Network: Roles, Norms and External Relationships in Ordinary Urban Families*. New York: Free Press.

Bouchet-Valat M. (2013). Patterns and Trends of Educational and Occupational Homogamy: Evidence for France Based on Yearly Surveys (1969–2011). Spring conference of the Research Committee on Social Stratification and Mobility (RC28), Trento (Italy), May 18, 2013.

Bouglé C. (1897). Qu'est-ce que la sociologie? *Revue de Paris*, 3(32): 533–555.

Bourdieu P. (1979). *La distinction*. Paris: Editions de Minuit.

(1980). Le Capital social, Notes provisoires. *Actes de la Recherche en Sciences Sociales* 31: 2–3.

Boyd D. (2007). Why Youth (Heart) Social Network Sites: The Role of Networked Publics in Teenage Social Life. In David Buckingham (ed.) *Youth, Identity, and Digital Media Volume*. Cambridge, MA: MIT Press, 119–142.

Brooks R. (2002). Transitional Friends? Young People's Strategies to Manage and Maintain Their Friendships during a Period of Repositioning. *Journal of Youth Studies* 5(4): 449–467.

Burt R. S. (1984). Network Items and the General Social Survey. *Social Networks* 6: 293–339.

(1987). A Note on Strangers, Friends and Happiness. *Social Networks* 9: 311–331.

(2004). Structural Holes and Good Ideas. *American Journal of Sociology* 110: 349–399.

Campbell S. W. (2015). Mobile Communication and Network Privatism: A Literature Review of the Implications for Diverse, Weak, and New Ties. *Review of Communication Research* 3(1): 1–21.

Cardon D. (2010). *La démocratie internet. Promesses et limites.* Paris: Seuil.

Castrén M. A., Maillochon F. (2009). Who Chooses the Wedding Guests, the Couple or the Family? Individual Preferences and Relational Constraints in France and Finland. *European Societies* 11(3): 369–389.

Coleman J. S. (1988). Social Capital in the Creation of Human Capital. *American Journal of Sociology* 94: 95–120.

Degenne A., Forsé M. (1999). *Introducing Social Networks.* London: Sage.

Degenne A., Fournier I., Marry C., Mounier L. (1991). Les relations sociales au cœur du marché du travail. *Sociétés Contemporaines* 5: 75–98.

Degenne A., Lebeaux M.-O. (1991). L'entraide entre les ménages, un facteur d'inégalité sociale? *Sociétés Contemporaines* 8: 21–42.

(2004). Does Social Capital Offset Social and Economic Inequalities? Social Capital in Everyday Life. In Henk Flap and Beate Völker (eds.) *Creation and Returns of Social Capital: A New Research Program.* New York: Routledge, pp. 51–73.

(2005). The Dynamics of Personal Networks at the Time of Entry into Adult Life. *Social Networks* 27(4): 337–358.

Duck S. (1991). *Friends, for Life: The Psychology of Personal Relationships.* London: Harvester Wheatsheaf.

Dunbar R. I. M. (1993). Coevolution of Neocortical Size, Group Size and Language in Humans. *Behavioral and Brain Sciences* 16(4): 681–735.

(2016). Do Online Social Media Cut through the Constraints That Limit the Size of Offline Social Networks? *Royal Society Open Science* 3: 150–292.

Eisenstadt S. N., Roniger L. (1984). *Patrons, Clients and Friends: Interpersonal Relations and the Structure of Trust in Society.* Cambridge: Cambridge University Press.

Elias N. (1991 [1987]). *The Society of Individuals.* Oxford: Blackwell.

Emirbayer M. (1997). Manifesto for a Relational Sociology. *The American Journal of Sociology* 103(2), 281–317

Federico A. de (2003). La dinámica de las redes de amistad. La elección de amigos en el programa Erasmus. *REDES* 4(3): 1–44.

(2008). Amitiés Européennes. Les réseaux transnationaux des étudiants Erasmus. *Informations Sociales* 147, 120–127.

Feld S. L. (1981). The Focused Organization of Social Ties. *American Journal of Sociology* 86(5), 1015–1035.

(1997). Structural Embeddedness and Stability of Interpersonal Relations. *Social Networks* 19, 91–95.

Feld S. L., Suitor J., Hoegh J. G. (2007). Describing Changes in Personal Networks over Time. *Field Methods* 19, 218–236.

Ferrand A. (2005). Réseaux de discussion hétérogènes et pluralisme cognitif. *REDES* 10(2). www.redalyc.org/pdf/931/93101003.pdf.

(2007). *Confidents. Une analyse structurale de réseaux sociaux.* Paris: L'Harmattan.

Ferrand A., Federico A. de (2006). Methods of Social Network Analysis. In Graziella Caselli, Jaques Vallin, and Guillaume Wunsch (eds.) *Demography: Analysis and Synthesis.* Cambridge, MA: Elsevier Academic Press, pp. 745–764.

Ferrand A., Mounier L. (1994). Social Discourse and Normative Influences. In A. Spira, N. Bajos, and the ACSF Group (eds.) *Sexual Behaviour and AIDS*. Dartmouth: Aldershot, pp. 140–148. http://halshs.archives-ouvertes.fr/halshs-00257614/fr/.

(1996). Talking about Sexuality: An Analysis of Relations between Confidants. In M. Bozon and H. Leridon (eds.) *Sexuality and the Social Sciences*. Dartmouth: Aldershot, pp. 265–288.

Ferrand A., Mounier L., Degenne A. (1999). The Diversity of Personal Networks in France: Social Stratification and Relational Structures. In B. Wellman (ed.) *Networks in the Global Village: Life in Contemporary Communities*. Boulder: Westview Press, pp. 185–224.

Fischer C. S. (1982). *To Dwell among Friends: Personal Networks in Town and City*. Chicago: The University of Chicago Press.

(1993). *America Calling: A Social History of the Telephone to 1940*. Berkeley: University of California Press.

(2009). The 2004 GSS Finding of Shrunken Social Networks: An Artifact? *American Sociological Review* 74(4), 657–669.

(2011). *Still Connected: Family and Friends in America since 1970*, New York: Russell Sage Foundation.

Forsé M. (1997). Capital social et employ. *L'Année Sociologique* 47, 143-181,

Forsé M., Chauvel L. (1995). L'évolution de l'homogamie en France: Une méthode pour comparer les diagonalités de plusieurs tables. *Revue Française de Sociologie* 36(1) 123–142.

Freeman L. C. (1978). Centrality in Social Networks Conceptual Clarification. *Social Networks* 1, 215–239.

(2004). *The Development of Social Network Analysis: A Study in the Sociology of Science*. Vancouver: Empirical Press.

Freeman L. C., Thompson C. R. (1989). Estimating Acquaintanceship Volume. In Manfred Kochen (ed.) *The Small World*. Norwood: Ablex Publishing, pp. 147–158.

Furlong A., Cartmel F. (2007). *Young People and Social Change: New Perspectives*. Buckingham: Open University Press.

Galland O. (2007). *Boundless Youth: Studies in the Transition to Adulthood*, Oxford: The Bardwell Press.

Gartrell C. D. (1987). Network Approaches to Social Evaluation. *Annual Review of Sociology* 13, 49–66.

Geoffray M. L. (2012). *Contester à Cuba*, Paris: Dalloz.

Godechot O. (2000). Plus d'amis, plus proches? Essai de comparaison de deux enquêtes peu comparables. Document INSEE, no. 0004.

Granovetter M. S. (1973). The Strength of Weak Ties. *The American Journal of Sociology* 78, 1360–1380.

(1974). *Getting a Job: A Study of Contacts and Careers*. Cambridge, MA: Harvard University Press.

(1983). The Strength of Weak Ties: A Network Theory Revisited. *Sociological Theory* 1, 201–233.

(1985). Economic Action and Social Structure: The Problem of Embeddedness. *The American Journal of Sociology* 91(3), 481–510.

Grossetti M. (1998). Communication électronique et réseaux sociaux. *Flux* 29, 5–13.
(2004). *Sociologie de l'imprévisible. Dynamiques de l'activité et des formes sociales*, Paris: Presses Universitaires de France.
(2006). L'imprévisibilité dans les parcours sociaux. *Cahiers Internationaux de Sociologie* 120, 5–28.
(2008). Proximities and Embedding Effects. *European Planning Studies* 16(5), 613–616.
(2010). Réseaux sociaux et ressources de médiation. In Vincent Liquette (ed.) *Médiations*. Paris: CNRS éditions, pp. 103–120.
Grossetti M., Barthe J.-F. (2008). Dynamiques des réseaux interpersonnels et des organisations dans les créations d'entreprises. *Revue Française de Sociologie* 49(3), 585–612.
Grossetti M., Barthe J.-F., Chauvac N. (2011). Studying Relational Chains from Narrative Material. *Bulletin de Méthodologie Sociologique* 110, 11–25.
Grossetti M., Bès M.-P. (2001). Encastrements et découplages dans les relations science – industrie. *Revue Française de Sociologie* 42(2), 327–355.
Haines V. A., Hurlbert J. S., Beggs J. J. (1996). Exploring the Determinants of Support Provision: Provider Characteristics, Personal Networks, Community Contexts, and Support Following Life Events. *Journal of Health and Social Behavior* 37(3), 252–264.
Halbwachs M. (1992). *On Collective Memory*. Chicago: The University of Chicago Press.
Hampton K. N., Sessions L. F., Her E. J., Rainie L. (2009). Social Isolation and New Technology. How the Internet and Mobile Phones Impact Americans' Social Networks. *Pew Internet and American Life Project*. www.pewinternet.org/files/old-media//Files/Reports/2009/PIP_Tech_and_Social_Isolation.pdf.
Hargittai E. (2007). Whose Space? Differences among Users and Non-users of Social Network Sites. *Journal of Computer-Mediated Communication* 13(1), 276–297.
Héran F. (1988). La sociabilité, une pratique culturelle. *Économie et Statistique* 216, 3–22.
Herpin N., Déchaux J. H. (2004). Entraide familiale, indépendance économique et sociabilité. *Économie et Statistique*, 373, 3–31.
Hess B. (1972). Friendship. In M. Riley (ed.) *Aging and Society*. New York: Russell Sage Foundation.
Hill R. A., Dunbar R. I. M. (2002). Social Network Size in Humans. *Human Nature* 14 (1), 53–72.
Hofstra B., Corten R., van Tubergen F., Ellison N. B. (2017). Sources of Segregation in Social Networks: A Novel Approach Using Facebook. *American Sociological Review* 82(3), 625–656.
Kadushin C. (1968). Power, Influence and Social Circles: A New Methodology for Studying Opinion Makers. *American Sociological Review* 33(5), 685–699.
Kahn R. L., Antonucci T. C. (1980). Convoys over the Life Course: Attachment, Roles and Social Support. In P. B. Baltes and O. Brim (eds.) *Life-Span Development and Behavior*, New York: Academic Press, pp. 253–86.
Kalmijn M. (2003). Shared Friendship Networks and the Life Course: An Analysis of Survey Data on Married and Cohabiting Couples. *Social Networks* 25, 231–249.

Katz E., Lazarsfeld P. F. (1955). *Personal Influence*. Glencoe: Free Press.

Eckert J. K. (1980). *The Unseen Elderly: A Study of Marginally Subsistent Hotel Dwellers*. San Diego: Campanile Press.

Killworth P. D., Russel B. H. (1978). The Reversal Small World Experiment. *Social Networks* 1, 159–192.

Klein I. K., van Tilburg T. (1999). Broken Ties: Reciprocity and Other Factors Affecting the Termination of Older Adults' Relationships. *Social Networks* 21, 131–146.

Kobayashi T., Boase J. (2014). Tele-Cocooning: Mobile Texting and Social Scope. *Journal of Computer-Mediated Communication* 19(3), 681–694.

Krackhardt D. (1992). The Strength of Strong Ties: The Importance of Philos in Organization. In N. Nohria and R. G. Eccles (eds.) *Networks and Organization: Structure, Form, and Action*. Boston: Harvard Business School Press, pp. 216–239.

Lahire B. (2011). *The Plural Actor*. Cambridge: Polity Press.

Laumann E. O. (1973). *Bonds of Pluralism: The Form and Substance of Urban Social Networks*. New York: John Wiley & Sons.

Lazega E. (2001). *The Collegial Phenomenon: The Social Mechanisms of Cooperation among Peers in a Corporate Law Partnership*. Oxford: Oxford University Press.

Le Gall D. (1998). Family Conflicts in France through the Eyes of Teenagers. In Renata Klein (ed.) *Multidisciplinary Perspectives on Family Violence in Europe*. London: Routledge, 79–109.

Lee C., Scherngell T., Barber M. J. (2011). Investigating an Online Social Network Using Spatial Interaction Models. *Social Networks* 33, 129–133.

Leeuwen M. H. D., van Maas I. (2005). Endogamy and Social Class in History: An Overview. *International Review for Social History* 50 (Supplement), 1–23.

Lenhart A., Smith A., Anderson M., Duggan M., Perrin, A. (2015) "Teens (2015). Technology and Friendships." Pew Research Center, August, 2015. www .pewinternet.org/2015/08/06/teens-technology-and-friendships/.

Leslie L., Grady K. (1985). Changes in Mothers' Social Networks and Social Support Following Divorce. *Journal of Marriage and the Family* 47, 663–673.

Licoppe C. (2003). Two Modes of Maintaining Interpersonal Relations through Telephone: From the Domestic to the Mobile Phone. In J. Katz (ed.) *Machines That Become Us: The Social Context of Communication Technology*. New Brunswick: Transaction Publishers, pp. 171–186

Licoppe C., Smoreda Z. (2005). Are Social Networks Technologically Embedded? How Networks Are Changing Today with Changes in Communication Technology. *Social Networks* 27(4), 317–335.

Lin N. (2001). *Social Capital: A Theory of Social Structure and Action*. Cambridge: Cambridge University Press.

Lopata Z., Maines D. R. (eds.). (1981). *Research in the Interweave of Social Roles: Friendship*. Greenwich: JAI Press.

Lubbers M. J., Molina J. L., Lerner J., Brandes U., Avila J., Mc Carty C. (2010). Longitudinal Analysis of Personal Networks: The Case of Argentinean Migrants in Spain. *Social Networks* 32, 91–104.

Luhmann N. (1979). *Trust and Power*. Chichester: Wiley.

Marin A. (2004). Are Respondents More Likely to List Alters with Certain Characteristics? Implications for Name Generator Data. *Social Networks* 26, 289–307.

Mark N. P. (2003). Culture and Competition: Homophily and Distancing Explanation for Cultural Niches. *American Sociological Review* 68(3), 319–345.

Marry C. (1983). Origine sociale et réseaux d'insertion des jeunes ouvriers. *Formation-Emploi* 4, 3–15.

(1984). Les jeunes et l'emploi, force et faiblesse des liens forts. In L. Coutrot and C. Dubar (eds.) *Cheminements professionnels et mobilités sociales*, Paris: La Documentation Française, pp. 300–324.

Marsden P. V. (1987). Core Discussion Networks of Americans. *American Sociological Review* 52(1), 122–131.

(1988). Homogeneity in Confiding Relations. *Social Networks* 10, 57–76.

Matou P., Todo Y., Ishikawa T. (2014). Emergence of Multiplex Mobile Phone Communication Networks across Rural Areas: An Ethiopian Experiment. *Network Science* 2(2), 162–188.

McPherson M., Smith-Lovin L., Brashears M. E. (2006). Social Isolation in America: Changes in Core Discussion Networks over Two Decades. *American Sociological Review* 71, 353–375.

(2009). Reply to Fischer: Models and Marginals: Using Survey Evidence to Study Social Networks. *American Sociological Review* 74(4), 670–681.

Mead G. H. (1934). *Mind, Self, and Society*. ed. Charles W. Morris. Chicago: The University of Chicago Press.

Mercier P.-A., de Gournay C., Smoreda Z. (2002). Si loin, si proches: liens et communications à l'épreuve du déménagement. *Réseaux* 115, 121–150.

Mercken L., Snijders T., Steglich C., Vartiainen E., de Vries H. (2010). Dynamics of Adolescent Friendship Networks and Smoking Behavior. *Social Networks* 32, 72–81.

Merton R. K. (1949). *Social Theory and Social Structure*. New York: Free Press.

Mesch G. de, Talmud I. (2000). *Similarity and Quality of Social Relationships among Adolescents*. Haifa: The University of Haifa.

Milardo R. M. (1982). Friendship Networks in Developing Relationships: Converging and Diverging Social Environments. *Social Psychology Quarterly* 45(3), 162–172.

Milgram S. (1967). The Small World Problem. *Psychology Today* 1, 61–67.

Miller McPherson J., Smith-Lovin L., Cook J. M. (2001). Birds of a Feather: Homophily in Social Networks. *Annual Review of Sociology* 27, 415–444.

Mizuko I., Baumer S., Bittanti M., Boyd D., Cody R., Herr B., Horst H. A., Lange P. G., Mahendran D., Martinez K., Pascoe C. J., Perkel D., Robinson L., Sims C., Tripp L. (with J. Antin, M. Finn, A. Law, A. Manion, S. Mitnick, D. Schlossberg, Sarita Yardi) (2009). *Hanging Out, Messing Around, Geeking Out: Living and Learning with New Media*. Cambridge, MA: MIT Press.

Mok D., Wellman B., Carrasco J. (2010). Does Distance Matter in the Age of the Internet? *Urban Studies* 47(13), 2747–2783.

Molina J. L., Lerner J., Gómez Mestres S. (2008). Patrones de cambio de las redes personales de inmigrantes en Cataluña. *REDES* 15, 50–63.

Mollenhorst G., Völker B., Flap H. (2008). Social Contexts and Personal Relationships: The Effect of Meeting Opportunities on Similarity for Relationships of Different Strengths. *Social Networks* 30, 60–68.

(2014). Changes in Personal Relationships: How Social Contexts Affect the Emergence and Discontinuation of Relationships. *Social Networks* 37, 67–80.

Moore G. (1990). Structural Determinants of Men's and Women's Personal Networks. *American Sociological Review* 55(5), 726–735.

Morgan D. L., Neal M. B., Carder P. (1996). The Stability of Core and Peripheral Networks over Time. *Social Networks* 19, 9–25.

Mounier L. (1999). A quoi peuvent servir les relations sociales des jeunes? *Agora* 17, 47–62.

Nie N. H. (2001). Sociability, Interpersonal Relations, and the Internet: Reconciling Conflicting Findings. *American Behavioral Scientist* 45(3), 420–435.

Padgett J., Ansell C. (1993). Robust Action and the Rise of the Medici, 1400–1434. *American Journal of Sociology* 98, 1259–1319.

Paik A., Sanchagrin K. (2013). Social Isolation in America: An Artifact. *American Sociological Review* 78(3), 339–360.

Paine R. (1970). Anthropological Approaches to Friendship. *Journal of the Institute of Man* 1, 139–159.

Park N., Lee S., Kim J. H. (2012). Individuals' Personal Network Characteristics and Patterns of Facebook Use: A Social Network Approach. *Computers in Human Behavior* 28, 1700–1707.

Paugam S. (2012). The Paradox of exclusion: Crossed Considerations on the Contemporary Forms of Broken Social Links. In Marc Humbert and Yoshimichi Sato (eds.) *Social Exclusion: Perspectives from France and Japan*. Melbourne: Trans Pacific Press, pp. 20–31.

Perrin A. (2015). Social Networking Usage: 2005–2015. Pew Research Center. www.pewinternet.org/2015/10/08/2015/Social-Networking-Usage-2005-2015.

Portes A. (1995). *The Economic Sociology of Immigration: Essays on Networks, Ethnicity and Entrepreneurship*. New York: Russell Sage Foundation.

Prouteau L., Wolff F.-C. (2003). Les services informels entre ménages: une dimension méconnue du bénévolat. *Economie et Statistique* 368, 3–31.

Rainie L., Wellman B. (2012). *Networked: The New Social Operating System*. Cambridge, MA: MIT Press.

Rivera M. T., Soderstrom S., Uzzi B. (2010). Dynamics of Dyads in Social Networks: Assortative, Relational, and Proximity Mechanisms. *Annual Review of Sociology* 36, 91–115.

Rosenfeld M., Thomas R. (2012). Searching for a Mate: The Rise of the Internet As a Social Intermediary. *American Sociological Review* 77(4), 523–547.

Russel Bernard H., Johnsen E. C., Killworth P. D., McCarty C., Shelley G. A. (1990). Estimating the Size of Personal Networks. *Social Networks* 12(4), 289–312.

Russel Bernard H., Shelley G. H., Killworth P. (1987). How Much of a Network Does the GSS and RSW Dredge Up. *Social Networks* 9, 49–61.

Schnettler S. (2009). A Structured Overview of 50 Years of Small-World Research. *Social Networks* 31, 165–178.

Shanyang Z. (2006). Do Internet Users Have More Social Ties? A Call for Differentiated Analysis of Internet Use. *Journal of Computer-Mediated Communication* 11, 844–862.

Silver A. A. (1989). Friendship and Trust As Moral Ideals: An Historical Approach. *European Journal of Sociology* 30, p. 274–297.

Simmel G. (1990 [1900]). *The Philosophy of Money*. London: Routledge.

Simmel G., Wolff K. H. (1950). *The Sociology of Georg Simmel*. Glencoe: Free Press.

Small M. L. (2013). Weak Ties and the Core Discussion Network: Why People Discuss Important Matters with Unimportant Alters. *Social Networks* 35, 470–483.

(2017). *Someone to Talk to*. Oxford: Oxford University Press.

Small M. L., Vontrese D. P., McMahan P. (2015). How Stable Is the Core Discussion Network? *Social Networks* 40, 90–102.

Small M. L., Sukhu, C. (2016). Because They Were There: Access, Deliberation, and the Mobilization of Networks for Support. *Social Networks* 47, 73–84.

Smits J., Ultee W., Lammers J. (2000). More or Less Educational Homogamy? A Test of Different Versions of Modernization Theory Using Cross-Temporal Evidence for 60 Countries. *American Sociological Review* 65(5), 781–788.

Smoreda Z. (2008). Sociabilités ordinaires, réseaux sociaux et médiations des technologies de communication. PhD thesis, Université Paris-Est.

Sola Pool I. de (1978). Contacts and Influence. *Social Networks* 1, 5–51.

Tazé S., Ferrand A. (2007). Les savoirs profanes sur le sida: des incertitudes rationnelles aux certitudes relationnelles. *Sociologie Santé* 26, 31–48.

Terhell E. L., Van Groenou B. M. I., Van Tilburg T. (2007). Network Contact Changes in Early and Later Post-Separation Years. *Social Networks* 29, 11–24.

Verbrugge L. M. (1977). The Structure of Adult Friendship Choices. *Social Forces* 56(2), 576–597.

(1979). Multiplexity in Adult Friendship. *Social Forces* 57(4), 1286–1309.

Vincent-Buffault A. (1995). *L'exercice de l'amitié. Pour une histoire des pratiques amicales aux XVIIIe et XIXe siècles*. Paris: Seuil.

Völker B., Flap H. (2001). Weak Ties As a Liability: The Case of East Germany. *Rationality and Society* 13 (4), 397–428

Watts D. J., Strogatz S. H. (1998). Collective Dynamics of "Small-world" Networks. *Nature* 393(1), 440–442.

Wellman B. (1979). The Community Question: The Intimate Networks of East Yorkers. *The American Journal of Sociology* 84(5), 1201–1231.

Wellman B., Frank O., Espinoza V., Lundquist S., Wilson C. (1991). Integrating Individual, Relational and Structural Analysis. *Social Networks* 13, pp. 223–249

Wellman B., Leighton B. (1979). Networks, Neighborhoods, and Communities. *Urban Affairs Review* 14(3), 363–390.

Wellman B., Wong R. Y., Tindall D., Nazer N. (1997). A Decade of Network Change: Turnover, Persistence and Stability in Personal Communities. *Social Networks* 19, 27–50.

Wellman B., Quan-Haase A., Witte J., Hampton K. (2001). Does the Internet Increase, Decrease, or Supplement Social Capital? Social Networks, Participation, and Community Commitment. *American Behavioral Scientist* 45(3), 436–455

White H. C. (2008). *Identity and Control: How Social Formations Emerge*. Princeton: Princeton University Press.

Willmott P. (1986). *Social Networks, Informal Care and Public Policy*. London: Policy Studies Institute.

Wrzus C., Hänel M., Wagner J., Neyer F. J. (2013). Social Network Changes and Life Events across the Lifespan: A Meta-Analysis. *Psychological Bulletin* 1, 53–80.

Zhao S. (2006). Do Internet Users Have More Social Ties? A Call for Differentiated Analysis of Internet Use. *Journal of Computer-Mediated Communication* 11, 844–862.

Index

STRUCTURAL ANALYSIS IN THE SOCIAL SCIENCES

CPSIA information can be obtained
at www.ICGtesting.com
Printed in the USA
LVHW042337161020
669015LV00004B/225